LONG SHOTS

Other books by Bronwyn Sell

Kiwi Heroes
Law Breakers and Mischief Makers

LONG SHOTS

The **greatest underdog stories** in **NEW ZEALAND SPORT**

Bronwyn Sell & Christine Sheehy

ALLEN&UNWIN
SYDNEY·MELBOURNE·AUCKLAND·LONDON

Allen & Unwin
Level 3, 228 Queen Street
Auckland 1010, New Zealand
Phone: (64 9) 377 3800

83 Alexander Street
Crows Nest NSW 2065, Australia
Phone: (61 2) 8425 0100
Email: info@allenandunwin.com
Web: www.allenandunwin.com

A catalogue record for this book is available
from the National Library of New Zealand

ISBN 978 1 877505 41 6

Internal design by Nick Turzynski
Set in 12/17 pt Newzald by Midland Typesetters, Australia
Printed and bound in Australia by Griffin Press

10 9 8 7 6 5 4 3 2 1

For Marion, Betty and Mary.
Booklovers all.

CONTENTS

It's more often than not the unlikely happening in sport, the underdog getting up against all odds, which results in tears being shed.

Ian Smith, former New Zealand cricketer

INTRODUCTION

THE POWER OF THE UNDERDOG

THE UNDERDOG STORY has captivated the human psyche for millennia. From David and Goliath and *The Little Engine that Could* to Frodo Baggins and Rocky Balboa, stories of the nobody who prevails capture our attention unlike any other tales.

It's not just something we appreciate with our minds; it's something we feel smack in the middle of our chests.

Perhaps we New Zealanders value a good underdog story more than most. Almost any tale of international success by a Kiwi is an underdog story. By virtue of our country's size and comparative lack of resources, we rarely go into any endeavour as a favourite, unless we happen to be wearing a black shirt and carrying a rugby ball.

We've all experienced moments when we've felt small and powerless. We love to believe that the underfunded, underrated, unheralded everyman or everywoman can prove the doubters wrong, through determination, hard work and self-belief. Perhaps such stories give us hope that we too can realise our dreams, and restore our faith that the world is fair and full of opportunity.

There's evidence that this response is innate. American psychologists once got a group of people to watch a rudimentary animation with four sequences. In the first sequence, a circle rolled steadily along a flat line. In the second, it rolled up a hill, slowing its pace as if it were struggling. In the third, a second circle passed the original circle on the incline, at speed. In the fourth, the second circle bumped the slower circle on the way past, knocking it back down the hill. 'We were not at all sure what kind of results we would get,' recalled the psychologists, Scott T. Allison and George R. Goethals, in their book *Heroes: What they do and why we need them*. 'After all, these were simple geometric shapes displayed on a computer screen. Why should participants like a circle or root for a circle at all? These circles were clearly not living things, and we included no instruction suggesting that participants view them as alive.'

The findings stunned them. The participants liked the circle more when it struggled than when it didn't. They liked it even more when it was passed by the other circle. And they felt so much sympathy and liking for it when the second circle bumped it that they became 'visibly agitated'. They told the researchers that such an aggressive act directed towards an underdog was 'out of line and unacceptable'. 'The underdog phenomenon is such a powerful part of our thinking that we anthropomorphically ascribe human traits of courage and strength to inanimate objects that resemble heroic underdogs,' said the professors.

Nowhere is the underdog story more prominent than in the sporting arena. New Zealand's sporting history is rich with tales of the unknown outsider who has taken on the world, or the written-off veteran who's come back to reclaim glory. Ever since the late nineteenth century, when we started taking on the world at sport, we've hurried to the street newspaper vendor for the latest news about our heroes, crowded around the wireless in a hush, or leapt to our feet and screamed at the television in the dead of night in darkened living rooms.

As the sports world grows more competitive and professional, athletes specialise from an ever younger age and train relentlessly, and richer countries pour money into elite athlete development, it may be harder for the Kiwi long shot to prevail. But that just makes the occasions on which they succeed even more special.

For this book, we've cherry-picked some of the most inspiring sporting underdog stories in our country's history, from the 'rustic yokel' who took on the Europeans at their own game in the 1928 Tour de France to the nationally scorned sportsman who kicked himself and New Zealand to glory in the 2011 Rugby World Cup. It's not an exhaustive catalogue of every Kiwi sporting underdog story—no book would be big enough for that. It's a selection of the stories we found most compelling, regardless of time period, or sport, or any other variable. Any gaps are unintentional.

This book is about sportspeople, but it's not just a sports book. This is sport as a microcosm of human endeavour; its themes are universal—effort and struggle, self-belief and sacrifice, ingenuity and courage in the face of daunting odds, cutting criticism, lack of money, tragedy, grief, illness, injury and disability. Sometimes it's not about winning a medal or a trophy but about athletes pushing their boundaries further than they thought possible and reaching goals they once only dreamed about. We've been inspired by researching and writing these stories. We hope you feel inspired by reading them.

1

HARRY WATSON

The 'rustic yokel' who took on the world's best

As THE RMS *OTRANTO* rolled into another wave, Harry Watson's bicycle wobbled and slipped sideways off the training rollers and onto the deck of the ship. The 24-year-old Cantabrian dismounted in disgust, seized the rollers and, to the amusement of his Australian teammates, Hubert Opperman, Percy Osborne and Ernie Bainbridge, threatened to throw the whole contraption overboard into the frigid Atlantic Ocean.

After a month at sea, the man they dubbed 'The Mile Eater' was desperate to feel the road beneath his wheels again. In just ten weeks Watson and his companions would become the first team from an English-speaking country to take part in the world's longest and most prestigious cycling race, the Tour de France. The four men would race against the world's greatest long-distance cyclists over 5377 kilometres (some 1700 kilometres longer than today's Tour).

In 1928 cycling was a popular spectator sport, and the men's quest to take on the pinnacle of professional cycling had captured the public imagination. Newspapers on both sides of the Tasman had led a joint fundraising campaign for the team that would race under both the wattle leaf and the silver fern but would be known as the Australian team. 'Tell New Zealand that I will do my best and will endeavour to uphold the great name that my country has in France,' Watson wrote in a letter home, as the ship neared the French port of Toulon.

The four men went straight to a basic training camp near Versailles, where they trained six mornings a week, cycling 65 to 145 kilometres a day. Sometimes they rode with the French Olympic cycling squad, who ridiculed the antipodeans for their fat balloon tyres. Later, in his autobiography, Opperman said he and his teammates looked like 'rustic yokels' next to the Europeans. They soon adopted French-style saddle positions, narrow tube tyres, berets and plus fours.

Before long the campaign began to unravel. The team's local sponsor, French bicycle manufacturer Ravat-Wonder hadn't supported a cycling team for many years and failed to provide essential supplies. The manager assigned to the team spoke no English, and according to Watson, knew little or nothing about bicycles and cycling: 'He told us we didn't really need a masseur, he told us all sorts of things about cycling racing which a fellow usually learns when he first commences to ride a bike, and he seemed to know so little about the requirements for a 3000-odd mile race that we were left to our own devices.'

The men finally received their fixed-wheel French bicycles,

custom-built by Ravat-Wonder, just four weeks before the start of the Tour. Watson wasn't impressed with the complicated machines. As with all racing bicycles of the era, to change gears the rider had to stop, undo the wing nuts on the rear wheel and manually shift the chain. Watson knew their lack of familiarity with the bikes would cost valuable race time. Tyre changes were taking them almost twice as long as their European counterparts.

Worse was to come. Most of the European teams were made up of eight to ten 'road cracks'—cyclists who had been specifically trained for the event. Before leaving Australia, the antipodeans had been told they would join up with French cyclists to make a full team, but it soon became clear there would be no additional riders. Ravat-Wonder claimed French cyclists would not ride with them, but it was widely believed the true reason was the company's reluctance to foot the bill.

It was a devastating blow. Not only did the four have little experience of the treacherous alpine roads on which the Tour was traditionally won, but with a smaller team they'd be at a significant disadvantage over flat terrain, too. Thanks to a controversial rule introduced in 1927, most of the flat stages were run as team time trials, to encourage riders to keep up a thrilling but exhausting pace. Larger teams could conserve energy by riding as a pack and drafting behind their teammates, and could help each other with punctures or gear failure. In addition, for the first time in the Tour de France, teams were to be allowed to substitute injured or exhausted cyclists at the twelfth stage, further diminishing the chances of small teams with no substitutes. Opperman wrote that it was like pitting 'four men against ten in a tug-o-war'. The chances of the team making it to the finish line were slim. 'The papers thought that we would be lucky if we got as far as the Pyrenees,' Watson later told the press. 'It was only the thought that we had been sent away by public subscription that kept us going.'

Days before the Tour began, a correspondent for Sydney's *Referee* newspaper visited the men at their training camp. She wrote a scathing attack on Ravat-Wonder and the Australian organising committee, describing the men's circumstances as 'nothing short of murder'. 'When Australians feel disappointed that their representatives . . . have not carried off all before them . . . let them blame those who sent the cyclists, without insisting on better contracts, precisely stated, rather than the unfortunate riders themselves, forced to race under such impossible conditions.'

But the plucky team had won the support of the French press and the public, who remembered the courage of the Anzac soldiers in France during the Great War a little over a decade before. Crowds cheered as they passed through villages on training rides. 'To hear our own accented names picked up and cheered melted our reserve and . . . we waved and smiled and surreptitiously wiped our eyes,' wrote Opperman of their last days before the Tour. 'The instinctive internal cringing which accompanied thoughts of distances, mountains and the [time trial] team stages was replaced by an inspired "We who are about to die salute you" spirit.' The Alcyon team (which included the previous year's winner, Luxembourg's Nicolas Frantz) also came to their aid, offering invaluable tips and techniques for operating the gears on their unfamiliar bicycles.

Watson and his teammates were determined to see the race through. 'We realise the task ahead of us is stupendous,' wrote Opperman to the Australian press on the eve of the race, 'but we are determined to strive every inch of the 3338 mile journey . . . You can depend that, if it is humanly possible, we will all finish.' That night Watson received a cablegram from New Zealand prime minister Joseph Coates: 'Best wishes from New Zealand for success in the forthcoming contest. Kia ora.'

At 9.20 a.m. on 17 June 1928, the team began their long journey, pedalling down the historic rue du Faubourg-Montmartre to the cheers of thousands of spectators, and then out of Paris towards the coast. French critics predicted the 'insufficiently manned team of Australians' would be back in Paris within three days. Instead, they made a strong start, finishing the third day with Watson, Opperman and Osborne placed seventh, eighth and ninth. By then the field had already dropped from 169 to 138.

The cyclists raced for eight consecutive days, covering more than 1600 kilometres, before the first rest day. In these time trial stages, the teams started ten minutes apart, so the antipodeans couldn't check their pacing against the larger teams. Opperman later recalled that it was 'most disheartening to see their big squads riding in perfect formation, steaming past our small contingent as we struggled to hold their speed'.

Race rules required the cyclists to finish each stage within fifteen per cent of the winning time or face elimination from the Tour. Punctures and crashes were common, and their lack of experience with the French equipment further delayed Watson and his team-mates. They felt they were fighting for their existence every day.

But as the race gathered momentum, so did French affection for the team. As the tight-knit group entered a village the cry would go up, 'Voilà, les Australiens!' By now, Tour director Henri Desgrange, who had introduced the controversial rule changes, was so impressed he announced that the following year each team would be identified with a nationality rather than a trade sponsor. 'Thank you, Australians,' he wrote. 'You have shown us the solution for the future.'

It was cold comfort for Watson and his companions. 'We didn't care what Desgrange did the following year,' wrote Opperman, who held Desgrange partly to blame for his team's disadvantages. 'If he had broken his neck, and the race had been stopped out of respect, we would have considered he had not paid too high a price for any relief to our sufferings . . . Our feet were swelling and tender under the daily repetition of miles, the pedal plates pressed like crusts on a sore tooth. We became saddle-chafed and on the buttocks large blind furuncles grew larger every day, drawing lurid verbal resentment as we bounced over the never-ending cobbles.'

As they approached the Pyrenees, the team made a determined attack, leading the field for 100 kilometres and finishing just four and a half minutes behind the dominant Alcyon team, to the delight of the French press. *L'Echo des Sports* described their performance as Homeric and sensational. 'The most conspicuous feature of the Tour was the consistency, ability and pluck of the Australians.'

But as they had anticipated, the alpine sections proved the greatest challenge. Long days in the saddle ascending snow-clad mountain passes as high as 2400 metres required early starts. Sometimes the cyclists set off at midnight, jolting and swaying up narrow dirt tracks in pitch darkness, without headlights. Yet going up was the easy part. The descents over rough tracks strewn with rocks and potholes were perilous and terrifying. The Australasians jammed their rudimentary brakes on hard as they skidded into hairpin turns and slid towards steep drop-offs, only to hear shouts of '*Attention!*' as the European cyclists hurtled past, bikes swinging wildly between cliff and abyss. 'The riding of the Europeans down the steep slopes of the Pyrenees was a revelation to us,' Watson later told the press. 'Coming to a steep down grade, we would end up not knowing the turns, but the French and Belgians would charge downhill at over 40 miles an hour and skid round corners in a manner that must take years of practice. It was on these hills that we lost so many hours that we were practically out of the race.'

On the twelfth stage, from Marseille to Nice, the pace increased as fresh substitute riders joined the other teams. The Australasians were now the only team consisting solely of their original riders, and it became even harder for the flagging men to finish within the daily time limit. On Stage 13, Watson's crank broke and he spent an hour searching for someone to weld it together. They were lucky to sneak in on time.

However, the support of the French crowds, which sometimes included expat Australians, and the team's belief in the task they were there to accomplish spurred them on. In every town an ovation greeted them. 'Often at the end of a long tedious journey—dog tired, weary and sick of our jobs—we were stimulated by the chorus of Australians who urged us on with the familiar "coo-ee" and not infrequently, the Maori war-cry,' Watson told journalists. 'Believe me, it made our task a whole lot easier.'

The four were sleep deprived, sick and struggling. Watson was suffering from the crippling stomach cramps and diarrhoea of dysentery, and Bainbridge, who had battled influenza in the early stages of the Tour, was covered in angry boils and weeping gravel rash, which made restful sleep almost impossible. When Osborne was struck head-on by a car one day, he lay sprawled across the bonnet thinking, *I hope to God I've broken my leg, too, and I won't have to ride any further.*

At one point, Watson grumbled to Opperman as they rode alongside each other, 'I feel as if I've been riding since I was born.'

Osborne overheard and added, 'And I wish I'd never been bloody born.'

The most gruelling day was yet to come. Stage 14 was a 329-kilometre haul over the Hautes-Alpes from Grenoble, taking in four major alpine climbs including the 2550-metre snow-capped Col du Galibier before descending to Evian on the shores of Lake Geneva. The day was hot and dusty, and marred by punctures and crashes. Bainbridge eventually struggled into Evian in 70th place. The 37 year old was spent. He was severely sleep deprived, covered in agonising sores and acutely aware that another 2000 kilometres lay between him and the finish line in Paris. After consulting a doctor, he decided not to sign the daily *controle* sheet, indicating his withdrawal from the Tour.

Watson was also in a wretched state. He was dehydrated, and the dysentery prevented him from taking on sufficient calories. He was so weak that at times he had to push the bike uphill or sit for a time by the roadside. When he arrived in Evian, in last place, he'd been in the saddle for seventeen hours and 37 minutes. As he crossed the finish line he collapsed, falling off his bicycle. But he was determined to see it through. 'Many times during the race, especially during the periods when I was suffering from stomach trouble and felt like quitting, the thought of the Prime Minister's message from the people of New Zealand spurred me on to fight it out to the finish,' he later told journalists.

After a day's rest, Watson, Opperman and Osborne embarked on the final eight stages of the Tour. Their grit and determination continued to impress the public, making them more popular than the leading Alcyon team. When they arrived in Charleville, at the conclusion of the nineteenth stage, 10,000 people were waiting in a velodrome decked out with Australian and New Zealand flags.

As the group raced towards Dunkirk, the old cobblestone roads caused violent vibrations in both bicycle and rider. It was slow going, and on one occasion Osborne came close to exceeding the time limit. Again, the Alcyon team came to their aid, offering each man a pair of tyres specifically designed to ease the jarring on that leg of the Tour.

On the final day—the hottest of the Tour—the remaining 41 riders set out early from Dieppe. They kept a slow pace for the first 150 kilometres before stopping together at the first feeding station. The leading 33 then rode as a group towards Paris, Watson among them. Thirty kilometres from the finish, he punctured. After replacing his tyre, he was unable to catch up with the pack for a strong final finish. Even so, the remainder of the race was unforgettable for the young Kiwi; mile upon mile of cheering fans crying, '*Vive les Australiens!*' As each of the three remaining antipodeans entered the velodrome in the Parc des Princes, they received a boisterous welcome from the crowd of 70,000 that eclipsed even its cheer for the winner, Frantz.

Opperman, Watson and Osborne were exhausted and emaciated but euphoric. They'd finished 18th, 28th and 38th overall, respectively. Only one quarter of the starting field had completed the race. More than 120 riders had dropped out or been disqualified.

Along with a devastated Bainbridge, the three returned to Versailles to rest and recover. With lucrative sporting contracts on offer, Opperman decided to remain in France, but Watson, Osborne and Bainbridge were ready to head home.

When the trio arrived in Sydney, Watson was outspoken about the team's lack of support. 'Never again under the same conditions,' he said. He believed that with the right financial backing and a team of seven or eight riders, they could have won several stages. 'My principal grievance was that we didn't get a fair go.' When he arrived home in Christchurch, on 12 October 1928, he was met by a crowd of supporters, including his wife, Kitty, cradling their newborn son. He'd been away from home for almost eight months.

Watson continued his long-distance racing career in New Zealand and Australia, using the experience and knowledge he had gained in France to win seven national road championships between 1929 and 1935, and setting records that endured well beyond his retirement. He never returned to race in Europe, or in the Tour de France.

The format of the 1928 Tour is still considered one of the toughest in the race's history, and time trials and substitute riders were abandoned in 1929. The story of the brave 'Australian' team went down in Tour de France lore. By the time Watson died, in 1996, aged 92, only one New Zealander had produced a better result in the Tour de France: Netherlands-born Tino Tabak, who came eighteenth in 1973.

2

THE 1929 SOUTHLAND RUGBY TEAM

'We were told we'd get a hiding'

EVEN FOR MINNOWS, the Southland rugby team that challenged Wairarapa for the Ranfurly Shield in 1929 were understrength. Most of their players were new to representative rugby, they'd left home without their two All Blacks, their star goal kicker and one of their best forwards, and they were dogged by influenza and injuries. It surprised no one when they suffered three straight losses on the way up north for the challenge, including wallopings from Canterbury and Wellington. After the Wellington loss, one of their managers deserted them. *The Evening Post* reported that Southland were badly outclassed in the match and their veteran captain, train driver J.R. 'Wampy' Bell, appeared to be past his best. 'Apart from one or two heady moves [Bell] could do little against the virile Wellington men . . . The Southlanders gave no indication of having forces that will seriously worry the Shield holders.'

Since Shield matches had begun, in 1904, Southland had won the 'log o' wood' only once, in 1921, and had lost it two games later. Wairarapa, meanwhile, were winding down for the season after their ninth straight Shield victory, against the Canterbury side that had destroyed Southland.

Wairarapa had eleven All Blacks in their starting fifteen, including their legendary captain Bert Cooke, whose performance against Canterbury had been lauded by one journalist as 'genius'. Cooke had dominated so many Shield wins that in some circles the trophy was nicknamed the 'Cooke Shield'. The Southland challenge would be the 100th Shield match ever played, and Cooke reputedly announced beforehand that he planned to cement his team's place in history with an unprecedented thrashing of the southerners. At that time, Wairarapa held the ignominious record for suffering the biggest loss in Shield history, having gone down 14–77 against Hawke's Bay in 1926, with Cooke on the team. Cooke was so determined to eclipse that record with a 70-odd-point victory over the challengers that several people approached his opposite player, second five-eighth Gil Porter, at the team hotel to say they felt sorry for him. 'In the end I was hostile,' recalled Porter, who was in his second year at representative level, while Cooke was in his seventh. 'We were told we were going to get a hiding.'

When Southland had planned the tour, they'd pinned their hopes on their three star players joining them for the Shield challenge, but their union reportedly didn't see the point of throwing more money at a series that was proving disastrous and kept the players at home. Only one reinforcement made it: forward

Ron Bird. 'When Ron Bird arrived, he had the fire and devil in him that our pack needed,' Porter later told *Southland Times* journalist Lynn McConnell, who authored the union's history. 'The others had promised to come north for the match but when they didn't it gave us a little extra backbone.'

They needed it. On the day of the match, 31 August, *The Evening Post* declared that Wairarapa's winning streak was likely to be increased before the close of the season. Cooke, who had the Shield on display in his menswear shop in Masterton's main street, didn't even bother to take it to Carterton for the challenge.

An *NZ Truth* reporter remarked that a Wairarapa victory was the biggest certainty ever to walk onto a football field. 'Considering that Canterbury had beaten the visitors by a 20 point margin, and Wellington had won as they liked three days previously, Wairarapa's comfortable win over Canterbury gave every justification for the widely held belief that Southland could not hope to seriously extend the Shield holders.'

When Southland ran out onto the Carterton Showgrounds in their maroon kit, they hadn't even decided on a goal kicker. With his star kicker a no-show, and given the team's pitiful kicking record on tour, Bell had told his second- and third-best kickers, Porter and Frank Anderson, to figure it out among themselves. 'Whichever of you has the best chance to take the shot, take it.' Porter hadn't taken a kick all tour but had spent the previous day practising in a paddock with Anderson, on Bell's orders. Neither had they had a team talk. 'They weren't thought of in those days,' recalled Porter. 'I don't think there was any particular build-up to the game . . . but we were all tuned up for it.'

Immediately, Southland set such a pace that Wairarapa appeared to be standing still. But the home team made the first attack, bringing the ball towards the Southland tryline and forcing an error, but missing the subsequent penalty kick.

Porter and his forwards amped up the pressure, and, twelve minutes into the game, his team won a free kick two metres inside halfway. 'Have a shot,' Bell told him. Porter was confident with the distance—shorter kicks were his bugbear—and duly booted it between the posts for three points. A minute later, Wairarapa gave away another penalty. Again Porter lined it up. Buoyed by his earlier success, he kicked a beauty of a goal.

As the game continued, a battle emerged between Porter and Cooke. 'The first time I got the ball I just ran at Cooke and he wouldn't tackle me,' Porter later recalled. 'At the first tackle he just jumped on my back and I kept on running. I ran at him every chance I could after that. When he ran, he tried to get between me and [Southland centre] Frank Townsend, and I just tackled him all day. Every time he tried to get past, he would accelerate to get through the gap but I tackled him.'

About twenty minutes into the game, the ball went into a Southland scrum. As it reached halfback A.W. 'Tubby' Holden, Bell launched into a decoy sprint down the blindside. Holden dummied the captain's way then fired a huge pass to Porter on the open side. 'Pot!' Holden yelled—an order for a drop kick at goal, worth four points.

The dummy move bought Porter time to collect himself. He fired off the kick, lost his footing and landed on his rump. But the ball went over. To everyone's surprise, Southland were up 10–0.

Wairapara seemed to wake up to their predicament. Under pressure, the visitors were penalised for an illegal tackle. The home side converted the error into three points, and shortly afterwards their backs set off on a charging run. Bell unsuccessfully tried to intercept the ball rather than tackle, which left Wairarapa with an overlap against which the last defender, Porter, was helpless. The Shield holders scooted in for the try, worth three points. Bell apologised to Porter and said it wouldn't happen again. The conversion missed, but Southland's lead was shorn to 10–6. 'Within ourselves we knew we were doing well but our supporters in the grandstand must have had the horrors,' said Porter.

Wairarapa's star back line began looking dangerous. They set up another attack, but Townsend scooped up a dropped pass and tore away. As he went down in a tackle he passed to wing Brian Mahoney, who scored. Porter's conversion rebounded off the posts.

The challengers' 13–6 lead didn't hold for long. Wairarapa returned charged up after half-time, and it took them just eight minutes to level the scores, with a drop goal and a penalty. Their renewed energy backfired when Bird was taken in a late tackle. Porter landed the penalty. Back in the lead, Southland went on attack but were stymied by solid defence. With ten minutes to go, Porter ran the ball up the field. Cooke and another defender caught him in a tackle, but momentum carried him to within a metre of the tryline. He offloaded to Bird, who scored. Porter's kick was disallowed, but they were up 19–13.

'The home side then exerted every effort,' one newspaper reported. 'Wairarapa made many fierce rushes, but the defence stood solid.' Finally, Wairarapa broke through with a try by All Black Clinton Stringfellow. It wasn't converted, leaving them three points behind. They continued to pound the opposition line. Minutes before full-time, Cooke made a brilliant run, with Stringfellow on his outside and only the Southland fullback, H.W. 'Biff' Norris, to overcome. With Wairarapa just needing a draw to retain the Shield it looked certain it would remain in Cooke's shop. As Cooke passed, Norris got a finger to the ball, just hard enough to deflect it away. Wairarapa were still attacking when time sounded. Southland had won by a fingertip.

'The tension was nerve-wracking,' wrote *Southland Times* rugby correspondent Albie Keast. 'The impossible was turned into the possible, and as the final bell went about sixty voices in the crowd of 4000 opened up a roar which must have been heard in Southland. The scene that followed was a memorable one. Managers, emergencies, supporters, local well-wishers and even pressmen dashed out onto the field in a wild stampede and for a minute went mad with excitement. It was a great day, not only for Southern rugby, but for Southland. Southland had lifted the Shield, and in doing so astounded the rugby world.'

A Wairarapa reserve was promptly despatched to the main street of Masterton to fetch the Shield from Cooke's shop in time for the after-match function. Once Cooke had got over the shock, he approached Porter and shook his hand, telling him he'd never spent so much time on the ground in a match.

'It was just one of those days,' Porter told McConnell. 'We started off on the right foot and they didn't lift their effort until too late.'

The *Dominion* reporter blamed the upset on Wairarapa's complacency. 'It is the unexpected that turns the tide of the battle, and over confidence is always disastrous. Both these had a lot to do with the defeat of Wairarapa.' The *NZ Truth* called the home side's performance 'as lively as stale ginger beer' and declared that Southland deserved the surprise win. 'That they would win was an idea not even lightly entertained and it can therefore be readily understood that the result of the game was nothing less than a sensation.'

Southland won its next three Shield challenges before going down 3–12 to Wellington in Invercargill in September 1930.

3

BILLY SAVIDAN

It's not over till it's over

WITH DAYS TO GO until the New Zealand team sailed to Canada for the inaugural British Empire Games (now the Commonwealth Games), Auckland runner Billy Savidan still didn't know if he'd be on the ship.

Savidan was the country's fourth-choice track and field athlete for the small 1930 Games team and had never attempted a six-mile race, the distance he'd be running on the opening day if he made the team. The 28-year-old stonemason had plenty to prove. He'd taken up running seriously only after he'd been forced as a teenager to give up a jockey apprenticeship because he'd put on too much weight. He'd been snubbed by Olympic Games selectors two years earlier despite being in the best form of his life, having won national titles in shorter distances and cross-country. He'd also spent years playing second fiddle to 1920s New Zealand track sensation Randolph Rose. When Rose had come out of retirement a few months earlier to beat Savidan in a three-mile race, an *Auckland Star* columnist had said the 'great' victory showed Rose was still the better man.

Faced with limited funding, and with the Great Depression starting to strangle New Zealand, athletics officials had decreed that if Savidan's supporters couldn't raise his money on his behalf, he'd be left behind. They figured they had better chances in javelin thrower Stan Lay, sprinter Allan Elliott and field all-rounder Ossie Johnson. As the RMS *Aorangi* was being prepared for the journey at the Auckland docks, Savidan's fundraising campaign was still £40 short of its £135 target.

Then, three days before the deadline, two Auckland men described by *The Evening Post* as 'enthusiastic amateur sportsmen' pledged to cough up the £40. As they scrambled to produce the money, Savidan waited for the national officials to confirm his inclusion. Two days passed with no word. On the eve of departure, as the team assembled for a civic farewell in Auckland, the regional official in charge of Savidan's campaign made an announcement to the press. 'It was only at eleven o'clock this morning, exactly 24 hours before the time of the team's sailing that we were given a definite statement that Savidan was to go to the Games,' he said. 'We have to give a cheque for £100 tomorrow and the balance has to be found within fourteen days.'

On 1 July 1930, Savidan boarded the *Aorangi*. At 11.15 a.m., with a flutter of handkerchiefs from the crowd and three blasts from the liner's whistle, the ship burst through 1000 coloured streamers and set off. Savidan had overcome his first challenge. More were to come.

For eighteen days, in choppy seas, Savidan trained as best he could on the rolling ship's 230-metre C Deck. The team arrived in Canada at the same time as a month-long heatwave.

Despite the unfamiliar conditions Savidan's build-up was promising. A few days before the opening ceremony he ran a fast six-minute time trial in 40-degree heat, relying on the stamina he'd built up through his systematic training. 'After a month he was as dark as mahogany,' wrote journalist Norman Harris. 'His eight stone 13 pounds was all bone and muscle. But the New Zealanders did not know what were his chances of winning. Savidan himself had never talked a lot; now he made no predictions for the race.'

Savidan's event was scheduled for the early evening of 16 August—the opening day of the Games—in Hamilton, Ontario. He spent a good deal of the afternoon walking in the opening parade at the stadium, in searing heat, and standing to attention listening to speeches and royal telegrams.

At 5 p.m. he fronted up for the race in his uniform of black shorts and singlet with the silver fern on his chest. He was the only Australasian in the line-up, which was a disadvantage because it left him short of running allies. The other athletes—from Canada, England and Scotland—could run as teams, taking turns to set the pace, sheltering in each other's slipstreams and setting up their fastest runners for the win. He'd also never raced on a hard cinder track. And he'd never even watched a six-mile race, let alone competed in one.

For the first half of the race, Savidan settled in the middle of the field as the English and Scottish runners hustled for the lead, setting a blistering pace. The Canadians ran as a pack at the back of the field, planning a late surge when the visitors flaked in the heat. Near the halfway point Savidan made a charge. The two strongest English runners thwarted him, and the Scots followed. He fell back.

As the Canadians had hoped, the leading runners began to tire, and their pace slipped. Savidan powered to the front. 'With his long, strong stride and low-slung arms, he was moving with the deceptive speed of a U-boat,' reported Harris.

The English pack immediately boxed him in—one in front, one outside him and one on his heels—trying to break his rhythm. He slowed, let them pass, then swung out and tore ahead. For a lap they chased, but the New Zealander's fitness was too great. As Savidan launched into the final two miles, only one other runner appeared to remain in the race—Englishman Ernie Harper, one of the favourites. Savidan and Harper began lapping the Canadians, whose game plan had imploded under the hectic pace.

'Savidan was moving along without the slightest appearance of being distressed, and as he swung along, the crowd commenced their cheering, which did not finish until the end of the struggle,' wrote the *Auckland Star*'s Games correspondent, Philippe Sidney de Quetteville Cabot.

An official held up a sign to Savidan with the number one on it—the signal that he had one lap to go. Some of the 15,000-strong crowd also saw it, and cheered. Savidan let loose. 'I'll make dead sure of this,' he told himself.

He pulled further and further ahead, burning up every last drop of his physical and mental reserves, determined to leave knowing he'd run the hardest race of his life. He charged around the lap, tore through the last bend, sprinted down the straight and crossed the finish line in a desperate rocking stride, nearly 300 metres ahead of Harper. He staggered to a halt, standing unsteadily with his hands on his hips, wondering vaguely why they hadn't put tape out for the winner.

Over his panting and the thundering of his heartbeat he heard yelling: 'Another lap! Another lap!' A gun fired—the signal that the leaders were entering the last lap. Dazed, Savidan looked at the lap sign. It still showed the number one. The official had blundered a lap ago, raising the wrong sign. 'From one of my easiest races it turned into my hardest,' Savidan said, later. 'I had stopped dead at the finish line, and I had to get moving again. The field was closing in.'

Harper had eaten up two-thirds of Savidan's lead and was just coming onto the straight. Savidan lurched back into the middle of the track. 'He managed to drag himself into motion again,' wrote Harris. 'He could scarcely move. He felt sick and weak. He was gulping for air, almost in tears with the shock.'

The crowd leapt to its feet, shouting at him to keep going. Harper, realising what had happened, saw his chance of gold and picked up his pace. 'Savidan's head went back, he almost overbalanced backwards,' wrote Harris, 'and then he swayed forward, almost toppling over. And so he staggered on in swaying surges—a Chaplin-like figure, only it was frightening instead of funny. At the end of the straight he staggered badly, and he weaved right over to the outside of the track. The fence appeared to bring back to him a sense of direction and on he fought again around the bend towards the bottom of the finishing straight.'

With 100 metres to go, Harper closed in. Screaming spectators leapt the fences. At the bottom of the straight, Savidan appeared to stop and peer along the track. The crowd fell silent. 'Then he gathered himself at last and began to beat his way down the straight,' wrote Harris. 'He was going to do it, and the crowd broke loose with a roaring, shouting, cheering ovation. He came on mechanically, no expression on his face, all the way down the straight until he had broken through the white tape.'

Savidan stumbled on blindly past the finish line, his legs working of their own volition. Ossie Johnson ran over from the long jump and Allan Elliott leapt a fence to get to him. One on either side, they held him up and walked him to a halt. He had to be propped up on the medal dais to be presented with the first ever gold medal of the Empire Games. He'd come within a minute of the long-standing world record, despite his rest stop and nightmare last lap.

In the *Auckland Star* de Quetteville Cabot declared he 'could never wish to see a finer effort' than Savidan's. 'No competitor more deserved the honours ... It was a fitting triumph to the New Zealander's persistence and ability, but as everyone of that huge crowd stood with bared heads as the band played "Land of Hope and Glory" and the New Zealand flag flew aloft as part homage to outstanding prowess, I paused to think of those loyal admirers of sport who, in the face of a reproachful indifference and unsatisfactory arrangements, finally made it possible to send abroad one who, in every sense, would bring the greatest credit to any country in the world. It was Savidan's day, and therefore New Zealand's day.'

Later, in the changing rooms, Savidan turned to Johnson. 'Did I win?' he asked.

'Of course. Can't you remember?' replied Johnson.

'I can remember heading for the tape,' said Savidan.

Savidan shut himself in the shower, and crumpled. 'I saw black and collapsed for the first time in my life,' he said, later. When he revived, he staggered back to his teammates. 'I think I'm going mad,' he said. They dressed him, took him back to the emptying stadium and walked him around the track to keep his circulation going. 'It took me weeks to get over the strain,' he recalled. 'I was really fooled in that race. It was a good job I didn't step off the track when I stopped—otherwise I would have been disqualified.'

Two years later, he placed fourth in the 5000 metres and 10,000 metres at the Los Angeles Olympics—after again enduring a battle for selection—but he always rued his non-selection for the 1928 Amsterdam Olympics. 'I was at my peak. I never really did find out why I didn't get picked,' he told journalist Joseph Romanos many years later.

By the time he retired, in 1937, at the age of 35, Savidan had won three national one-mile titles, seven three-mile titles and six ten-kilometre cross-country titles, and set—and reset—New Zealand records in each event. He died in 1991, aged 89. One of his records stood until 2002.

4

NORMAN READ

The spectator who dreamed of glory

IN 1956 A DISAPPOINTED Norman Read bought himself a spectator's ticket for the 50 kilometre racewalk at the Melbourne Olympic Games. The 25 year old had missed out on selection for both his native Britain and his adopted homeland, New Zealand, despite being the latter's fastest racewalker. Watching the action from the stands would be humbling, but at least he could cheer for his good mate Bill Baillie, who looked a sure bet for Olympic selection in middle-distance running.

Portsmouth-born Read had first discovered racewalking as a child, during World War II, when he was evacuated to the town of Steyning, in Sussex. Steyning's big annual event was an Easter Monday walking race that involved almost everyone in the town.

Though Read played other sports, including cricket and rugby, he was soon hooked on racewalking.

Racewalking is a technically rigorous sport with strict rules that forbid loss of contact with the ground. In 1956, the rules specified that the athlete's back toe could not lift until the front heel touched the ground, and the front leg had to be straightened 'for at least one moment'. Fouls are spotted and enforced by observers along the course and can lead to disqualification. The distinctive pelvis-swivelling, heel-and-toe movement has often been ridiculed, with one American commentator famously comparing the sport to 'a contest to see who can whisper the loudest'. But Read loved the technical discipline and the challenge of maintaining precise form while moving at speed.

Physically, Read was an unlikely athlete. He was splay footed and at fifteen had been diagnosed with scoliosis, or curvature of the spine. For the next six years he had worn a brace that he removed only for sleeping and competing. Nonetheless, he had won several junior national walking titles and dreamed of racing at the Olympics.

His career took a backward step when he emigrated to New Zealand in 1953 and discovered there were no roadwalking races in his new country. Long-distance walking was Read's forte, and he struggled with the comparatively short track races. In his first two seasons his best result was a definitive third in a three-man race.

By 1956 roadwalking had grown in prominence inter-nationally, and in that year a New Zealand roadwalking championship was held for the first time. Read took national titles in the 20 kilometre and 50 kilometre events but was passed over by both the British and the New Zealand Olympic selectors. He wasn't well known in New Zealand, and his best time for the

50 kilometre event was 30 minutes slower than the world record, set that year.

Read wasn't prepared to give up. In May, six months before the Olympics were due to take place, he moved to Melbourne, determined to prove he was worthy of the silver fern in the very city the Games would take place. He found work as a gardener and spent all his spare time training on the planned Olympic route.

In September he took the Australian 50 kilometre title on the Olympic course in a time just two minutes short of the Olympic record. He'd proved he could compete at Games level, and the selectors could no longer discount his abilities. Two weeks later he was named in the New Zealand team. He would not need that spectator's ticket after all.

His elation was tempered when questions were raised over the eligibility of such a recent migrant to represent New Zealand. The matter was referred to the International Olympic Committee, and his selection was approved only after an anxious wait.

A few nights before the race, Read had a vivid dream. He was dressed in his black singlet and shorts, eyes raised, arms and hips swinging rhythmically as he closed in on the leader, Russia's Yevgeniy Maskinskov. At the 45-kilometre mark, Read passed Maskinskov and strode away to the finish line in first place.

When awake, Read harboured no such ambitions. He didn't think he had a chance of winning against the world's best. His fastest time was well short of many of the European competitors and still 25 minutes slower than the world record. His goal was simply to finish in the first dozen.

He almost didn't start at all. Before the race, the officials and the 21 competitors assembled in a dressing room tucked deep within the labyrinthine passages beneath the grandstand of the

Melbourne Cricket Ground. 'I decided to have one more nervous one while we were all in the dressing room,' Read later recalled. 'When I came back, they'd gone. I panicked and raced around trying to get to the track. I made it with two minutes to spare. When I came running out, the crowd all laughed.'

With the help of some good-natured teasing from his competitors Read soon relaxed. His plan was to maintain a consistent pace throughout the race. He'd calculated that he'd need to complete the opening two-and-a-half laps of the cricket ground in two minutes per lap to keep up with his competitors. To his surprise he found himself leading the pack out of the stadium. 'To me that seemed crazy,' he told broadcaster Murray Deaker in 1993. 'I felt that any fool could lead out—it was leading in that really counted.'

He eased up on the pace, dropping in with the pack. It was 31 degrees, with blistering heat radiating from the surface of the road and a north-westerly blasting waves of hot air over the competitors. As they made their way down St Kilda Road and out towards the eastern edge of the city, the walkers rose and dipped over the numerous hills that made the course one of the toughest ever raced in an Olympics.

Read walked conservatively, content to let the others set the pace. The conditions were trying, but after six months of training he knew every inch of the out-and-back Olympic course. He also knew he could handle the heat. He just had to remain patient.

At fifteen kilometres he was in fifth place. By the halfway mark he'd moved up to third, as the heat began to wear down his competitors. Soon after the turn he learned that one of the leaders had been disqualified, putting him in second place. With no Australians in the running, local spectators began cheering for Read, who'd become a familiar sight on the route. 'The crowd . . .

were very encouraging and they kept telling me I was doing well, that I was going faster than the leader,' he recalled. He found this hard to believe, but the undulating course prevented him from seeing the walker in front to confirm the news.

At 35 kilometres Read finally sighted the leading man. It was Maskinskov. Read began his charge. By 40 kilometres he could see he was making progress. At 42 kilometres he crossed to the other side of the road to pass Maskinskov in a low-key manner, hoping to avoid reigniting the Russian's competitive spirit. The two matched strides for the next three kilometres, but Read slowly inched ahead.

By 45 kilometres—just as in his dream—a smiling Read had taken an 82-second lead. All he had to do was hang on until the finish line. He kept his pace steady, maintaining his focus and his form as the spectators cheered, 'Come on, Kiwi!'

Back at the Melbourne Cricket Ground, the 117,000-strong crowd strained to see who would be first home. In New Zealand, fans gathered around the wireless as announcer Lance Cross declared, 'And there's the black uniform—and listen to that crowd.'

When Read entered the stadium and caught sight of the roaring, waving crowd, he smiled broadly. 'I was tingling all over,' he told Deaker.

To the spectators, Read appeared just as fresh as at the start of the race. He waved to the crowd, maintaining his energetic form as he paced around the track. He felt as if he were walking on a cloud. 'Today I saw Kiwis crying,' wrote Noel Holmes in the *Auckland Star*. 'They were grown men and they wiped their eyes unashamedly as below them a slight black figure pounded his way round the oval track of the Olympic stadium, heel and toe, heel and toe.'

As Read crossed the finish line, he raised both hands, waved once more and began to run, then dance in delight. He'd taken New Zealand's fourth ever Olympic gold with a winning time of four hours, 30 minutes and 42.8 seconds.

He stayed beside the track to clap home Maskinskov two minutes and fifteen seconds later, and then the bronze medallist, Sweden's John Ljunggren. He greeted both men with a hug and a kiss. Only six of the 21 competitors completed the course in less than five hours, and another six failed to finish at all.

Read ran to the stands to greet Baillie, who leaned over the fence railing and embraced him. After missing out on selection, Baillie had taken Read's spectator's ticket.

Asked by a journalist whether he was British or a New Zealander, Read declared, 'I'm a Pommie Kiwi and proud of it.'

As he stood on the dais and the New Zealand flag was raised to the tune of 'God Save the Queen', he cried and kissed his medal. Thoughts rushed through his mind: *Here am I, the lad from Steyning in Sussex who immigrated to New Zealand, and here am I at the top position in the world.* He later told Deaker, 'It was incredible and very difficult to accept and to believe. In fact, after I finished that night I never slept, I just couldn't believe that here was I an Olympic champion. But I've said many times since, when I look back on it, I guess I was lucky. I happened to win an event one Saturday afternoon.'

Read added a Commonwealth bronze medal to his collection, at the Kingston Commonwealth Games, in 1966. He died from a heart attack in 1994, aged 62, while competing in a cycling race at Pirongia.

5

PETER SNELL

'He'll never get anywhere'

ON A BALMY SUMMER MORNING in Rome, four runners lined up in the Stadio Olimpico for an 800 metres heat at the 1960 Olympic Games. The result appeared a foregone conclusion: the first three would qualify for the next round. American Ernie Cunliffe was ranked third in the world in that distance, and Christian Wägli from Switzerland fifth. Hungarian István Rózsavölgyi was the reigning 1500 metres world champion. Several other athletes had been scratched.

Next to this intimidating trio stood an introverted 21 year old from the tiny New Zealand town of Te Aroha. Peter Snell had raced outside New Zealand only once in the past, had switched from tennis to running just two years earlier and had been on crutches a year before, recovering from a stress fracture to his tibia. After his first practice run on the track in Rome, he'd vomited in the dressing rooms. His running shoes were made by his coach, an unknown Auckland shoemaker named Arthur Lydiard. He was ranked 26th in the world, and just a few years earlier his only claim to athletics fame had been as the third-best runner at Auckland's Mount Albert Grammar School.

His broad physique seemed unpromising for a middle-distance runner. The world record holder and gold medal favourite, Belgian Roger Moens, once said about Snell; 'He'll never get anywhere with his build—he's too heavy.' A *Sports Illustrated* journalist later wrote, 'The usual runner is like a Jaguar. Snell is a Sherman tank—with overdrive.' Up in the broadcasting box, the BBC commentator was dismissive. 'This is ridiculous,' he was reported to have muttered. 'A four-man field and you can write down the first three names before the race starts.' Snell was the conspicuous absentee from the list.

Even back home in New Zealand, nobody expected much. The attention was focused more on Snell's teammate and fellow Lydiard protégé, 5000 metres contender Murray Halberg. When Snell's Olympic selection had been announced, the coach of overlooked athletics champion Marise Chamberlain had bitterly pointed out that Snell had only once run an official qualifying time. Over the same distance, Chamberlain had twice beaten the Olympic women's standard. 'I was very much under the radar,' said Snell, later, 'certainly a dark horse. I was up against all the best athletes from these big countries and I was just … the small-time New Zealand boy.'

Snell, however, quietly harboured hopes of making the final, encouraged by his pioneering coach. A key facet of Lydiard's method was to build endurance in middle-distance runners by having them run long distances in training. 'The New Zealand coaches were very critical of what I was doing, quite derisive in fact,' Lydiard said, afterwards. 'They scoffed at an 800 metre man running marathons.'

After New Zealand officials refused to take Lydiard to Rome for the Olympics, his athletes and their supporters had fundraised to get him there. Even then, he wasn't allowed in the Games village. He found lodgings five kilometres away and cycled or ran back and forth, meeting his runners outside the village gates.

One thing, at least, had worked in Snell's favour. Within days of the start of racing, the officials had changed the rules to include a quarterfinal, which meant two races on the first day instead of one, with semifinals on the following day, and the final the next. Lydiard was delighted. 'This', he told Snell, 'is going to be a test of stamina and you are probably the only athlete prepared to stand four races in three days.'

The heat began. Wägli led until the straight, when the tall bloke in the black singlet passed him to comfortably take the win, in a personal best time. Even Snell's teammates were taken aback.

That afternoon, with the temperature soaring, Snell limbered up for the quarterfinal. The big name in the line-up was Moens. In the first lap, Snell appeared lost in the back of the field. Gradually he moved up, battling weariness. Just over halfway, he surged ahead to take the lead. Moens challenged. Snell glanced behind. They were clear of the rest of the field, so he eased up and crossed the line in second place, knowing it was enough to qualify for the semifinal.

Afterwards, New Zealand chef de mission Harold Austad approached Snell, the following day's semifinal on his mind. 'Well, Peter, tomorrow's the big day, eh?'

Unblinking, Snell replied, 'No, Mr Austad. The day after tomorrow is the day.' His mind was already on the final.

Snell and Moens met again in the semifinal. This time, Snell sought to unsettle Moens and didn't let up, crossing the line first in a time that would have been good enough to take the gold in any previous Games. The earlier semifinal that day had been even faster, with Jamaican George Kerr breaking the Olympic record and retaining his position as the quickest 800 metres runner so far that year.

Despite his solid lead-up, Snell was widely expected to finish last in the final. 'I was not worried,' Lydiard said, later. 'I knew that we had reached the point where Peter's stamina would be the deciding factor. There were only six in the final and Adidas gave gifts to five of the finalists. They didn't consider Peter a medal prospect, so they didn't give him a pair. So the other five runners went out on the track wearing nice new Adidas shoes for the race, while Snell wore the plain white shoes I had made for him before we left New Zealand.'

(Snell's recollection differed: 'After my third elimination success, the representatives of Adidas wasted no time in reaching me with samples of their latest model. Undeniably, with their world-dominating experience, it was a far superior shoe to the one I was wearing but not for a moment did I entertain the idea of making a change. I'd become attached to those Lydiard shoes.')

For the final, the athletes were led 'like gladiators', according to Snell, halfway around the track to the start. Up in the press seats, American crooner Bing Crosby made a surprise appearance. He gestured with his pipe down to the track. 'Who's the big guy in black?' he asked an American journalist.

'Oh, that's Snell from New Zealand,' came the reply. 'He's run okay so far but the pressure will get to him here. He hasn't a show.'

Snell had drawn the unfavoured outside lane. The gun fired. He sprinted hard to the back straight, to the point he could break the lanes, and settled into fourth place.

'The crowd noise was so overpowering I didn't hear the time or the bell,' he later recalled. 'The pace was pretty hot and I began to feel it. In the middle of the back straight on the second lap I was supposed to make a race-winning move, but couldn't do it. At that point I felt I couldn't win. They were going too fast and I didn't have enough left. I stayed on the pole line and ran with the field, without attempting a decisive break. Moens came past and I could have tried to follow, but I didn't. I don't know why. I was so inexperienced I didn't realise that everyone would be feeling the pace, not just me. Sure enough, as we hit the straight, runners began dying out there. They were fading and gaps were opening up. It gave me renewed life.'

He stuck to the leaders, who ran four abreast into the final bend, leaving him no space to sneak through and no time to pass on the outside. His only chance was for them to split up. 'We swung into the straight. The runners spread out to make their drives to the tape. Suddenly I could see a way through. I discovered a gap in front of me and I edged past the fading pacemaker, Wägli. Here was a chance for third. Then only Moens and Kerr were in front of me and I had a clear run to the tape ahead. I realised I'd improved to a chance for second and put everything into a final sprint.'

Moens, in the lead, was unaware of Snell's break on the inside—he was busy checking for Kerr over his right shoulder. '[Kerr] was about three or four metres back,' Moens later recalled. 'I closed my eyes and I thought, "Roger, this time it's you—the Olympic champion." I opened my eyes and I saw Peter Snell to my left.'

Snell sensed Moens was slowing. 'With only 20 yards to go, I suddenly felt I could win. All I remember from that point is hurling every ounce of effort into the finish and flinging myself forward.' He ran the last half a yard with his eyes shut. 'The finishing line flashed past. I tottered about 10 yards and wrapped my arms round a convenient post in a feeling of exhaustion. I didn't know where I'd finished. I was just so delighted with my own performance I didn't care whether I was first or second.'

In the stands, Lydiard's view of the track had been obscured. New Zealand athlete Les Mills, sitting next to him, said, 'I think Peter won that.'

Out of Snell's sight, Moens collapsed and wept. When Snell was finally able to leave the security of the post, runners began to offer their congratulations. Among them was Moens.

'Who won?' asked Snell.

'You did,' said Moens.

A disbelieving Snell looked up at the scoreboard, waiting for confirmation. 'Finally up it went, "PG Snell NZL",' he recalled. 'When I saw those words, I felt a chill down my spine.' He'd won from Moens by 0.2 seconds and had broken the Olympic record— set the previous day by Kerr.

In the tunnels leading to the stadium, Halberg waited for his 5000 metres final. A few stragglers walked in from the arena with bewildered looks on their faces.

'Who won the 800 metres?' Halberg asked.

They shook their heads, incredulous. 'Snell,' they said.

The news energised Halberg. 'I couldn't believe it,' he wrote in his autobiography. 'That for me was the last piece of the jigsaw. I consciously remember a thought pattern, saying to myself, "Pete's won it, so can I."' And he did, creating a golden Olympic hour for New Zealand. After his win, Halberg collapsed beside the track, only vaguely aware of Snell leaning over him to check he was okay.

'I feel like I've been riding since I was born.' In 1928, New Zealander Harry 'The Mile Eater' Watson and his three Australian teammates battled sleep deprivation, sickness, inexperience and meagre resources as the first team from an English-speaking country to take on the Tour de France. The 1928 race is still considered one of the most gruelling in the event's history. (Bibliothèque nationale de France, courtesy of the New Zealand Sports Hall of Fame, Dunedin)

The courage and determination of the Australasian team won the support of the French crowds. In every town, Watson and his companions were greeted by an ovation, and cries of 'Vive les Australiens' spurred them towards the finish line. (National Library of Australia, vn3802604)

Southland winger Len Stubbs closes in for a tackle on Rawi Cundy in his side's David and Goliath battle against Wairarapa in 1929. The All Black-studded Wairarapa rugby team were so confident of shrugging off Southland's Ranfurly Shield challenge that they didn't even bring the shield to the game.
(*The Otago Witness*)

Dazed, Billy Savidan crosses the finish line to take out the first ever gold in an Empire Games. An error by a race official nearly cost him the win—and his health. (NZ Sports Hall of Fame)

Looking as fresh as when he started the race, Norman Read strides towards the finish line in the 50 kilometre racewalk at the 1956 Melbourne Olympics. (NZ Sports Hall of Fame)

Wearing the silver fern, Aucklander Billy Savidan sets off for the six-mile race in the 1930 British Empire Games in Hamilton, Ontario, Canada. Savidan squeaked into the New Zealand team for the Games with hours to spare. (NZ Sports Hall of Fame)

Peter Snell, a previously unknown runner from Te Aroha, blazes past a stunned Roger Moens of Belgium to win the gold medal for the 800 metres at the 1960 Rome Olympics. (John G. Zimmerman/Getty Images)

In 1962 Burt Munro became the sensation of Bonneville Speed Week when he set an American 55 cubic inch (900 cc) record of 178.971 mph (288 kph), with his Munro Special, a 42-year-old modified Indian Scout motorcycle equipped with a homemade streamliner. (Getty Images)

The New Zealand coxed four rowing team went to the 1968 Mexico Olympics as spare rowers for the favoured eight. They came home champions. Clockwise from left, cox Simon Dickie, Warren Cole, Ross Collinge, Dick Joyce and Dudley Storey. (NZ Sports Hall of Fame)

Ignoring the pain from badly burned hands, Denny Hulme leads his McLaren team to victory in the 1970 Can-Am series. Hulme had vowed to ensure the team's survival following the death of his teammate, close friend and fellow Kiwi Bruce McLaren. (Alvis Upitis/Getty Images)

Christchurch swimmer Jaynie Parkhouse celebrates her unexpected win at the 1974 Christchurch Commonwealth Games, with fellow gold-medal winners Richard Tayler (athletics) and Mark Treffers (swimming). (*The New Zealand Herald*)

Alexandra mechanic Peter Petherick stunned even himself when he bowled his way into the record books after his surprise inclusion in the New Zealand cricket team for their 1976 Pakistan tour. (*Otago Daily Times*)

The New Zealand men's hockey team (in white) weren't favoured to make it out of the pool round in the 1976 Olympic Games at Montreal. After a series of hard-fought battles, they made it to the top of the medal dais. (Getty Images)

Pioneering jockey Linda Jones (née Wilkinson), aged eighteen, rides Scots Bard to victory by a neck at the Bay of Plenty Racing Club's 1970 Powder Puff Derby. (*The New Zealand Herald*)

Digby Taylor prepares for the launch of *Outward Bound*, the 51-foot yacht he built in a boatshed in Auckland's Herne Bay for the 1981–82 Whitbread Round the World Race. (Alan Sefton/*Auckland Star*; courtesy of Digby Taylor)

The Whitbread fleet departs Auckland's Waitemata Harbour on Boxing Day 1981, bound for Mar del Plata, Argentina. (Paul Estcourt/*The New Zealand Herald*)

(New Zealand's only other medallist at that Games was another Lydiard athlete, Barry Magee, who won bronze in the marathon.)

Lydiard, for one, wasn't surprised by Snell's victory. 'He was unknown to the world, but not to me.' That night, he wrote in his journal, 'Snell's mental approach to the race and lack of nervous tension were remarkable.'

Snell not only repeated his feat at the 1964 Tokyo Olympics—winning the gold in the 800 metres—but doubled it, by also winning the 1500 metres. In 2000 he was officially named New Zealand Athlete of the Century. In his dazzling career, he also broke six world records, ran the first sub-four-minute mile in New Zealand—in a world record time—and won double gold in the 1962 British Empire and Commonwealth Games. Some of his New Zealand records still stood more than half a century later.

Lydiard's training system became the world standard for middle-distance runners, influenced every subsequent generation of New Zealand athletes and was credited for launching a worldwide jogging boom. Many years later he told a reporter Snell was the greatest middle-distance runner he'd ever seen. 'Sometimes I think of what he could do on those tracks and I just shake my head. He had bounce off the ground. He got life out of any surface, grass and shale. He had strength and speed, real speed, and that's why I place him above all the great ones. He just burned people away, he had so much power.'

Having proven himself, Snell retired from competition in 1965, aged only 26 and after just six years of international competition. 'Once you have acquired the knowledge of what a human being can make himself do, it becomes a powerful force in anything you aim to accomplish,' he wrote, presciently, in 1965. A decade later he embarked on an academic career in sports medicine in the United

States, leaving behind a job in sales and promotions for a cigarette company. Though he'd been an unpromising school student, he went on to earn a doctorate in exercise physiology and to take up a fellowship in the University of Dallas, in Texas, where he remained well into his seventies.

Snell always rated Rome as his best performance. 'I gave it everything and couldn't have done any better. Rome was absolutely thrilling, a disbelief-type thrilling. I was 21 and not much more than four years earlier I was third in my high school 880 yards, and by quite a large margin.'

6

BURT MUNRO

The pursuit of one good run

SHIELDING HIS EYES from the late summer sun, Burt Munro looked out across a blinding-white plain so vast he could almost see the curve of the earth. Waves of heat shimmered up from the salt crust, creating the mirage of a lake in the distance. It was August 1956. The 57-year-old speed freak, motorcycle salesman and self-taught engineer from Invercargill had jogged two and a half miles in 40-degree Utah heat to watch the German NSU motorcycle team attempt a world speed record on the Bonneville Salt Flats.

The 30,000-acre lake bed had been the scene of world record speed attempts since the 1930s. It flooded each winter then dried out in the harsh spring and summer sun, leaving a firm, smooth-as-concrete surface with excellent tyre grip. The Bonneville Speedway was a fifteen by ten mile strip on which the salt lay six inches thick, surrounded by plains of deep mud covered by a salty veneer that trapped any vehicle that went too far off course.

Standing on the salt watching Wilhelm Herz reach 210.64 miles (339 kilometres) per hour, the fastest speed ever recorded on a motorcycle, was one of the most astounding experiences of Munro's life. He turned to his new mate, timing official Roscoe Turner, and declared, 'Whatever I'm going to do in my life on a motorcycle, this is it.'

In the spring of 1920, at the age of 21, Munro had first laid eyes on an Indian Scout motorcycle, parked at the back of the Criterion Hotel in Invercargill. She was beautiful with her simple lines, soft red paint and tan leather seat. He could tell she was a goer, and he went straight to the local dealer to slap down his £140 of savings.

One month later, he drove away on his brand-new 37-cubic-inch (600-cc) motorcycle fresh off the ship from Massachusetts. Her official top speed was 50 mph, if he leaned over the handlebars. But like all his motorcycling mates, Munro tinkered constantly with the engine. He knew he could get more power out of her, so he taught himself the art of machining and mould making, creating all his components by hand. By the early 1930s he was pushing the Indian past 90 mph in races, compensating for her tiny brakes by dropping one foot to the ground and sliding into a turn when he wanted to stop, a crowd-pleasing move that became his trademark.

Sometimes his ideas worked; sometimes they didn't. The engine blew up hundreds of times, and Munro was hurled into skull-cracking, cartwheeling, teeth-shattering crashes. Each time, he'd simply start again, often with his head or his hands in bandages, and usually after an attempt to finish whatever race he was in. Some said he was delusional; others said he was crazy. But as long as he was working on his 'motorsickle', he was happy. In January 1940 he set his first New Zealand speed record, travelling 120.8 mph on his 20-year-old Indian, now known as the Munro Special.

He had other motorbikes over the years, but none meant as much to him as the Indian. His devotion to her even put strain on his twenty-year marriage to wife Beryl. The couple separated in 1945 when he announced plans to move his motorcycle into the front room.

With their four children grown and the family farm sold, Munro worked odd jobs until 1948, when he dedicated himself full time to his motorcycle. He built a concrete-block garage with one window and put a single bed in the corner and his ramped motorcycle stand in the middle. Along one wall, a collection of broken parts lay on a shelf marked 'Offerings to the God of Speed'. Rainwater was diverted into an open barrel and used equally for dousing newly cast pistons and filling the kettle to make suspiciously metallic-tasting tea. He began an overhaul of the Indian, often working sixteen-hour days and cranking the engine at all hours, to the annoyance of his neighbours.

By the mid-1950s, Munro was growing frustrated with New Zealand's speed trial possibilities. The conditions on Southland's Oreti Beach were too fickle, and every time he felt he'd done well at the Christchurch road speed trials, the timing equipment failed. All he wanted was one good run, one chance to test his life's work and see just how fast he could make her go. So in 1956, when a friend from the Southland Motorcycle Club announced plans to compete at Bonneville Speed Week, Munro decided to go along for a look. He felt instantly at home on the salt flats, swapping yarns with fellow motorcycle enthusiasts, record breakers and speed freaks.

Some were professional racers with large entourages; others were amateurs on shoestring budgets. Journalist Bill Bagnall was incredulous that Munro could have ridden a 1920 Indian Scout at an unofficial top speed of more than 130 mph and interviewed him at length for the popular *Motorcyclist* magazine. Munro made friends with officials and racing legends such as Marty Dickerson and Rollie Free. The latter famously set a record of 150.313 mph at Bonneville, stretched horizontally over his motorbike dressed only in red swimming trunks.

Munro returned home invigorated, inspired by the speeds achieved with the teardrop-shaped streamliner shells he'd seen at Bonneville. He resolved to build his own, eventually opting for an unconventional long and low fish-shaped design, after watching goldfish flash across the pond at Invercargill's botanic gardens. He built the aluminium shell by hand, placing each panel over a small bag of sand and beating it with a hammer to achieve the proper curvature. It took five years, and then, on the first test run, he discovered the shell was too tight to properly control the bike. It was time to start again, this time with fibreglass.

'He did everything the hard way,' Turner told filmmaker Roger Donaldson, who made a documentary about Munro in 1971, and later a feature film based on Munro's life. 'If you offered him the Douglas Long Beach Aeroplane Plant to work in, he'd rather gather a set of pliers, a hammer and a screwdriver . . . proving it could be done his way and work just as good.'

By 1962, Munro had the engine going well, but he knew the real test of his homemade streamliner would be the bike's stability at high speed. He'd need to go over 160 mph in a controlled area to prove his design and it was too dangerous to attempt such speed on the bumpy New Zealand roads. It was time for Speed Week in Utah.

The phrase 'on the smell of an oily rag' could have been coined for Munro. He began what became a familiar pattern of working his passage across the Pacific by washing dishes or doing odd jobs. On arrival in Los Angeles he bought a 1940 Nash with a cracked windscreen for $50, ripped out the back seat, installed a piece of ply and a mattress and, armed with a ten gallon drum of oil, hit the road for San Francisco to meet the cargo ship carrying the Indian.

The ship was delayed, and his only hope of collecting the bike in time for Speed Week was to carry on to Seattle, the vessel's first American port of call, some 850 miles over the mountains to the north. En route, the Nash lost first gear. As he coasted down the steep mountain roads, he would open the driver's door to act as an air brake, much to the surprise of oncoming traffic.

In Seattle, customs officials demanded a $10,000 bond to release the 'high-performance' motorcycle. Munro charmed his way up the customs hierarchy, eventually consulting a sympathetic lawyer who listened to his long tale, found a loophole and persuaded officials to release the bike, sending him on his way with 'the best of Scottish luck'.

The Nash crawled over the majestic Cascades, a mountain range extending from British Columbia in Canada to northern California. On the descent into eastern Washington state, the trailer came loose from the coupling, causing car and trailer—and Indian—to swing all over the road. Munro made a temporary fix with a pair of vice-grip pliers. Later, the bonnet flicked up, blocking his vision. He wired it shut, unwiring it every 100 miles to top up the leaking oil. On one stop he propped up the bonnet with the dipstick, as usual, only to absent-mindedly slam the bonnet shut afterwards, shooting the dipstick straight through the radiator. On another occasion, the clutch blew out, smashing into his foot and making it swell badly.

In all, Munro faced fifteen major problems with the Nash and considered it as big a challenge as his speed trial. But everywhere he went people were fascinated by his unusual streamliner, and his audacious dreams distracted a highway patrol officer from issuing a fine, and a lawyer and a mechanic from issuing bills.

By the time he arrived in Bonneville, Munro had travelled the greatest distance of any competitor. He felt anything but confident. His home-made streamliner looked rough and ready next to the sleek, futuristic and parachute-equipped designs of the professional teams. At 4300 feet (1300 metres) in altitude, the dry atmosphere reduced an engine's power by fifteen per cent of its power at sea level. Temperatures climbed above 40 degrees, and the wind could blow from any direction. Riders had to tweak the carburetion to suit the conditions, learn how their streamliner shells behaved at high speeds and come to grips with timekeeping and distance protocols.

Munro had seen how hard it was to attempt high speeds in an untried streamlined shell. He had no ambitions of setting records. All he wanted was one good run.

First, he had to pass a technical inspection. As he lined up, Free pointed out a patch of tyre where Munro had cut back too much tread, leaving the nylon cords exposed. 'They won't allow that,' said Free. 'You'll have to get another tyre.'

'Not a problem,' said Munro, and he proceeded to ensure the bare patch was on the ground every time he stopped.

The next issue was his clothing. Not fire resistant, said the officials. 'I got married in these pants,' protested Munro. 'Everybody knows wool is great for resisting flame . . . Besides, it's my flaming skin and bones, so what's your bloody problem?'

With the inspectors' reluctant sanction, Munro went on to

prove he could handle the bike with a low-speed run. American Motorcycle Association official Earl Flanders cast a curious eye over the home-made streamliner, which Munro planned to enter in the 55 cubic inch (900 cc) class. 'From memory that [record is] well over 170 miles an hour,' he said. 'You really think your old scooter can run anywhere near that?'

'I reckon we might,' Munro replied. 'We ran close to 150 on a road near home before we ran out of room.' He tucked his sandshoe-clad feet far into the streamlined shell, lying over the lowered and lengthened frame of the motorcycle so the curve of his back formed the top of the shell's fish shape. At 40 mph the bike began weaving by up to 18 inches (45 centimetres). Munro thought he'd be on the next boat home, but he pushed it up to 95 mph in second gear and, to his surprise, passed the handling test.

The following day he lined up for his qualifying run. He was still learning how to ride the new streamlined shape, and Free was worried about the weaving and the tyres. At high speed, centrifugal force can expand a rubber tyre by as much as two centimetres, and the Munro Special had less than one centimetre of clearance between the tyre and the frame. Free urged Munro not to go too fast. Munro disregarded the warning, averaging 174 mph in the qualifier, which was faster than the American national record.

The next morning, Munro pulled up for his record attempt. Dickerson and Free gave him a running push start and he was away, roaring over the salt at 179 mph. In the unfamiliar white environment, with no landmarks other than a black line and mile markers, Munro got lost. He continued six miles past the end of the nine-mile track, stopping only when his motor conked out.

Two spectators gave him a push-start back to the end of the track, where Dickerson and Free were waiting to refuel the tank and send him off on the return journey. Munro took off without raising the landing gear. As he fiddled with the lever, the engine almost died. He grabbed the clutch but gave too much throttle, and the bike slipped broadside on a near 90-degree angle.

Dickerson started to run. 'I figured he's going to be rolling like a cigar down the track,' he told Donaldson, later. Instead, Munro seized the clutch once again, gave some more throttle and swung broadside the other way. Free put his head in his hands, but Munro kept the bike balanced, straightened it up and stepped on the gas. 'I stood there with my mouth hanging open and my eyeballs popping out in disbelief,' Dickerson recalled. 'I said, "Earl Flanders should have seen this—if he ever thought this guy couldn't ride."'

But Munro made another error. After travelling just two miles he mistakenly thought he was entering the timed stages and opened up the engine to 180 mph. The front tyre started to rub against the frame, and fine rubber dust flew off, coating his goggles and every exposed part of his face. The engine was too fragile to race at full bore for long, and by the time he reached the actual timed stages, some three miles later, he'd already burned through a piston, and the exhaust pipe was scorching his leg. Disoriented, he decided to keep going until the bike stopped or blew up. He flew through the first timed mile at 178.5 mph, the second at more than 160 and the third at 145. Still he kept going, speeding through the finish line on one cylinder.

By the time Dickerson and Free reached the spectator area, there was no sign of Munro. 'I think he's gone back,' Free remarked. 'Back to whatever planet he came from, because he sure as hell ain't from this one!'

They found him more than two miles beyond the pit area, lying on his back in the shade of the bike. It was 42 degrees and had been even hotter inside the shell. He had severe chemical burns on his left leg caused by spilt fuel combined with the heat of the engine.

'The salt was very cool,' Munro told Donaldson. 'I was peeling the flesh off this leg in big hunks and throwing it on the salt . . . I had burned 60 square inches of my leg—cooked it. They told me I'd averaged 178 mph coming back. I said, "I don't believe it but if it's true, I'm never coming back and going through this again."'

The timekeepers ruled that Munro didn't qualify for a record because of a technicality. His supporters were furious, fellow competitors complained on his behalf, and newspapers and magazine editors took up the issue. But Munro was already thinking about what he could do to improve his speed. As soon as his leg was dressed, he worked non-stop for 48 hours, rebuilding the engine, raring to have another go.

Munro and his 42-year-old motorbike had become the sensation of Speed Week. Two young women working for trade suppliers noticed his frugal lifestyle and organised a whip round, presenting him with $350 and the Sportsman of the Year trophy engraved with 'Owner of the World's Fastest Indian'. To the women's horror and the crowd's amusement, Munro rewarded each with a fat smooch on the lips.

The Indian's engine proved too tired for another record attempt that week, but Munro stayed on, determined to sort out the stability issues. He built a steel mould, melted down 22 old batteries and created a lead brick to add weight to the front of the shell. 'I might as well have cut my throat then and there,' he said, later.

As soon as the bike was started, it began to wobble. Munro's solution was typical: add more speed. 'At 150 mph . . . I thought I'm a goner. I was getting heart shock—we're all scared to die when you can see it facing you—and she was snaking two-foot-six, leaving a five-inch-wide track. If it hadn't been a tight fit in the streamliner, I'd have been flung out . . . I figured I was going to die . . . So to save my life, I gave her full throttle and held it like that for another mile and a half.'

It made no difference. When he finally managed to slow the machine to 100 mph, he sat up, shifting the centre of gravity and at last the bike went straight. 'When my friends got down there I was laughing like hell . . . and I said, "Well, I should have been dead long ago, but I'm so pleased to be alive I can't help laughing!"'

Back home in Invercargill that Christmas, he received a letter and certificate—thanks to the lobbying of his supporters—confirming that his earlier run had indeed broken the American 55 cubic inch (900 cc) record, with a speed of 178.971 mph (288 kph). But Munro wasn't done yet. 'I think if a thing's worth doing, it's worth finishing,' he told Donaldson in 1971. 'I'm never going to give up till I get a good run . . . It's effort and concentration that makes life worthwhile—and nice ladies around are a big help.'

He set about rebuilding the engine and the shell. There was only one place to test his refinements at speeds of 170 mph: Bonneville. He arrived in San Diego in July 1963 to discover the cargo ship was late again. He bought an old Chrysler, drove to Vancouver and found that the Indian's crate had been crushed beneath a heap of fertiliser, which had cracked the shell across the handlebars and tail. He towed it to Bonneville and got to work.

On his qualifying run, it seemed as if he'd at last overcome the stability problems. Thrilled, he had high hopes of topping 200 mph. His speed trial began well. As he approached the end of the first timed mile, travelling about 195 mph, the motor blew up without warning. The damage was severe. Bonneville was over for 1963.

Munro spent 2000 hours rebuilding the motor. 'I just do it for the sport and the enjoyment, and to improve my work, to test what I've done, see whether it was right or wrong,' he told Donaldson. 'Anyone can buy a bike and go fast these days. I think there's a lot more in it and it's a lot more enjoyable to develop a slow machine to go fast . . . Riding it is only one hundredth of the experience.'

He returned to Bonneville in 1964, but bad weather rendered the track too rough to be usable. The same happened in 1965, but he went out on the salt anyway, only to break a vertebra and dislocate his spine.

For Speed Week in 1966, Munro decided to enlarge the capacity of the engine and move up to the 61 cubic inch (1000 cc) class. Before the end of the first timed mile, something upset the aerodynamics of the shell and it started to shake and weave. He was going faster than ever before, but the bike was out of control. Remembering his heart-shocking run of 1962, he sat up to shift the centre of gravity. The chief timekeeper remarked that he was going well over 200 mph. 'By this time the bike was snaking over the salt,' Munro later recalled, 'and if I hadn't sat up then I'd be killed because if you get thrown off your bike at this speed the salt just grinds through everything on you, down to the bone, provided you didn't break your neck or break a limb . . . You might skate for half a mile, depending on the frictional efficiency of your body.'

As he sat up, a blast of air tore the goggles from his face and almost lifted his crash helmet from his head. Blinded by the air and salt thrown up by his front wheel, he rode by instinct. He continued for seven miles, running into the rough four times and missing a steel pylon by just twenty centimetres. When he finally managed to slow the bike, he couldn't find the landing gear and it flopped on its side, sliding across the salt and badly wrenching his shoulder. The shell was split from cockpit to tail.

'Look at her—I'm done for 1966,' Munro told his supporters. But then he remembered some wire in the back of his borrowed panel van, and they set about hammering and wiring the Indian back together, out of sight of the officials.

To qualify for a record, Munro had to make his return within the hour. Once again, he was travelling more quickly than he ever had before until the first timed mile, when the bike started to wobble, building up to a half-metre weave. He lifted his head and his goggles whipped off. Blinded again, he kept the throttle open, shooting a mile and a half past the pit area before crashing and tearing his right shoulder. He'd achieved another American record of 168.066 mph (270 kph) for streamlined motorcycles in the 61 cubic inch class.

Thirty records were broken at Speed Week 1966, but none earned as many column inches as Munro's. His fame came not from his speeds but from the fact they were achieved by a 67-year-old man on a 46-year-old Indian Scout with many original components. But Munro was disappointed with his performance. He believed he'd been travelling much faster than the record suggested. Now he'd hit 200 mph—and some said he'd been travelling as fast as 212 mph— his ambition for one good run had been replaced by the desire to have his speed officially recorded at that level.

For once, Munro took a cautious approach. He knew the bike was capable of doing 200 mph, but he also knew that unless he could improve the stability, any large increases in power or speed could be fatal. Each incremental rise in speed would change the aerodynamic forces on the motor, frame and shell. Components that were perfectly stable at 170 mph would react completely differently at 200 mph, and as he had made the size and power of the engine greater, some parts had become more and more fragile.

The following year, at the age of 68, he hit 184 mph in his qualifying run, but a piston seized due to a split cylinder. Back at the motel, he thought his 1967 attempt was over until he spotted a cast-iron downpipe on the outside wall. He quickly procured a section and used it to replace the split cylinder. Later that week, he increased his official record by 15 mph to 183.58 mph, a record that still stood nearly half a century later. He was awarded the Top Record Breaker trophy and voted American Motorcyclist of the Year.

Munro made more than ten trips to Bonneville, where he was the oldest man both to make record attempts and to break a record. He once said that some of the bikes at Bonneville had cost thousands of dollars, 'whereas mine only cost a few months of hard work . . . well, 45 years'.

With trial and error, he'd augmented the power of the Indian Scout's engine to seven or eight times that of the original, modifying the original side-valved 600 cc V-Twin engine to a 1000 cc overhead valve. Although he never had an officially timed run of 200 mph, he did make a qualifying run of 191 mph in 1969, the highest speed ever recorded on an Indian.

When Munro died, at home, in January 1978, his car was loaded up ready to drive to Auckland for a motorcycle show. The pursuit of 'one good run' had been his life's work—not the glory of medals or records, but the satisfaction of taking his bike as fast as it could possibly go. He once said, 'You can live more in five minutes on a motorcycle in some of these events I've been in, than some people do in a lifetime.'

7

THE 1968 NEW ZEALAND COXED FOUR

'The funniest-looking crew you ever saw'

FOUR MONTHS BEFORE the 1968 Mexico Olympics, four men and a baby-faced teenager slid a skiff into the Avon River at Christchurch. It was their first time in a boat together, and not all were happy about it. The four oarsmen had been passed over for the New Zealand rowing eight, the country's big Olympic hope. For rowers of that era, being selected for the eight was the pinnacle of the sport—the equivalent of pulling on an All Blacks jersey. They were well aware that this four was an afterthought—they were spare rowers invited to the pre-Olympics training season only in case someone had to withdraw from the eight. With funding and coaching concentrated on the eight, and with the notoriously fickle national selectors to convince, there was no guarantee the unfavoured four would even get to the Olympics.

Only one of the crew, Dudley Storey, had any real international racing experience. Dick Joyce had been rowing for just four seasons. Stocky Warren Cole had been told by a sports science expert that he didn't have the physique for rowing and should stick to swimming. Cox Simon Dickie was only seventeen, freshly plucked from his school rowing team after champion first-choice cox Alan Boykett was killed in a boating accident on Wellington Harbour. Joyce had been with Boykett that day and had desperately searched the murky water for his friend before police ordered him to hospital to be treated for cuts to his face. 'Alan was a great cox,' he said, later. 'His loss was a huge blow.'

That winter day in Christchurch, the crew's minds weren't on the job when they pushed out into the river in a borrowed boat, with borrowed oars. They promptly toppled out, right in front of the Avon Rowing Club. 'Someone didn't put the oars on properly, and that's how we fell out,' the fifth crewman, Ross Collinge, later told journalist Peter Bidwell for the book *Reflections of Gold*. 'The oars floated out of the gates. It would normally be the first thing that you would check on getting into the boat. It was our own fault, a basic novice mistake. I went home for a break not long after, and I said to my wife, Valerie, "I don't want to be in the four, I want to be in the eight."'

Olympic rowing coach Rusty Robertson evidently had as much faith in the four as they did in themselves. 'When they got together, they were they funniest-looking crew you'd ever seen,' he said. Assistant coach Ted Lindstrom called them 'rubbish' and a 'rebellious bunch'.

Despite their shaky position in the squad, the four had left families and jobs to be in Christchurch for the twelve-week training session. Storey and his wife had rented a $5-a-week house on the banks of the Avon that was earmarked for demolition. 'We'd take a deep breath and run down the hall from the kitchen to the bedroom and leap under the covers.'

They took jobs while in Christchurch, to get by. Cole would get up at 7 a.m., cycle seven kilometres to work and back, and start training at 3 p.m., a mixture of gym work, running and rowing. 'All the guys worked,' he later recalled. 'They worked hard—they had to support either themselves or their families. There was no other way of living—there were no other financial benefits.' They also had to fit in fundraising, holding raffles in pubs, organising copper trails and even going door-to-door asking for twenty cent pieces, watching curtains flicker and doors remain closed. It was a hard slog through a foggy, rainy, cold winter.

The men struggled to hit their stride. They were told they simply didn't look right in the boat. Their motivation flagged. During one particularly messy training, Lindstrom called across the river, 'For Christ's sake, you're wasting our time, just stop, will you? This boat is getting worse.' The skiff drew to a halt, and Lindstrom, who'd been doing most of the coaching while Robertson concentrated on the eight, asked why they were going so badly.

Joyce and Collinge admitted they were struggling to follow the stroke rhythm of the man in front of them in the boat. Said Joyce, 'We go 20 or 30 strokes and we get a glimmer of how we should be going, and then it crashes out.'

'It's not working, it's getting worse,' Collinge remarked, adding a few curses. 'I feel like going home.'

Lindstrom made a couple of seating changes. They seemed to

work, and the team began concentrating on building rhythm and speed. When Joyce suggested another position swap, however, Robertson flatly forbade it. It put the rowers in a difficult spot. 'Robertson was always the boss,' Joyce told journalist Joseph Romanos. 'When he said "jump", it wasn't a question whether you jumped but how far. He commanded fantastic respect. He was very good technically.'

One weekend, while Lindstrom was laid up in hospital for an operation and Robertson was away at a wedding, the team secretly experimented with different configurations. Collinge assumed the key position of stroke—the rower closest to the stern, who sets the rhythm. They went for a series of long rows and at last began feeling comfortable.

When Robertson returned, they nominated the forthright Joyce to break the news. 'We've done some experimenting over the weekend and we all think the boat is going a lot better,' he ventured. 'We're not trying to usurp your authority, and we'll change back to what you had before, but we still believe the boat is better now.'

Robertson said nothing, but he didn't look happy. He remained silent as he followed them down the river in the training boat. Collinge related the plan for the return home to Dickie. When they arrived back, 'Rusty brought his boat in, and stomped off into the dark, still without making any comment,' Joyce later told Bidwell. 'As we hauled our boat into the shed we wondered what to do now. We were left thinking at least he didn't say no. But there was still a strong feeling we were in the shit. We'd done things directly against Rusty's instructions, and we knew if we didn't make them work, we'd never wear the black singlet again.

'Rusty was God to us. He had established quite a reputation for getting excellent results with his crews, and what we'd done was tantamount to treason. We'd thumbed our noses at him. We just got on with it, and he never mentioned [it]. For quite some time we felt we were there very much under sufferance.'

Despite the tension, they trained hard, still harbouring dreams of making the eight and securing their Olympic passage. As they progressed, Robertson decided to mix things up. He split the eight into a bow four and a stern four, and raced them against the coxed four, for practice. As he expected, the teams from the stronger eight dominated—initially. But the four knuckled down. Eventually, they began to win.

One day, after a win by the coxed four, Robertson made what Joyce considered to be a provocative comment, and Joyce let rip: 'Today we beat the stern four more times than they beat us. Next week we're going to beat them every time, and just watch us do it, and then, sir, we're going to ask you why we aren't in the bow of the eight. Good morning, sir.'

Two weeks out from the announcement of the New Zealand Olympic team, the four raced the entire eight over a long stretch of the Avon and led almost the whole way. '[The eight] got us right at the very, very end,' recalled Storey, 'but we said to ourselves, "We now know that this is fast. We now know!" Because they just couldn't get past, no matter what they did, and that was a very fast eight. They were set for a medal.'

Storey lobbied for the teams to be reconfigured, believing the four had proven themselves to be the stronger rowers and deserving of promotion. He got the next best thing—an assurance that the four were no longer just considered spares, and their team would not be cannibalised for the eight. In early July, during a nervous gathering at the Avon club, the coxed four heard their names read out by the Olympic selectors over the radio, alongside the eight.

There was still the question of money. While funding for the higher priority eight was assured, the rowing community scrambled to cover the four. Though they made it with days to spare before departure, funds didn't stretch to a ticket for Lindstrom, the four's main coach. The crew felt that Robertson was focused on the eight, and Lindstrom's exclusion left them largely on their own. (Robertson later told Romanos he'd known the four were as good a crew as the eight and had spent equal time with each team.)

Coach or no coach, the crew were determined. 'The boys were absolutely focused in their desire to win and that became an extraordinary motivation,' Dickie said. 'It was a step into the unknown. Except for Dudley, none of us had really raced internationally, and we knew we had to get it right straight away. Rusty was very good—he talked the guys through what might have been a lack-of-belief threshold.'

The members of the New Zealand Olympic team were among the first athletes to arrive in Mexico City, to allow their bodies to acclimatise to the potentially dangerous elevation. Medical staff told some of the rowers they'd be lucky if everyone came back alive.

The crew eased themselves into training and continued to gain confidence. But when a member of the eight, Mark Brownlee, developed health problems, Joyce was subbed into the bigger crew. His replacement struggled to fill a position he was unfamiliar with, and Joyce continued to train with the four on the sly. It meant an exhausting four training sessions a day for him. When Robertson found out, several days later, he said it couldn't continue. 'I will do it honestly for as long as it is necessary to keep both boats on the water,' replied Joyce. 'Please don't ask me to make a decision one way or the other, because you know what the four has been through together to get here, you know that you have said that you would not sabotage the four for the eight, you know where my loyalties lie and, frankly, you might not like my answer.' Brownlee was promptly returned to the eight, and Joyce rejoined the four.

Storey, meanwhile, was fighting stiffness and agonising pain in his left elbow. The team's doctor, he recalled, 'had this big horse needle, which he jammed in between the bones of the elbow. He said it could be a waste of time.' It worked.

When they lined up for their heat, it was their first race as a team, and Dickie's first big race out of a school uniform. They were warned to take it easy because of the altitude. They figured they couldn't afford to. They went out strong and finished first. 'We didn't want to get sucked into what the medicos were saying,' recalled Storey. 'The problem was, when we got to the end we were so shagged we couldn't get out of the boat. But nobody knew that because the other little strategy that we had was that regardless of what happens, when we hear the bell go at the end, we've just got to keep on rowing to the dock. We're not going to stop. Just don't stop. Another 200 metres, all we have to do is just keep rowing.' They made it to the dock and sat in their boat for twenty minutes before they could gather the strength to climb out. But they knew they had a winning strategy—they just needed to refine it.

In the semifinal, again they started strong. After overcoming a challenge from Italy, they hung on for another win.

Despite the back-to-back wins, they weren't favoured for the final—their heat and semifinal had been relatively slow. Robertson missed their pre-final team meeting because he was with the eight. By the time he turned up, they told him they'd already settled on their strategy.

As they lined up for the race of their lives, Storey was thinking, *We know we're fast, and all we have to do is bury these people somewhere down the course.* Once more, they started hard, figuring no other team would be crazy enough to match them, given the altitude. 'We took a risk and that was what you had to do if you wanted to achieve these goals,' said Cole. They kept up the relentless pace. At the halfway mark, Joyce chanced a look around. 'I realised that all we had to do was not blow up and we had the race.'

But though they looked steady and controlled, their bodies were anything but. Collinge vomited violently onto Storey's back. Joyce pushed himself so hard that he fell into a semi-conscious state. 'By the last 400 metres I'd worked myself to the stage where I couldn't hear the crowd or the coxswain,' he recalled. 'I felt like I had a giant hangover, and I was struggling to get the necessary oxygen to come to the surface. I just wanted to be allowed to go to sleep . . . You grey out. You can do it in a boat. The cox steers it. It's not like a runner running off the track or a cyclist running into a lamp post.' In his haze, he didn't notice when they crossed the finish line. He couldn't even process his teammates' voices over the roaring in his ears. Finally, his brain registered Cole's voice. 'Hey, you bastards. We won that race.'

Their bodies ached. Collinge's hips and even his teeth gave him mysterious pains. Their arms had turned a ghostly white; their legs were purple. But they'd won gold. 'We'd gone to Christchurch as individuals, and we were all broke,' Collinge told Bidwell. 'We built up a camaraderie that got us home when the chips were down. On that day we were invincible. We got to the stage we didn't care who we were racing, we were so confident. Our timing and blade work were perfect. I'd had dreams about the race long before the Games, and we'd won.'

It was New Zealand's only gold of the Mexico Games and first ever Olympic rowing gold. The crew's celebrations were dampened by the disappointing fourth placing of the eight later that day, after a final so tough that three of the Kiwi rowers were stretchered off the water, one for intravenous saline.

Robertson didn't attend the four's medal ceremony. Dickie put this down to his humble nature. 'He wanted his boys to have the moment to themselves.' Joyce felt that the New Zealand rowing administration's reaction to the four's success was strangely muted. 'We were the leftovers, the spares for the eight, yet here we were winning gold. What we did was almost an embarrassment.'

Four years later at the Munich Olympics they were determined to prove their success had been no fluke. Joyce and Dickie won gold in the eight, and Storey and Collinge took silver in the coxless four. 'It was so satisfying when we pulled it off,' said Joyce. But the champion coxed four never raced together after Mexico, leaving a perfect record: three races, three wins and an Olympic gold.

8

DENNY HULME

'Stuff that, I'm driving'

IF THE 1960S were New Zealand's dream decade for motor racing, the 1970s got off to a nightmare start.

New Zealand entered the new decade with two drivers in the top echelons of the sport: Denny Hulme, the prickly Pongakawa-raised son of a Victoria Cross winner, and Bruce McLaren, the son of a Remuera service station owner who overcame a painful hip deformity as a child. Separately, they'd impressed the world with their international debuts in the early 1960s. In 1968 they came together to spearhead the McLaren team, forming one of the most dominant pairs in world racing.

Hulme, nicknamed 'The Bear', was a notoriously gruff man of few words, while McLaren was outgoing and friendly to a fault; but they developed a tight friendship and great mutual respect. 'Bruce was just genuine,' Hulme once said. 'There was no bullshit. He wouldn't sit and waffle. He was successful just by being natural.'

Two horror crashes within weeks of each other ended the dream run and threatened to destroy the McLaren team. On 12 May 1970, Hulme was driving in a practice session at Indianapolis when his fuel cap opened. He was into his second lap, cranking the engine to about 290 kph, when he noticed fuel along the left-hand side of the car, beside the windscreen. Something then washed backwards and forwards in the pedal box, and onto his feet. It was methanol, which burns with a shimmer rather than a flame and cooks skin on contact. It poured over the bodywork and into the cockpit.

Hulme braced as a hairy turn approached. A helmet and Nomex fire suit protected his head and body, but his hands felt like they were shrinking in their leather gloves. In fact, they were burning, the leather fusing to his skin, but with the car travelling at speed he had no choice but to hang on to the wheel.

His seat heated up—the fire had got in under it. Every time he braked, more fuel sloshed out, intensifying the invisible inferno. As he roared around the track he managed to set off the car's fire extinguisher, but the flames merely flinched for half a second. He passed a stationary fire truck, going too fast to stop. His best chance was to make it to the next one, and—somehow—park beside it.

As the fire worsened, black smoke billowed up. Hulme lost visibility. A cloud of burning fuel enveloped him. He'd have to leap for it. He bumped the car out of gear and jumped—but the seat belt yanked him back down. He'd forgotten to undo it. He forced his burning hands to navigate the clip. 'I had to talk really hard to myself to undo that seat belt,' he said, later.

With the burning windscreen folding down in front of him,

raw fuel coating the left-hand side of the car and another turn approaching, he leaned on the roll bar, figuring his only chance was to jump far enough out to the right to avoid getting clobbered by the rear wheel. The car began to turn. The ground was passing by more quickly than he'd expected.

He slid back into the car to hit the brake again. His foot and clothing caught fire. The car was still going about 110 kph, but with his overalls ablaze, he was out of options. He leapt out at a 45-degree angle. As his foot touched the ground he felt like he was being ripped in half. He collapsed and rolled. Another car zoomed past. He came to a stop and managed to pull himself to his feet and run towards the fire trucks that were descending on the car. By the time he got there the flames were out.

At the track side, a doctor began to unzip Hulme's left-hand glove but stopped when he realised how serious the burns were—second degree and covering the backs of his hands and the tops of his feet. Hulme was rushed to hospital. 'There is no hair missing off the back of my hands, but there sure is a lot of skin missing,' he told motoring journalist Don Grey.

While he lay in hospital with his hands in splints, Hulme missed the Indy 500 but vowed he'd be back in the car within a month for the first race of the Can-Am series, at Mosport, Ontario. McLaren and Hulme had dominated the prestigious North American event for three years running, and the pressure was on to produce another win, which would net enough prize money to see the team through that season's Formula One bid. Without a good result, they'd struggle financially. The doctors 'just sort of laughed' off his vow, Hulme recalled. When they realised he was serious, they advised him not to race. He'd been lucky not to lose several fingers, he was likely to need skin grafts, and he'd injured his back in the jump.

Exactly three weeks after Hulme's crash, Bruce McLaren set off around a track in Sussex, England, testing a new car for the Can-Am. Under a pristine blue sky, he revved up the orange MD8, nicknamed the 'Batmobile' for its fins. He did a warm-up lap then let it rip, the sound of the exhaust audible from all parts of the track. His team, waiting in the pit, heard the car slow and brake. Then, silence. In the distance, smoke plumed into the sky.

Nobody had seen the crash. The bodywork had broken free under aerodynamic pressure. In a split second, McLaren had lost control, left the track at 260 kph and slammed into a concrete-reinforced abutment. He died at the wheel, aged 32.

Hulme's wife, Greeta, broke the news to him at their London home. He had just returned from having his burns treated by a specialist in Harley Street. Greeta drove him to the McLaren home in Sussex, where the team members were gathering.

New Zealand motoring journalist Eoin Young, who also made the pilgrimage to the McLaren house that day, called team manager Phil Kerr to report that the legendarily stoic Hulme was in a terrible state. He'd broken down and wept helplessly. 'He won't listen to anyone and you may be the only person he can talk to.'

When Kerr arrived, he walked around and around the back garden with his distraught driver. As well as grieving for his best mate, Hulme was worried about the future. 'What is the team going to do? How are we going to cope?'

Young later recalled, 'He had handled the huge pain and shock of the Indianapolis incident in a way that we put down to Denny's toughness, and to a degree I think this was true. But when news of Bruce's death came through . . . even the traditional Hulme family courage wasn't sufficient.'

In the days following McLaren's death, the drivers, mechanics and other staff came together. Even as they grieved, they had to make decisions about the team's immediate future. The first challenge was the Can-Am, which was due to start twelve days after McLaren's death. 'Denny, who had been so wracked with grief on the day Bruce died, was showing enormous courage and determination and had clearly made up his mind he was going to adopt a leadership role,' Kerr recalled. 'Despite his hands needing another six weeks of treatment, he decided he was driving. We said, "You can't!"'

'Stuff that,' Hulme replied. 'I'm driving at Mosport.'

After McLaren's funeral in Auckland, some journalists began to write the obituaries for the McLaren team, claiming Hulme's injuries would force his retirement and the team wouldn't survive without its two superstar drivers. 'But the sceptics weren't privy to what was taking place within the confines of McLaren Racing,' Kerr said, in his autobiography. 'They didn't know about Denny's courage and leadership and the example every team member had been shown less than a day after the accident ... It was Denny who helped us deal with our grief. He had gained strength from somewhere and decided he would lead by example. Bruce had left a remarkable and indelible legacy, and we as a team were going to carry on undaunted.'

They got through the fortnight in a trance. As the Can-Am opener approached, Hulme was in no state to drive but felt obligated not to quit, for the sake of the team. 'And that meant trying to do something tangible for Bruce, no matter what it took or how much he suffered, which was indicative of the sort of individual he was,' Kerr told journalist Richard Becht. 'He just had such immense courage.'

The day after McLaren's death, Hulme had grabbed a spare steering wheel and practised getting his injured fingers around the rim. He managed it okay with his right hand, but his left hand had suffered worse injuries and wouldn't cooperate. The skin was puffy and tender, and the blisters were prone to burst if he tried to close his fingers. He couldn't even hold a knife and fork.

When day dawned on the first Can-Am race, he had no feeling in his left hand, which was, in his words, 'bandaged like a boxer'. He carried a DIY medical kit with him so he could lance any blisters with sterile needles and reapply bandages and antiseptic if necessary. Easing on his gloves was agony. 'I should never have been driving,' he later admitted to motoring photographer Dave Friedman. 'The doctors were extremely concerned about the possibility of infection in my hands. If it hadn't been for the team situation at the time I wouldn't have been out there.' To ensure he could control the wheel, he forced the fingers of his left hand to fold around the rim of the steering wheel like a claw, with the help of the mechanics, leaving his right hand to do all the work. If the left hand came off the wheel during the race, getting it back on would be near impossible.

He led the race until about the halfway mark before intense pain in his hands forced him to ease off. He came third, with the win going to his American teammate Dan Gurney, the ring-in for McLaren. The crowd poured over the fences and lined the kerbs to give Hulme a huge ovation as he returned to the pits.

Gurney was in awe. 'I don't know how Denny managed to drive that car with the terrible pain that I know he was in. A lesser man couldn't have done it, but Denny was so focused on keeping the team together that he was able to block all of the bad things out.' Greeta Hulme vividly recalled the aftermath of that race, and of the races that followed: 'After he'd been driving in a race for two hours, he'd come into the pits and nobody was allowed to touch him . . .

Ever so slowly, he'd pull the gloves off and all the bandages and skin would come off, too. It was just like raw meat. But it was something he had to do. You had to stand by and be patient. Let him be.'

As the season progressed, the rougher tracks especially gave Hulme hell. He'd have to hook his hand round the wheel even tighter so the additional vibrations didn't knock it off. The skin was so tender that paper cuts would draw blood. For days after a race, his hands would buzz with pins and needles. The tip of the index finger on his left hand was particularly painful. It would bleed during a race and was topped by what he thought was a thick scab; it turned out to be a protruding bone. He figured it might eventually need an operation, but for the moment he had a team to save. 'Still,' he wrote in a motoring column, 'my problems were relatively minor ones—it just felt great to be in a racing car again.' He was, he said, 'doing it for Bruce'.

Not only did he hang on to become the winning driver in the Can-Am series that year—dedicating his victory to Bruce McLaren—but he came third in the Mexican Grand Prix and fourth in the overall Formula One drivers' championship standings. Most importantly, for Hulme, the McLaren team proved it would not only survive without its figurehead but continue to dominate world racing. To this day, it remains one of the most successful Formula One teams.

Hulme died in 1992 of a heart attack while racing at Bathurst. He was 56. He'd won eight Formula One Grands Prix and remains New Zealand's only Formula One champion. After his death, Becht wrote that Hulme's determination to continue McLaren's legacy in 1970 'should, and will, stand as the most monumental tribute to the man's bravery and loyalty to a friend'.

9

JAYNIE PARKHOUSE

From teenage nobody to hometown heroine

EYEBROWS SHOT UP when the final swimmer was announced for the New Zealand Commonwealth Games team in 1974. Christchurch schoolgirl Jaynie Parkhouse was, by her own admission, in poor form and was a distance swimmer entered in a sprint event. Given that no New Zealand female swimmer had won gold in either a Commonwealth or an Olympic games, what chance was there for a seventeen year old picked last for a sixteen-strong squad?

She'd competed as an overwhelmed sixteen year old in the 1972 Munich Olympics, where she hadn't made it out of her heats or even swum a personal best. Since then she'd struggled to regain her form and had nearly quit the year before the Commonwealth

Games. 'I had a really bad year in 1973,' she later said. 'I didn't swim well at the trials or the nationals. I couldn't even get a placing. It got to the stage where I was tossing up whether to even keep going.'

Her father, Pic Parkhouse, who'd taught her to swim and coached her since she was a young child, convinced her to stick with it for another year. 'Give it one more go,' he said. 'The Games are in Christchurch.'

She took his advice, though she couldn't see herself as a medal contender. 'I was lucky to get selected. The Games were in my home town and it was cheap to have me there, otherwise I might not have made it.'

When a Christchurch *Press* journalist suggested her selection was more to do with her father's position as a squad coach than her likelihood of success, something clicked in her. 'When you read that about yourself, you can either get really annoyed and quit, or you can dig your heels in and say, I'll show you, which is probably what I did,' she later told Radio New Zealand. 'It really made me determined to prove [the journalist] wrong and get into it.'

Parkhouse and her father knew she needed to improve her sprint if she were to justify her selection, given that her only event at that stage was a sprint relay. He drilled her on a new kicking style—a sprinter's pace of three kicks per arm circle, instead of one. In the pre-Games swimming squad camp, she improved so much she won selection for all the freestyle events and broke the New Zealand record for the 800 metres. 'I was quietly determined to prove those critics wrong and once in camp I started to swim well again,' she said, later. 'I was motivated by all sorts of things . . . fear of failure, letting myself down, letting other people down. These things always seem so important to you when you're young.'

Outside the camp, her improvement went largely unnoticed. She wasn't expected to win anything in a Games that was tipped to be dominated by a powerhouse Australian contingent. Australian coach Forbes Carlile predicted that his team would pick up all the freestyle golds.

On the first day of competition, Australia duly won gold in the 100 metres women's freestyle, with Parkhouse acquitting herself well with a fifth place in an event that wasn't her speciality. After swimming two sprints that day—the 100 metres heat and final— she slogged through an 800 metres freestyle heat and qualified for the final, fourth fastest in a quick field. She'd smashed her own New Zealand record, but the three top-rated Australians had finished faster. The smart money was on two young Australian sensations, reigning world record holder Jenny Turrall (Carlile's pick for gold), and Sally Lockyer, who had set a new Games record in the heats. Backing them up were Queenslander Rosemary Milgate and Canadian star Wendy Quirk.

'I really was not expected to do anything much at the Games,' said Parkhouse, in an interview to mark the 30th anniversary of the Games. '[But] going into the final I was a lot more confident than going into the heats because I'd improved on my best time by about 22 seconds. That in itself gave me incredible confidence. I knew I could go faster, and I had this really great feeling that I could do something special in that race. I was really thinking probably more about swimming my own race, bearing in mind that I had the world record holder and two other Australians who were almost as fast beside me, and that I would just be hanging onto them as best I could.'

She visualised how the race would play out, and ate a lot of Peanut Slabs. 'I would dream about this fabulous race—I didn't know you called it visualisation, back in the seventies. I used to play it over and over in my mind, like a video. I would turn fourth at the last length and sprint home and then I would touch the wall and I would win.'

The race began just as the pundits had predicted, with the three Australians and the Canadian setting the pace. After the first 100 metres, Parkhouse trailed the field. By the 200-metre mark, she'd settled into fifth. In those days swimmers rarely wore goggles, so, given her position near the edge of the pool, she had only a rough idea how she was doing—but it also meant the Australians were largely unaware of her presence.

Parkhouse stuck with her race plan, keeping pace with the leaders. With 300 metres to go, she nudged out the Canadian. She got into a good rhythm and felt comfortable. She could see that she was in a line with the three Australians. *Oh, heck*, she thought. *Who's going to make a move?* Up in the stands, surrounded by Australian supporters, her future husband, Craig Hudgell, scribbled in his race programme that Parkhouse would win. Her mother, sitting beside him, worried that the Australian fans would see the prediction.

Parkhouse turned into the last length in a close fourth place. She surfaced into a deafening roar from the crowd and unleashed her secret weapon. 'I knew I had that kick at the end and I just kept my rhythm,' she later told Radio Live. 'I knew I could pull off a fast finish, I just sprinted with that fast kick.'

The home crowd leapt to its feet and began clapping rhythmically. The media contingent feared *Press* swimming reporter Kevin Tutty would topple out of the media box in his excitement. In the stands, Hudgell shouted, 'That's my girlfriend!' Parkhouse's Kiwi teammates shouted chants from the sidelines, matched by their Australian rivals. The uproar shook the building and filtered into the water, spurring Parkhouse on.

Little separated the top four in that last length. Turrall, who had turned first, led until the halfway point, chased by Lockyer and Milgate. Then Parkhouse began to charge, the water boiling white in the wake of her kick.

'It's Turrall now, with about 25 metres to go,' said the television commentator. 'And on the far side Jaynie Parkhouse is starting to move up. The New Zealand girl is coming up on the outside. This is a tremendous finish, Turrall on this side, Parkhouse on the far side . . . and Parkhouse is coming through. Parkhouse is going to touch first—and she does. Turrall is second and third is Milgate. What a sensational finish. Jaynie Parkhouse of New Zealand . . . can hardly believe it. She's taken the world record holder. What a superb finish by the New Zealand swimmer. And the crowd in this stadium are standing up everywhere and applauding this girl.'

Parkhouse spun around to read the scoreboard. She'd won by four-hundredths of a second. 'I kind of knew I'd won but just had to check. It was incredible.' She clung to the lane rope. Her broad smile was caught on camera and became an enduring symbol of the Christchurch Games. 'I visualised myself winning that race for a long time, and touching just by a fingernail. It might have been a bit of a fantasy at the start but it turned out to be real at the end.'

She climbed out of the pool and found her father. He grabbed her hand, beaming, and they embraced. She felt vindicated after the criticism about her selection. 'For me to actually win the medal was a bit of a surprise to everyone . . . I felt a lot of things—relief, and pride that you had done it in New Zealand in front of your home crowd and your family.'

The Australian media called Parkhouse a 'New Zealand heroine'. A report in *The Canberra Times* said the Australian swimmers were stunned. 'The Australian swimming team offered no excuses today for the defeat of Jenny Turrall, Rosemary Milgate and Sally Lockyer, beaten in a tactical race in which the three girls spent so much time watching each other that they neglected the other competitors.' Later, the Australian coach echoed the sentiment, saying that his three golden girls had forgotten the urgency of the situation. 'Jenny and Sally became so engaged in their own personal duel that they did not notice New Zealand's Jaynie Parkhouse, who sneaked through and won.'

Parkhouse denied the Australians a clean sweep in the individual freestyle events that year. She followed up her win with a bronze in the 400 metres freestyle, won by Turrall, and a respectable fifth in the 200 metres freestyle. She retired from swimming the following year.

Later, reflecting on her career, she said she was glad to have been able to win the gold medal for her father. 'A coach's life is not easy. He had dedicated his whole life to swimming. [He'd] been such an inspiration for me, and a great encourager and a fabulous coach all my career. To have done that for him, to see that come to fruition for him and for the whole of New Zealand was wonderful.'

10

PETER PETHERICK

'I wished like Christ I could go home'

YOU NEEDED ONLY to look at New Zealand's debut spin bowler for the First Test against Pakistan in October 1976 to guess that the selectors hadn't had a lot of choice.

Peter Petherick was a 34-year-old grey-haired, overweight mechanic from Alexandra who enjoyed his beer and his cigarettes and spinning a yarn or two. He'd made the jump to first-class cricket just the previous summer, with a call-up to Otago after the retirement of their number one off spinner. Before that, he'd turned out for his local Central Otago side on the infrequent occasions they played. But with four bowlers unavailable for the Pakistan tour, on top of the sudden death from cancer of wicketkeeper Ken Wadsworth, the selectors were forced to do some last-minute lateral thinking.

They still had veteran medium-fast bowler Richard Collinge and 25-year-old fast bowler Richard Hadlee, who was just hitting his stride. But they noted that the Pakistani team had brought extra spin bowlers into their squad at the expense of seamers, perhaps anticipating that the dry Lahore pitch would better suit spinners. New Zealand had played 21 Tests against Pakistan and had won only two, so they followed the home side's lead and Petherick got the unexpected call-up. He became one of the oldest players ever to debut for the national side.

Petherick, nicknamed 'Pizzle', was a true tail-end batsman and a dicey fielder, but since starting with Otago he'd developed a reputation for a classy off spin. In his fifth first-class match, earlier that year against Northern Districts, he'd taken nine wickets and conceded just 93 runs in the first innings, bowling 35 overs straight, and was unlucky not to get a tenth wicket. When Otago played India he'd bagged six wickets for 36 runs. It was said he could turn a ball square on any pitch. His top first-class score at the crease, however, was four runs, and he'd never hit a boundary.

As he waited for his Test debut, at Gaddafi Stadium, in Lahore, Petherick watched Richard Hadlee burn up the dry, brown pitch in front of the big crowd. The young rising star took care of three of Pakistan's best, and part-time off spinner Mark Burgess bowled another, to give the visitors a promising four wickets for 68 runs by lunch.

Hadlee became ill over lunch and spent most of the break vomiting in the dressing room. He battled on, but his weakened state put pressure on the less-experienced bowlers. Veteran Asif Iqbal started the afternoon's batting, alongside a newcomer for Pakistan, nineteen-year-old Javed Miandad, who was fifteen years younger than Petherick. In just 84 minutes the pair scored

100 runs. By the tea break the partnership was worth 161. After four hours they were up to 281, of which 96 were off Petherick deliveries. Miandad became the second-youngest player in history to score a century. He was having a dream debut, while Petherick's was a nightmare.

'We took a hell of a hammering,' Petherick later told *The Dominion Post*. 'It wasn't just me, all the bowlers got hit to all parts of the ground. They get in and you just can't get them out over there. I wished like Christ I could go home at times. Everyone was going for fives and sixes an over.'

Miandad, said Petherick, was all class. 'He wasn't afraid to give it a whack in those days. It didn't matter where you bowled to him. We were just hoping like hell for the wicket to do something a bit different.'

Finally, the pitch began to provide a bounce, which suited Petherick's bowling style. In his sixteenth over, he bowled to Miandad, who aimed for the fence but top-edged a pull shot and was caught by the ailing Hadlee at square leg. He was out for 163.

In came Wasim Raja, a left-handed batsman with a reputation for breathtaking stroke play. Petherick bowled. Raja struck it low and hard—straight back to Petherick. The Kiwis held their breath, aware of their new teammate's poor fielding reputation. Petherick held the catch.

All-rounder Intikhab Alam stepped up to the crease. 'The players were crowding the bat,' Petherick later recalled. 'As I went back to my mark I thought, "If I was Intikhab I would come down the wicket," and so I darted one in to him.' Caught off guard, the Pakistani dabbed at the ball. It rebounded off his glove, and Geoff Howarth, crouching at silly point, dived for it. He caught it in his left hand, just above the dirt.

'Everyone appealed and as I turned around to the umpire he was unmoved,' recalled Petherick. 'I thought he wasn't going to give it, but then his finger went up—only after Intikhab had walked . . . It was a good catch inches above the ground and that was that. I never even thought about the hat-trick.'

The hat-trick—three wickets in successive balls—had taken just a few minutes to complete. Hadlee called it 'magic', 'an incredible turn of events'. It did nothing to change the result—a three-Test loss—but it bowled Petherick into the history books in only his twelfth first-class game. He became the first New Zealander ever to bag a Test hat-trick, and only the second cricketer in the world to do so on debut, after England's Maurice Allom did it in 1930 against New Zealand.

Petherick joked with the New Zealand Press Association's correspondent at the match, Alan Graham, 'I always knew I would do it. I just gave them 97 runs to loosen up.' He later told *The Dominion Post*, 'At the end of the day I sat down in the shed and had a beer. Everyone just looked at me and said, "What have you done?"'

Petherick took two more wickets in that Test. By the time the series concluded, he'd taken the second-largest wicket haul for New Zealand, after Hadlee and equal to David O'Sullivan. After a series against India, he played his fifth and last Test, against Australia, at Eden Park in 1977, and made himself unavailable for a tour of England later that year after landing a job as a tyre company executive. 'Back then we didn't make any money from playing cricket and I had a reasonably high-paying job,' he explained. 'Looking back I probably should have just played cricket, but at the time it seemed the right thing.'

He retired from the sport at the age of 39, his first-class batting total of 198 runs just eclipsing the 189 wickets he'd taken. Petherick later found his forte in a different type of bowling. He switched to lawn bowls in 1984 and went on to become a national champion. Nearly four decades later, he remains the only New Zealander, and one of only three people in the history of international cricket, to take a Test hat-trick on debut.

He took home the ball he bowled to glory in the Lahore Test, but it went missing for a quarter of a century. In 2004 it was rediscovered, apparently in a cricket administrator's basement, and was eventually returned to him. 'It's been a long, long time,' he told *The Dominion Post*. 'So it's good to get it back . . . I think it's time it spent some time on my mantelpiece.'

THE 1976 NEW ZEALAND MEN'S HOCKEY TEAM

Blood, sweat and broken bones

AS THE NEW ZEALAND men's hockey squad trained for the 1976 Montreal Olympics, doubts hung over them and the entire national team. Several African nations had demanded New Zealand be excluded from the Games as punishment for sending the All Blacks on a government-sanctioned tour of apartheid-era South Africa earlier in the year. After the International Olympic Committee declared it had no grounds to ban New Zealand, African countries began to pull out of the Games. By the time of the opening ceremony, more than two dozen countries had joined the boycott.

On the domestic front, the selection of the New Zealand athletes was also embroiled in controversy. The unfavoured men's hockey team made up almost one-fifth of the 87 athletes named for the Games. Resentment brewed about the cost of sending such a large squad for an event in which the country had no hope of winning a medal, and calls went up for a review of their inclusion. 'One fact seemed clear,' wrote journalist Terry Maddaford, later. 'New Zealand men's hockey teams had been regular Games competitors, had occupied a disproportionately large part in the New Zealand teams forever trimmed by the amount of money available, and had never even scented a medal. Perhaps hockey at the Olympics was a luxury New Zealand teams could no longer afford?'

Forward Barry Maister, later the secretary-general of the New Zealand Olympic Committee, said the team's previous Olympics campaign, in 1972, had been a 'disaster'—they lost five of their seven games and were lucky to place ninth. 'I remember we sat around after that performance and said, "Hey, we are better than that. We are basically going to have the same group coming through and we are going to sweat blood for four years." And that's what we did.'

One of the strongest strikers in the squad, Ramesh Patel, later said the doubts over their selection fuelled their determination. 'But I think the biggest fuelling we had was the fact that we had a core of players who had a lot of experience. We had a very strong unit going in. That was our biggest driving force as a team—the coach, the manager and the players. We knew that we were capable of doing much better than what we'd produced previously. We didn't really have a weakness—all the players were pretty good, even the reserves. What we wanted to do was just to be the best we could and do better than any other New Zealand team had.'

The players largely ignored the naysayers and got on with their preparations while fundraising to cover some of the team's costs.

Their trainer, physical education lecturer and Arthur Lydiard devotee Brian Maunsell, set them challenging fitness regimes that involved running long distances to build stamina. Otago player Arthur Parkin would run up the 373-metre-high Signal Hill in Dunedin and back before breakfast, as well as pounding out long stretches in the hills around the city, sometimes with fellow student Lorraine Moller, who later won an Olympic bronze in the marathon.

Fitness was especially important for Montreal, because for the first time the hockey tournament was to be played on artificial turf instead of grass. Turf promised to change the dynamics of the game, making it faster and more precise. This was expected to work in the favour of the big names in the competition, who were considered technically superior. With no turf in New Zealand, the Kiwis practised on smooth concrete, their bodies taking a pounding from the unforgiving surface.

The team also experimented with new attacking tactics. Instead of advancing on the defence as a forward line, as was the traditional strategy, they would pass the ball around the mid-field like soccer players, drawing the opposition in to create gaps.

'We were underdogs,' recalled captain Tony Ineson. 'Before the tournament, people were looking at the strong European countries, the Indians and Pakistanis and the Australians. We wouldn't have figured on many lists . . . [but] we had all been well-coached in the basics. Our skills and technique were right up there and we were as fit or fitter than any team in Montreal. I'd say it was the best side I played in through my international career.'

'We were never really confident going into Montreal but we knew anything could happen,' goalkeeper Trevor Manning later said. For a man who'd sat on the reserves' bench throughout the previous two Olympic campaigns, just being at Montreal was a victory. 'You get to the opening ceremony and stand there and think, "I've made it." Everything else is a bonus [after] all the hard work, all the miles and training, everything you've done.'

The New Zealanders weren't given the luxury of easing into their campaign. In their first pool game, they took on the defending Olympic champions, West Germany. 'That was a win or draw situation,' said Manning, 'because the teams were so close that we needed a good start.' Through the first half, they kept the Germans scoreless. Seven minutes into the second half, Patel scored from a penalty stroke. The Germans equalised with twelve minutes to play, but the draw was an encouraging start.

Next up was Spain. The Spaniards scored first, but the New Zealanders fought back in the second half, scoring from another Patel penalty stroke to rack up another 1–1 draw. They expected to easily triumph in their next game, against lowly ranked Belgium, but had to fight hard for a 2–1 win.

Their performances were variously described, according to Maddaford, as 'unimpressive', 'lacking zip' and 'disappointing'. Ivan Agnew, a New Zealand reporter covering the Games, said they were labelled 'the dullest team in the competition, the team with the slowest forward line in the world'.

And then came Pakistan, their last game in pool play. The former world and Olympic champions had downed Belgium 5–0 and West Germany 4–2 and had drawn with Spain. They were looking like contenders for gold. They hammered New Zealand, 5–2. 'We were outclassed,' said Ineson. 'They were far too good.' A *New Zealand Herald* journalist at the Games, Brian Humberstone, wrote, 'There was a graceful flow to the Pakistanis' game, something which the considerably less mobile New Zealanders could never match. Pakistan already have a gold-medal look and appear to be the team to beat.'

By the close of pool play, New Zealand had won just one game, drawn two and lost one. They'd scored six goals and conceded eight. But the topsy-turvy results of the other games worked in their favour. Crucially, Spain had wiped out West Germany 4–1, while bottom-of-the-table Belgium had squeaked through for a surprise 3–2 win over Spain. Spain and New Zealand were tied at second in the pool. With only the first two teams qualifying for the semifinals, they were sent to a play-off. It was frustrating and fruitless, played under dreary skies. At full-time, the scores were locked at nil-all. The match went into fifteen minutes of extra time. Still the scoreboard remained blank. Patel badly injured his thumb but played on. They entered a sudden-death round—the first team to score would win. 'It became a really tense situation,' said Ineson. 'Our fitness came through, but even so it was very tight.'

The New Zealanders were awarded a penalty corner. The ball rebounded from the first shot at goal. Patel trapped it, took another shot and scored. The Kiwis had scraped out of their pool to book a semifinal against the Netherlands. They were guaranteed at least a fourth placing in the tournament, which would be the country's best hockey result in an Olympics. As the Netherlands were the on-form team of the tournament, having won all five of their pool matches, it seemed likely New Zealand would have to be content with fourth. But the gutsy Kiwis weren't ready to settle. 'We went into the semi-final pretty confident that we could do this,' said Patel.

They started well, forcing three penalty corners in the first fifteen minutes, but couldn't break through their opponents' defence. Instead, the Netherlands sneaked the ball into the corner of the New Zealand goal. As the Dutch centre-forward ran back to halfway, he shouted to his team in English, 'How many more, boys?'

The Kiwis fought back. Three minutes later, Wellingtonian Thur Borren charged down the right wing with the ball, crossed into the goal circle and flicked it past the Dutch goalkeeper.

For the rest of that half, and then the second, New Zealand searched for the decider. The Netherlands found themselves in the unfamiliar position of having to throw their resources into defence, with penalty corner after penalty corner awarded against them. But defend they did. Full-time came and went.

Disaster struck in extra time when a Dutch attacker drilled the ball into the New Zealand net. To the Kiwis' great relief, the umpire judged the shot to be dangerously high and disallowed the goal. Extra time ran out, with the score deadlocked. They'd been playing for 85 minutes. For the second time in two days, the Kiwis went into a sudden-death round. The first goal scored would be the difference between making the gold medal final or the play-off for the bronze.

Within a minute, the New Zealanders forced a penalty corner. They'd failed to score from the last seventeen corners of the match—they had to make this one count. The ball went to vice-captain Greg Dayman, playing in his third Olympics. He slammed it into the net, securing the win. 'To pull it off in extra time and to win that game, with the feeling of knowing you were going to have a medal made it pretty special,' said Patel.

The Dutch captain later told Ineson his team had under-estimated the Kiwis and had spent too much time looking ahead to the final. '[The win] was a hell of a thrill,' said Ineson, later. 'The Dutch were terrific hockey players and to beat them in such an important match was a real coup. The Dutch themselves couldn't believe how well we played.'

Australia beat Pakistan to take the other final slot. New Zealand hadn't beaten Australia in their last eleven matches, stretching back seven years. But the pressure was also on the Aussies. With the closing ceremony just days away, Australia had won only one silver and four bronze medals, their worst Olympic result in 40 years. The hockey final was their last chance for a gold.

The Australians were 'very cocky', said Ineson. In the Olympic village on the eve of the match, they hung notices on the Kiwi players' bedroom doors warning them they were about to get their wings clipped. On the day of the final, they put champagne on ice in their dressing room, anticipating their gold medal celebrations. *The Sydney Morning Herald* mocked up its front page with the headline 'Hockey in the Bag'. Australian team manager Keith Murton said he was pleased for New Zealand but considered Australia the favourites. 'The last time we met, Australia won 5–nil and I think we can win again.'

The New Zealanders refused to accept the odds. The night before the final, coach Ross Gillespie told them to ignore the little voice in the back of their heads that told them to back off, that they'd done enough. 'We developed a code word,' said Maister, 'and if we saw someone was flagging we would call it out, remind them to ignore the little voice.'

Agnew noticed that while the Australians were brazenly confident, there was nothing pretentious about the Kiwis. 'They knew their limitations, took their triumphs modestly, and kept plugging away trying to correct faults, improve their trapping and passing and, most of all, their success rate at penalty corners, which hadn't been a strong point. Tenacity and flexibility, rather than individual brilliance, were their strengths, and they had supreme confidence in their fitness and ability to cope under pressure.' In the bus on the way to the stadium, they were uncommonly quiet. 'Usually when we went along we'd be singing a few songs, stuff like that,' said Manning. 'We knew we were going to get a medal, but everyone was thinking about beating Australia and getting the gold.'

After just six minutes of play, in which Australia dominated, New Zealand was awarded a penalty stroke. The crowd and the players fell silent as Patel, still playing with an injured hand, lined it up. He flicked it. It soared over the goal. 'I knew when I had taken it that it was an absolute flop,' he later told Kent Johns of Radio Sport. 'It was soft as, it was slow as, and it was absolutely mistimed. It was pretty unfortunate. As I was running back, some of the players tapped me on the back and said, "It's okay, we're still going."'

The Australians took advantage of the wobble in the New Zealand team and assumed control of the match. The New Zealand television commentator called it a 'lifeless, tight, scrappy first 35 minutes'. Patel was aware they were playing stand-offish hockey. 'We let them come at us, which was a bit unfortunate.'

The Kiwis managed to hold the Australians goalless until half-time. In the dressing room during the break, Gillespie told them their first-half performance was the worst he'd seen from a New Zealand team. Decades later, Patel remembered the speech mostly for its volume. 'It was pretty harsh. When he gives a harsh team talk, you listen. He was saying, "If you can come off the field after playing like that and still be nil-all, a gold medal is definitely possible."'

They returned to the match fired up. In the first minute, Parkin missed a cross from Maister in front of an undefended Australian goal. The Kiwis launched a series of attacks and forced a couple of penalty corners but were unable to convert them into points. With 28 minutes to go, they were awarded another penalty corner. A trio of Canterbury teammates set themselves up, with John Christensen hitting the ball off the baseline, Maister stopping it and Ineson shooting. Ineson slammed it into the goal. 'It was something [we] had rehearsed thousands of times back in Christchurch,' Ineson later told a reporter. 'I'd equate it to [former All Black] Grant Fox and his place-kicking. It worked perfectly. That goal really changed the nature of the game. It was incredibly exciting, of course, to be in the lead in the final, but I was conscious that there was still a long time to go and I knew the Aussies would come back at us.'

Sure enough, the Australians became desperate, bringing the game into the New Zealand defensive circle again and again, and pounding at the goal. 'They threw everything at us,' said Ineson. 'For them, scoring a goal was now the only thing that mattered so they pushed everyone forward, and we had to absorb a lot of pressure. We seemed to be camped in front of our goal, defending furiously.'

Manning repelled attack after attack. With eleven minutes to go, the Australians were awarded a short corner. Manning ran out as fast as he could, as usual, and prepared for the shot. Australian forward Ian Cooke whacked the ball in thigh high, and Manning lifted his knee to block it. It hit his unprotected kneecap through a gap in his pad, smashing the bone. One report estimated the ball was moving at 160 kilometres per hour. 'Beautifully stopped by Manning,' enthused the New Zealand television commentator, not noticing the goalie was swaying. 'A magnificent save.'

A second later, Manning went down, hard. 'I dropped from the force of it,' he said. 'The pain gradually moved up my leg from my foot and when I tried to move my leg around I knew something was wrong.'

As he lay on the pitch clutching his knee, he knew he couldn't go off the field. Not only would it give the Australians a psychological advantage while unnerving the Kiwis, but the backup goalkeeper was relatively inexperienced and had never played in an Olympics. It wouldn't be fair to him. Manning figured he could last the remaining ten minutes. 'I was in quite a bit of pain,' he told Maddaford, afterwards. 'But I didn't want the Aussies to know too much—you didn't want an Aussie to know you were injured—and I didn't really know how serious it was. The adrenalin was pumping. Nothing was going to stop us.' After a minute, he pulled himself up. To convince the Australians he was still in peak form, he did a few squats. Though adrenalin masked the pain, he found he couldn't put weight on the injured leg.

The Aussies lined up for another corner. 'I just went out as far as I could to block the shot and hoped nothing ended up in the back of the net,' he recalled. He managed to repel the ball before collapsing again.

To Patel, every minute of that game felt like ten. Finally the crowd began shouting, 'Five, four, three, two, one.' Even before the siren sounded, the New Zealanders were celebrating. 'It was euphoria everywhere, a fantastic feeling,' said Patel. 'So fantastic that I think our minds must have gone numb. I threw my stick into the crowd, then thought, "What am I doing? That was my favourite hockey stick."' He didn't get it back.

The New Zealand manager, coach, reserves and supporters charged onto the field. As Manning's body began to cool down, the pain took over. He had to be helped onto the medal dais. It was New Zealand's second gold medal of the Montreal Games, following runner John Walker's win in the 1500 metres. 'To be standing there above Australia and Pakistan was phenomenal,' said Patel. 'It was a bit of a numb feeling on stage, hard to believe. It started to sink in a couple of hours later, what we had actually done. It was a pretty proud moment for everyone.' Ineson rejected suggestions the win had been a fluke. 'That would be unfair. We were a good team when we went to Montreal, and we raised our game further.'

Maddaford wrote, 'New Zealand has, over the years, known some great moments in sport, usually on the rugby field or running track. But here in Montreal perhaps the greatest of them all had unfolded, as eleven hockey players had overcome the impossible odds and snatched a gold medal.'

The Australians magnanimously arrived at the Kiwi dressing room with their champagne, and the rival teams celebrated their medals together. 'We sat together long into the night and it tasted even better because they had brought it,' said Maister.

Despite the gold medal, Ineson expressed regret upon returning home that the New Zealand Olympic team hadn't withdrawn from the Games. 'We worked hard to get to the Games and would have been brassed off, but we would have gone if called [home],' he told a reporter. 'We should have been called. We were all bitterly disappointed for the Africans when their governments took them away from Montreal.'

A week after the final, surgeons in New Zealand implanted wire into Manning's knee to hold it together. He later developed arthritis and walked with a limp, though sometimes his leg was so painful he could barely walk at all. In 2013, aged 67, he finally had a knee replacement. 'Yes, it has caused a lot of problems for me,' he once said, 'but in the end I got the gold medal, and they can't take that away from me.'

12

LINDA JONES

The 'wispy housewife' who challenged the racing establishment

THE CROWD ROARED as celebrated American amateur jockey Lotte Von Bromssen urged Royal Falcon down the final straight of the Bay of Plenty Racing Club's 1970 Powder Puff Derby, in Tauranga. Von Bromssen had ridden a perfect race. She'd taken Royal Falcon wide—very wide—but, glancing over her right shoulder at her nearest rival, she was sure she'd made a good call. Then, just 50 metres from the post, she glimpsed a flash of green on her left. Linda Jones (then Linda Wilkinson), an eighteen-year-old pharmacy assistant from Paeroa, was storming down the outside on her chestnut mount, Scots Bard. The American tried desperately to pick up the pace, but it was too late. Cameras flashed as Jones streaked ahead to win by a neck.

It was the first time Jones had donned jockeys' silks, and she was hooked. In 1970, women weren't permitted to race as licensed jockeys in New Zealand. The Powder Puff Derby was a novelty 'racing parade' for female riders. Although no betting was allowed, it gave the women an opportunity to experience race day conditions. That night, as a euphoric Jones showed the family her prizes—a powder compact, a dress, a Crown Lynn coffee set and nearly $20 in cash—she felt almost professional.

Jones had fallen in love with racing in her early teens, spending every spare moment at the Paeroa training track, mucking out boxes and galloping hack racehorses. That was where she first became aware of racing's gender divide and began to wish she had been born a boy. 'At pony club, as a child, and in a show-ring, girls competed against boys on equal footing,' Jones told her biographer, John Costello. 'But in racing, while I could ride track work with the boys, I could never be a jockey like them. Jockeys were men, or boys . . . that's the way it was and always had been.'

After leaving school at fifteen, Jones rose before dawn every day to ride track work for local trainer Alan Jones. Soon she was competing in gymkhanas and ladies' point-to-point races around Waikato and the Bay of Plenty—the only races she was allowed to enter—but it didn't occur to her to challenge the status quo. 'I was quite happy with the odd lady riders' race,' she told Costello. 'But I wanted as many of them as possible.'

Jones loved the thrill and competition of racing, and her impressive results prompted the invitation to the 1970 Powder Puff Derby. Other clubs followed Tauranga's lead in staging ladies' races at totalisator meetings, and a year after her marriage to Alan Jones in 1971, she took first place in the Paeroa Hot Pants Scurry—with a prize of a hotpants outfit.

Although women's races were popular with the public, many owners, trainers and jockeys complained they would only whet women's appetites for more racing opportunities. They argued that if 'jockettes' were allowed to ride, clubs would be landed with the expense of installing additional changing rooms. They claimed women weren't strong enough to handle hard-pulling horses and would never match the performance of top male jockeys.

Opportunities for women dwindled. In 1972, shortly after Jones won a barrier trial against professional male jockeys at Te Aroha, the Waikato District Committee declared women ineligible for barrier trials. Jones was indignant. 'You don't have to be a professional rider to ride in barrier trials,' she later told Costello. 'You can take a man or a boy off the street or out of the bar who has never ridden a horse . . . But a girl who might have ridden track work for years and competed under race conditions in a dozen lady riders' races is barred.'

By 1973, the Powder Puff Derby and other women's races at totalisator meetings had petered out. Jones began airing her views to trainers and journalists, arguing that women's strength and stamina would increase over time if they had as many opportunities to race as men. She believed that a rider was only as good as his or her horse, and that women deserved the right to try, irrespective of whether they would ever match their male counterparts.

Not all women riders agreed. 'Most of the girls are quite happy about the way things are going at the moment,' wrote one anonymous member of a women riders' club to racing publication *Friday Flash*. 'I think some lady riders are pushing their luck too far and too fast in trying to ride against men, and they will spoil it for others in the future.'

But Jones's views were strengthened by her exposure to the international racing scene. 'Leave the Dishes in the Sink—Linda's Gone Riding' ran a 1974 headline in Auckland's *8 O'Clock* sports newspaper, announcing that Jones was to compete in Australia's first international women riders' event, the Dame Merlyn Myer International Stakes. There she met two professional female jockeys from North America who were able to compete on equal terms with their male counterparts at home.

In 1975 the progressive Rotorua Racing Club staged a similar event, the Qantas International, attracting top women riders from the United Kingdom, Australia, Singapore and the United States. Jones won the tough and thrilling race by half a head and was once again struck by her competitors' tales of life as professional jockeys.

The final spur came in 1976, when Jones was invited to compete at the Lady Riders' World Championship in Sao Paulo, Brazil. Of the sixteen countries represented, only Australia and New Zealand didn't allow women to compete equally against men.

Jones returned home to Pukerimu more determined than ever. She was no longer content with women's races. She wanted fully fledged professional equality. Laid up with a broken jaw after being kicked by a colt, she studied the New Zealand Rules of Racing with her husband. They couldn't find a single rule prohibiting women from riding. The code merely stated that 'no jockey's wife or husband could race a horse', and that where appropriate 'masculine' could also be taken to mean 'feminine'.

With high hopes, 24-year-old Jones publicly announced her decision to apply to the New Zealand Racing Conference to become a probationary apprentice to her husband. Her application was rejected two months later, without explanation. She was crushed. She appealed, and the conference was required to provide reasons.

Jones, they said, was 'too old, married, not strong enough, and would be taking away a male jockey's livelihood'.

Meanwhile, Canadian professional jockey Joan Phipps arrived in New Zealand for the 1976 Qantas International. Stunned to discover women couldn't be licensed as professionals, she applied for an open licence to ride at totalisator meetings. Such licences were granted automatically to visiting male professional jockeys, but the racing conference deferred the decision until Phipps had left the country and then refused to consider it unless she returned. She was furious.

Shortly thereafter, Jones's appeal was dismissed. At the time she was in a neck brace, after cracking two vertebrae when she was thrown into the side of a shed by a nervous filly. Still determined, she resolved to take legal action. Meanwhile, her cause was gaining public momentum. In the *Sunday News*, Judy McGregor wrote a scathing attack on the racing conference's 'patently absurd' reasoning, pointing out that young boys weren't turned down as jockeys for lack of strength: 'The racing conference is an example of the old guard sporting administration noted more for its head being in the sand than compelling logic . . . If it is good enough for women to muck out stables, ride track work, own horses and train horses, it is damn well good enough for women to ride in races alongside men if they want to.'

When the racing conference deferred an application for a probationary apprenticeship by Vivienne Kaye—who at fifteen was neither old nor married, and whose strength at weight-for-age was vouched for by her trainer father, civil liberties campaigners entered the debate. The secretary of the Auckland branch of the Council for Equal Pay and Opportunity called for an investigation. Shirley Andrews, president of the Auckland branch of the National

Organisation of Women, wrote, 'It is hard to believe that an intact sample of Victorian male chauvinism exists in New Zealand ... If women jockeys were granted equal rights in the paddock it would follow that women should have equal rights throughout the clubs, district committees, right through to Conference level. This is the real threat the Racing Conference men are fighting and why irrelevant nonsense about age, strength, language, changing rooms and lavatories is trotted out when women wish to become professional jockeys.'

Women MPs raised the issue in parliament, and MP Marilyn Waring wrote to the racing conference advising that under forthcoming human rights legislation it would be illegal to deny women the right to jockeys' licences. The powerful racing conference had never before faced such pressure. In July 1977, at the annual conference of racing clubs, a motion was raised that where female riders met the criteria applicable to men, they should be duly registered as probationers. It was passed without dissent. By then four women had applications before the conference, but Linda Jones wasn't one of them. She was seven months pregnant.

Probationary apprentices were required to wait twelve months before competing, so in November 1977 it was Phipps—back in New Zealand for the Qantas International—who became the first woman to ride against male professionals in a tote meeting, and the first to win. Watching Phipps cross the line, Jones felt her own desire rekindle. 'I don't think I've ever yelled so loud.'

Jones returned to picnic racing on Boxing Day, when her daughter, Clare, was three months old. When she applied for her probationary licence a month later, the conference not only granted it but backdated it by six months, so she would be eligible to ride early in the racing season, which began in late winter.

On 12 August 1978, Jones finally made her professional debut at Matamata, bringing the crowd to its feet with a stunning run for third on an outsider. Within a week she'd won a 1600-metre maiden event at Te Rapa on Big Bickies. 'Jockey Mum's a Winner—Linda Grabs the Bikkies for Libbers', hailed the Sydney *Daily Mirror*, declaring that 'Linda's looks are not the only thing favouring her. She is a tough rider and the way she rode Big Bikkies [*sic*] in the race was a stunner.'

Jones's goal was to ride six winners by Christmas. She managed it in less than a month. Any lingering doubts over her abilities were put to rest at Te Rapa in October, when she brought home four winners in a single day. As she crossed the line for the fourth win, ahead by a length and a quarter, the crowd erupted—and so did the press. The 26 year old, described by *The New Zealand Herald* as a 'wispy Cambridge housewife', had silenced the last of the sceptics and ridden her way to a place in the record books.

Jones was becoming known for a unique empathy with horses that enabled her to coax exceptional results. By Christmas, she'd ridden 36 winners and was ranked second in the apprentice jockeys' premiership. Some racing clubs had done little to make it easier for the women. Jones often had to change in caravans or switchboard cupboards, and her winning streak caused resentment, with male jockeys teased for 'losing to a bird'. One male colleague grabbed her leg so hard it was later covered in bruises.

In January 1979 she made her Trentham debut while nursing a broken rib from a fall at Thames. Her presence attracted huge interest, with an army of supporters dubbed Linda's Legion wearing T-shirts emblazoned with 'Go Linda Go' and 'We Love Linda, Queen of the Turf'. On the opening day Jones didn't disappoint, winning two races and taking second place in the Wellington Cup. As she dismounted after her second win, the crowd gave 'three cheers for Linda'. She told the Melbourne *Herald*, 'It's been a great day but you must remember thousands of jockeys have ridden doubles in a day and, after all, I am a jockey even though I am a woman.'

On day two, Jones lined up Holy Toledo for the prestigious Wellington Derby. It was a tough race, with five horses battling it out down the final straight. As she whipped her grey colt up the outside, the chant went up: 'Go, Linda, go!' The five flashed over the line together. The crowd hushed as the judges called for a photo finish. Then the loudspeaker crackled into life: 'The 1979 Wellington Derby ... in a photo [finish], number twelve, Holy Toledo.' Pandemonium broke out. Jones had become the first woman in Europe, North America and Australasia to win a derby. At the presentation, an emotional Jones choked out her thanks then buried her face in her hands. Later that day, she won the Douro Cup. She was the sensation of the racing world.

On the final day, Jones saddled up Toni Renee, a slender hope for the 2400-metre New Zealand Oaks. On the home turn the group was tightly bunched, and Toni Renee trailed behind two flagging horses, forcing her towards the back. Another horse began improving on the outside, and Jones saw it was her only chance. She tried to go with the other horse, pushing Toni Renee up where there was barely room. 'One moment Toni Renee was there, but only just there ... not really going well enough to hold her place as the pressure went on,' Jones told Costello. 'The next moment she went down on her nose and I was flung over her head. I felt one horse hit me ... I'm not sure how many did.' A horrified crowd watched as at least three horses appeared to strike her. Toni Renee continued on with the group, and the race finished in near silence.

Jones was rushed straight to hospital with fractured ribs, severe bruising and a punctured lung. But the worst pain came from learning that her next three mounts had all won. 'I was lying under the X-ray and said, "Just let that thing fall on me,"' Jones recalled. 'I was so disheartened.'

She returned to racing a month later, but it wasn't until autumn that she regained some of her previous form. She then announced her intention to ride in Australia, beginning with the Manion Cup at Rosehill, in Sydney, on 31 March. Recognising the huge publicity Jones's visit would attract, the Australian Jockey Club held a special meeting on 9 March and, to enable her to compete, brought forwards plans to license female jockeys from 1 August. Legendary Australian trainer Bart Cummings was impressed by Jones's record but warned, 'One swallow doesn't make a summer and Linda's success doesn't necessarily mean a bunch of women jockeys would be an asset to the racing game.'

At Rosehill, Jones made history once again, as the first woman ever to ride professionally against male jockeys in Australia. She took third place, and the crowd and the media couldn't get enough. Her planned short visit turned into a six-week tour, with public engagements, radio and television appearances and many more rides, as clubs competed to attract her to their meetings. She became the first woman to ride a winner against men at a registered meeting in Australia, at the Labour Day Cup in Doomben.

For Jones, it was all about doing what she loved. She told Costello, 'I love race riding, even though I get frustrated and wild with myself when I'm riding badly. I love the thrills, the competition, the tension before a race, the satisfaction when you win . . . And I'd be lying if I said I didn't get a big thrill out of the glamour and the publicity and the fan mail.'

When her first season ended, on 31 July 1979, Jones had notched up 49 wins in New Zealand, led the first season apprentice list and was ranked equal tenth overall. She was awarded an MBE in the Queen's Birthday Honours, became the subject of a *This is Your Life* programme on Australian television and was named New Zealand Racing Personality of the Year.

But her professional career was destined to be short. In March 1980, she was thrown by a colt and suffered a broken pelvis, concussion and yet another cracked vertebra. This fall, the doctors advised, must be the last. Any more would likely result in paralysis. With a young family to consider, she reluctantly announced her retirement. Her professional career spanned eighteen months, of which she raced for only eight. In that time she took 65 wins and changed the face of New Zealand racing. By the early 2000s New Zealand had one of the highest proportions of female riders in the world, and by 2012 almost half of all apprentices were women.

13

DIGBY TAYLOR

The backyard boatbuilder who took on the world

As SAILORS AND SPECTATORS bustled around the racing yachts clustered at Auckland's Marsden Wharf in December 1977, one man in the crowd began some mental calculations. What would it take for an unknown and unconnected hobby sailor to win the world's longest, toughest and most demanding yacht race?

The yachts were on a stopover during the second Whitbread Round the World Race, a 27,000-mile circumnavigation starting and ending in Portsmouth, England, stopping in South Africa, New Zealand and South America. Along the way they would encounter mountainous seas, gale-force winds or no wind at all, whales, icebergs and gear failure. During the inaugural Whitbread, in 1973–74, three men had lost their lives as the fleet battled freak waves and rugged weather in the Indian and Southern oceans.

As crowds admired the mighty 77-foot sloop *Heath's Condor*, Digby Taylor found himself drawn to the smaller yachts, like the 56-foot *Gauloises II*, which had made an impressive showing on the first leg, from Portsmouth to Cape Town. Taylor was a keen offshore sailor with his own fibreglass business. He'd built his own yacht, the 33-foot *Delphin*, and had raced her to Nouméa and around Cook Strait and Auckland, accumulating a fine collection of trophies. For Taylor, winning the Whitbread was a sailor's ultimate dream. More than just a race, the Whitbread was an endurance test requiring courage, tenacity, strategy, fine seamanship and more than a little luck.

The 34 year old seemed an unlikely contender for a Whitbread challenge. He was a heavy smoker, was not well known outside yachting circles and lacked the influential connections capable of funding such a campaign. 'When I began talking to my friends and family of my desire to do the Round the World Race, I met with blank looks,' Taylor told writer Alan Parker. 'No one said to me that it was impossible for a private individual to take it on—rather their actions of dismissal were evidence of their real thoughts.'

The more Taylor considered it, the more he became convinced that the Whitbread was his 'big opportunity in life to really do something'. He'd studied the first two Whitbread races and noticed that smaller yachts had won six of the eight legs. He calculated that a 50-foot vessel had a good chance of taking out the top prize on handicap. But first, he'd have to find a way to finance the costs of building and campaigning a round-the-world racing yacht.

Taylor wasn't the only New Zealander with global racing ambitions. In April 1979, Peter Blake, a 30-year-old high-profile sailor, launched his own New Zealand Whitbread challenge. Blake had credentials and contacts. He'd sailed in both of the Whitbread races and had already secured the support of the Royal New Zealand Yacht Squadron and industrialist Tom Clark, of the Ceramco group of companies. Ceramco agreed to underwrite most of the cost of building *Ceramco New Zealand,* an impressive 68-foot aluminium sloop designed by the renowned Bruce Farr. The balance would be raised by public debenture, whereby New Zealanders could purchase a share in the boat for $500, to be repaid when the boat was sold at the end of the campaign.

For Taylor, raising the finances was a more complex and personal challenge. *Delphin* would have to go, and, after late-night discussions with his wife, Diane, so did the family home and the car. His father, Fergus, offered to sell the family's 46-foot motor launch, *Thetis.* Even so, Taylor was left with a total contribution of $30,000, a sum equivalent to the design fees quoted by one yacht designer and nowhere near the funds required to build a yacht and get it safely around the world.

In June 1979, Taylor met designer Laurie Davidson and shared his audacious idea. Davidson sketched a series of drawings and a sail plan for a broad yacht, fast off the wind but also strong upwind, which would be crucial on the first and fourth legs of the race. By October, Taylor had secured the use of a boatshed on the water in Auckland's Herne Bay just big enough to build Davidson's 51-foot design. It was painstaking, exacting work, but as word of Taylor's quest seeped out, keen sailors and boatbuilders began arriving at the shed, donating long nights and weekends to the project with no guarantee of a place in the crew.

Diane was now working full-time on the campaign, and life for the couple and their three children revolved around the boat.

'Digby would arrive home late in the evening for dinner, then get on the phone organising supplies,' Diane told Parker. 'Often, when it sounded quiet, a quick check would reveal an exhausted Digby fast asleep on the floor beside the phone!'

Twelve months later, in October 1980, *Ceramco New Zealand* was launched in a blaze of publicity. Dame Norma Holyoake, wife of the governor-general and former prime minister Sir Keith Holyoake, broke the ceremonial bottle of champagne over her bow, and 600 invited guests partied into the night.

The following day Taylor's boat slid quietly into the water at Herne Bay, with Diane doing the honours with the bubbly. Taylor had heard rumours of potential changes to the rules of the race and decided to launch the boat early in the hope that any new conditions would not apply to him. In the absence of a major campaign sponsor, she was named *Outward Bound* for the Anakiwa-based outdoor education programme with which Taylor's father had a long association. The programme was renowned for its adventurous spirit and for challenging New Zealanders to push beyond their limits.

The lack of a key sponsor was a concern, but, as Taylor later told journalist Richard Becht, 'Our best people were so involved in actually building and sailing the boat that we didn't have time to promote ourselves.' Nonetheless, news of the challenge spread via yachting magazines and word of mouth. At the mention of *Outward Bound*, companies began offering parts, freight and food at little or no charge.

Diane got to work provisioning 10,000 meals for the delivery trip and race, and Taylor began reviewing the 40 crew applications. After working on the boat for months and being repeatedly told not to get their hopes up, lawyer Mike Keeton, electrician Godfrey

Cray, chef Terry Flynn and nineteen-year-old boatbuilder Dale Tremain were delighted to be among those selected. The eight crew members were expected to join the challenge full-time and work unpaid for the duration. They were also asked to pay $2000 towards the challenge fund and a further $3000 if a sponsor wasn't secured. For some this proved a problem. '[Mike Keeton] came to me and said "I've managed to borrow $500 from the old man, I've got a Seiko watch and a ukulele. Do you think I could pay the rest back after the race is over?"' Taylor told Becht. 'That's just the way it was.'

The official blessing and launch party took place on 16 January 1981 at Half Moon Bay. *Auckland Star* yachting reporter Alan Sefton described the project as 'typically Kiwi, a do-it-yourself job involving a lot of individual drive and determination. It's a project that deserves to succeed.'

The first sail out into the Rangitoto Channel was promising. *Outward Bound* handled well and accelerated quickly off the wind. Prior to joining the challenge, a few of the crew had participated in races to Pacific islands, and one had sailed the Sydney to Hobart Yacht Race, but the rest of their experience was limited to the Hauraki Gulf. They needed to get in as much sailing as they could, to test different positions and fine-tune the yacht.

The race was a little more than eight months away, and there was still no major sponsor on the horizon. Taylor had pared back the budget to a strictly no-frills $120,000 but had no assets left to sell and his overdraft was causing concern. *Ceramco*'s campaign budget was reported to be $750,000.

The *Outward Bound* challenge committee decided to try a different approach, seeking several companies as co-sponsors. By March 1981, just three weeks before the planned departure date, only one company had taken up the proposal. But public support was rapidly growing. A group of dinghy owners noticed *Outward Bound* hadn't received as much publicity as *Ceramco* and organised a nine-hour sailing marathon, raising $4300 for the campaign. Taylor was touched by these efforts by complete strangers, but the deficit was still huge. No amount of *Outward Bound* T-shirts, bumper stickers, pens or sponsored miles would be enough to get her safely around the world.

The breakthrough came when Television New Zealand proposed a deal whereby it would provide advertisements thanking co-sponsors. Four more companies signed up, and just eight days before *Outward Bound* was due to leave New Zealand, Taylor finally got confirmation of the funds they needed. The budget would still be tight, but for the first time Taylor knew *Outward Bound* was a viable entry.

On 15 March 1981, the crew cast off the lines from Admiralty Steps in downtown Auckland for the 100-day journey to Portsmouth to begin the race. While *Ceramco* was shipped to England ahead of the start, the *Outward Bound* challenge couldn't afford the freight, and besides, the crew needed the sailing experience. Taylor's plan was to sail south of the Chatham Islands for a taste of the Southern Ocean, turn north before Cape Horn and sail up the west coast of Chile, go through the Panama Canal and cross the Atlantic to England. He believed the journey gave them an advantage. 'The delivery voyage allowed us to find out what was wrong with the boat, and ... to address it before it became a problem once the race started,' he told Becht. By the time they arrived in England, the crew knew every inch of the yacht, had weathered fierce storms and knew they could get along. Taylor was confident they were ready for the Whitbread.

The morning of 29 August dawned still and misty over Portsmouth. Wearing 'If anyone can a Kiwi can' T-shirts provided by the Dargaville Lions Club, the crew weaved through a dense wash of spectator craft to the starting area. The pressure mounted as the 29 entrants jockeyed for position. Competition was expected to be tight on the first 7000-mile leg, and a jump at the start could make a big difference down the line.

At precisely noon, the 150-year-old cannon at Southsea Castle fired a resounding boom. *Outward Bound* was one of the first across the line. As they passed a boatload of champagne-swilling *Ceramco* supporters with a 'C'mon Kiwi' banner, a cry went up: 'Three cheers for *Outward Bound!*' For Taylor, it was a great moment.

As they entered the Bay of Biscay, the wind dropped away and progress was frustratingly slow. Between watches, Taylor, Keeton and team doctor Richard Dinsdale studied the weather maps, plotting the positions of other boats and any weather information gleaned from daily radio calls. Dinsdale studied books published about previous Whitbreads, noting details about conditions that had prevailed in their current position.

Rounding the north-western tip of Spain at night in just three knots of wind, they spotted a ship in the distance. Over the next few minutes it grew bigger and closer, and it became apparent its crew hadn't seen *Outward Bound*. As the behemoth bore down on them, its huge wall of steel towered high above the yacht's mast, and the noise of the engines drowned out Taylor's air foghorn. There was nothing they could do. 'He was right on us,' Taylor told Parker. 'I was quite sure he would hit us, exactly between me, at the top of the companionway, and Matt [Smith] in the helmsman's cockpit ... It was just inevitable that Matt was going to end up going down the other side of the ship from the rest of us ... As she passed across our stern, I could have stepped out of the cockpit, reached over the lifelines and touched her. That's how close she was.'

The stunned crew continued on in silence.

Flynn, who had never used a sewing machine before joining the *Outward Bound* crew, was in charge of sail repairs. He spent many hours below deck in cramped conditions, painstakingly patching together torn spinnakers and sails. On one occasion, the halyard (or line) used to raise and lower the mainsail broke for the second time, sending the mainsail and boom crashing to the deck. To replace it they needed to send a man to the top of the 70-foot mast, but *Outward Bound*'s foresail halyards only reached 55 feet high. In 25-knot winds, the crew used these halyards to lift rigger Matthew Smith to 55 feet clutching a seventeen-foot spinnaker pole. He lashed the pole to the mast as high as he could reach, then used a line attached to the top of the pole to hoist himself higher and drop the new halyard down the mast. It was an ingenious but nail-biting solution that took five hours to execute in the rolling seas.

As they drew close to Cape Town, it looked as if they might win the leg or place on handicap. But expected westerlies didn't arrive, and they found themselves becalmed with a great high-pressure system stretching between the boat and the coast. 'I think it's called character building,' Taylor told Sefton by radio. 'If that's true I'll have a really good character by the time we make Cape Town.'

Outward Bound finally arrived in Cape Town placed sixth on handicap, one of the few yachts to have suffered no major damage. Of the 29 starters, 21 reported structural, equipment or rigging failure, and three had been forced to retire altogether. *Ceramco*'s mast had crashed down, and with it any hope of winning the overall trophy. Blake and his crew had fashioned a jury rig from the broken parts of the mast and rigging, but its inefficiency had forced them to sail an extra 1500 miles before reaching Cape Town.

The crew of *Outward Bound* enjoyed a three-week break, working on the yacht, playing squash, sightseeing, partying and sailing with new friends. Taylor spent time with Cape Town yachties, grilling them about local conditions in preparation for the start of the next leg. One experienced local told him that if conditions were light in the late afternoon he should hug the coastline as closely as possible rather than head out to sea.

On 31 October, Taylor's crew lined up for the challenging second leg. Tremain, however, didn't show. He'd gone out with local friends the night before and hadn't returned. At 2.30 p.m., half an hour before the start of the race, Taylor heard he was among a group of young people being held by police after an incident at a farewell party. Although there were no charges against Tremain, the police would not release him because they were contemplating charging others in the group. The start time came and went, and *Outward Bound* was soon the only Whitbread boat left in the marina. Finally, Taylor decided they'd have to sail without his youngest crew member. They crossed the line four hours late. Half an hour later, they got word by VHF radio that Tremain had been released, so they turned around.

They finally left the city five hours after the official start. As they set out from Table Bay into the dark, the wind dropped dead. Taylor remembered the local sailor's advice and, against the consensus of the crew, set a course close to the surf line, keeping the depth sounder on all night. The next morning they spotted a sail ahead. Incredibly, they'd caught up with the fleet and even overtaken a much bigger yacht. *Outward Bound* looked to be in the top six on handicap.

As they headed south, Flynn began a series of difficult sail repairs that continued for almost the entire leg, during which the yachtsmen faced winds gusting to 50 knots, snowstorms and nasty squalls putting strain on the gear. In anticipation of his birthday, Flynn declared 12 November a repair-free day—no sails were to be torn or blown out. At watch changeover that day, the crew gathered on deck, looking forward to the celebratory meal of spaghetti bolognaise and cask wine waiting down below. As they jibed from port to starboard tack, the spinnaker ripped. 'Here we were in the middle of nowhere,' recalled Flynn, 'cold as hell, fighting to get the kite aboard the yacht, rolling and pitching like mad, all singing "Happy Birthday".'

As they moved deeper into the Southern Ocean, the seas became rough and confused, and they sailed on the edge of control. The boat surfed, and sometimes broached, when a wave or a sudden gust caused the yacht to round into the wind and heel over with the mast almost level with the water.

Taylor took the boat as low as 55 degrees, much further south than the bigger yachts ventured. This was dangerous territory, but he judged it to be the fastest course for a boat of *Outward Bound*'s size. The crew all wore safety harnesses, for if a man went overboard there would be little chance of finding him in such seas, supposing he survived the shock of the freezing waters. They picked their way through fields of ice, watching for semi-submerged chunks, some of which were as big as houses. Although they saw as many as twelve icebergs in a day, they never spotted one at night, as skies were overcast and visibility was poor. It was so cold they could keep ice-watch for just ten minutes at a time. At changeover they slid on their stomachs across the frozen deck to avoid slipping over the side. They grew accustomed to sleeping in wet clothing, with steam rising above their sleeping bags.

As dawn broke after a particularly nasty cold snap, they discovered the boat was iced over. The sails and sheets were frozen stiff, and the winches had turned to blocks of ice. If a squall hit the boat, they'd be in real trouble. The crew boiled seawater and frantically chipped at the ice to keep the boat working until the temperature rose.

The wind began to increase and brought with it mountainous seas. Sometimes the waves were so big they threatened to flip the stern over the bow, so the crew had to luff up, turning towards the wind and letting the waves roll over the top, knocking the boat flat. Late one night, a vicious wave knocked Smith off the wheel and into the sea. He instinctively grabbed his lifeline, hauling himself in as the boat righted.

The storm blew out, leaving *Outward Bound* all but becalmed. The satnav and weatherfax malfunctioned, and it was impossible to get readings or use the sextant with the overcast skies. Taylor's estimated course took them too far south, costing precious time.

As they finally rounded the northern tip of New Zealand in more stormy conditions, they had a serious sail blowout and then got stuck in light winds off Cape Brett. They were despondent, realising that they would be arriving after midnight on 10 December 1981, in seventh place and more than eight days after *Ceramco*. Their hopes of putting on a strong performance for their supporters at home were dashed. It was a huge anticlimax.

But as they neared Kawau Island a boat lit up, and voices began cheering and yahooing. Just south of Tiri Passage, Taylor's family came alongside, and then other boats joined them, until there was quite an armada. 'The more boats that arrived, the less we could believe it,' Taylor recalled. 'At one stage I had to hand the helm over to Mike Keeton because the scene had become too much. I was shaking and the tears in my eyes were clouding my vision.'

By the time they rounded North Head, on their way to the finish line on the Waitemata Harbour, more than a hundred boats were escorting them. Suddenly, the waterfront burst into light. Prompted by live radio commentary, hundreds of cars aimed their headlights at the boat's reflective hull. Naked revellers jumped off Orakei Wharf. Flares were fired, horns and sirens sounded and cheers filled the night as *Outward Bound* crossed the line. It was 1.30 a.m. They'd completed a full circumnavigation, and half of the Whitbread was behind them. As they approached Marsden Wharf and saw about four thousand supporters waiting in the rain, they were overcome. 'None of us will ever forget this welcome,' Taylor told television reporters. For days, he cried every time he spoke about the remarkable homecoming.

On Boxing Day the crew assembled once again, in uniform Stubbies shorts. They made a promising start, keeping up with the maxi yachts as the fleet departed for Mar del Plata, in Argentina.

In 40-knot winds, the boat was surfing, accelerating with the power of the swell and plunging into the waves. They lost a spinnaker overboard on one of these dives, and the mainsail caught on a block, tearing right across the width and halfway up. It took Flynn thirteen days to repair the sail. Cracks appeared on three spokes of the steering wheel and had to be fixed. Taylor set up an emergency tiller, but it was too short to get enough leverage as the boat careered down the giant swells. The crew took apart the spinnaker pole, fitted it over the tiller and began learning to surf a 51-foot yacht with a slightly wobbly ten-foot steering pole, resulting in some wild rides. Taylor then set about repairing the wheel with fibreglass and ply, creating a small tent over the cockpit and using meths burners to cure the fibreglass. When the wheel was finally replaced, after twelve hours under emergency tiller, *Outward Bound* was still going strong and Taylor estimated they were in the top four.

As they rounded Cape Horn they passed around a magnum of champagne, then sailed straight into a 30- to 40-knot northerly, punching through near-vertical waves and dropping fifteen feet on the other side. *Outward Bound* finished the leg fourth on handicap. After 20,000 miles of racing, they were in sixth position overall. They were leading the race for the small boat trophy, but the 40-foot French yacht *Morbihan* was just three hours behind them on overall handicap; they had to beat her by eighteen hours to take the trophy.

They rested in Mar del Plata for five weeks and the unpaid crew were delighted when a 'spending money' cheque arrived from the members of the Royal Akarana Yacht Club. Taylor, meanwhile, was spending money he didn't have. He felt the fourth leg could be their chance. *Outward Bound* was strong upwind, and if weather conditions developed as predicted it could favour them. But the mainsail and number three headsail needed replacing, so he committed himself to the expenditure knowing that unless *Outward Bound* could be sold upon arrival in England he'd be in real difficulty.

On 27 February 1982, *Outward Bound* made a strong start from Mar del Plata, pulling ahead of *Morbihan* and keeping pace with some of the larger yachts for the first two days. The fourth upwind leg is considered the most challenging from a tactical perspective, and Taylor spent many hours hunched over his programmable calculator, trying to determine the best course. In the right conditions, *Outward Bound* had a chance of moving up a place or two.

But for all Taylor's mathematical calculations and strategising, the weather was one variable he couldn't control. Winds favoured the maxi yachts, which soon pulled ahead, while the smaller boats got caught in fluctuating conditions for a week and had to tack often to maintain a course. While the larger yachts seemed to breeze through the Doldrums, conditions grew progressively worse as the fleet passed through, penalising those further back. The yachts were now stretched over 3000 miles, with *Outward Bound* more than 300 miles ahead of *Morbihan*.

Finally Taylor and his crew got under way, sailing west of the Azores High, a calmed area of the North Atlantic, and heading towards England.

At last, they were in the English Channel, sailing at ten knots, with three knots of tide. Visibility was severely limited, the navigational systems gave conflicting reports, and for four hours the satnav gave no position. They were just hours from the finish line, but exactly how close was anyone's guess. When the satnav fix finally came, Taylor realised they'd already passed the Needles— the three distinctive chalk stacks at the western end of the Isle of Wight, signalling the entrance to the Solent strait and the approach to their final destination, Portsmouth—overshooting by seven miles. They dropped the spinnaker and jibed, heading back through the murk. It was gut-wrenching to watch a rival yacht sail past from behind and fly down the Solent.

The water was flat, but with 30 to 40 knots of breeze, they were soon sailing at almost fourteen knots. 'We rocketed through the Solent, past Cowes and the Medina River [on the Isle of Wight],' Taylor told Parker. 'Suddenly, wham, a great gust of wind coming down the valley from Cowes hit us broadside on. It was at least 50 knots ... We wiped out in a big way. A real, screaming, flat-in-the-water broach.

We came up again and carried on a bit then, wham, over we went again. We had to get the kite off and quick ... In our haste the halyard got away and we dropped the kite fair into the water. It was the first time we had ever done this, and we had to pick now ... I was forced to head upwind to stall the boat. With 700 square feet of main up in 40 knots of wind, it flapped wildly and it looked as though we would lose our mast ... In two minutes, just six miles from the finish, everything had gone mad. Finally we got control and headed off down the Solent ... Then, right at the finish, we did another hairy jibe around the mark at Fort Castle before we finally crossed the finish at midday.'

Outward Bound was thirteenth across the line, taking the small boat trophy and finishing the race in a remarkable fifth place overall on handicap. All four of the boats ahead were bigger, and all four skippers had done the race before.

Just twenty of the original 29 boats finished the race. *Outward Bound*'s main rival in its class, *Morbihan,* finished more than 50 hours after *Outward Bound,* in seventh place on handicap. *Ceramco* was the third-fastest yacht around the world but finished eleventh on overall handicap.

'The highlight of the whole race for me was that I wanted to sail against the best in the world,' said Taylor. '[We] have shown that New Zealand yachtsmen are competitive among the best.'

In 1982, Taylor was awarded an MBE for services to ocean yacht racing, proving, he declared, that 'you didn't need to have an education to have letters after your name'.

ANNE AUDAIN

'Outclassed and outraged'

'HAD SOMEONE TAKEN a good hard look at my class at school and tried to pick possible future athletic champions,' Anne Audain once remarked, 'I would surely have gone unnoticed.'

Audain was born Anne Garrett in 1955 with deformities in both feet—bony protrusions on the inside forefeet like giant bunions. She grew up in unrelenting pain aggravated by migraines and poor circulation in her legs. Surgery wasn't an option until her bones had grown strong enough to handle it, so the little girl from Otahuhu in South Auckland would walk the three kilometres to school barefoot, her weight on the outside edges of her feet to lessen the agony. When bare feet weren't an option, she'd wear shoes with sections cut out of them to ease the pressure. She was teased mercilessly.

Even so, she enjoyed sport and was an enthusiastic, if 'pretty hopeless', member of the Otahuhu Athletics Club. At thirteen she finally went under the knife. While recovering in hospital, she learned for the first time how to walk properly—in a straight line rather than with the pigeon-toed gait she'd developed.

Weeks later she started at Otahuhu's McAuley High School, wearing heavy plaster casts from toes to knees on both legs that cut into her swollen feet, and large 'rocker' shoes designed to teach her normal heel–toe movement. Other girls would steal her lunch as she ate or swipe the project she was working on, knowing she couldn't chase them. 'I can't say that my high school years were very pleasant because of all the teasing, but on the other hand my tormentors certainly gave me plenty of incentive to become quicker on my feet,' she recalled in her autobiography, *Uncommon Heart*.

When the casts came off after six months, sores and blisters covered her legs. But to Audain her feet looked perfect. She spent many hours walking or running through the shallows of Auckland's beaches and rivers to strengthen her muscles and improve her gait. 'The kids used to laugh at the way I walked,' she later told the *New Zealand Woman's Weekly*. 'Then they laughed when I started to run—but that just made me more determined.'

She returned to the athletics club, where she discovered a love for competitive running. Her parents couldn't bear to watch. 'They just couldn't understand why I wanted to run,' she told journalist Virginia Myers. 'They didn't stop me—I don't think they could have.'

A year after her surgery, barely fourteen and running barefoot, she surprised everyone by coming third in a one-mile race against some of Auckland's top senior athletes. Then she came second in an Auckland championship half-mile, behind one of the country's best runners, Anne Smith, whose coach, Olympic silver medallist Gordon Pirie, told Audain's parents she had great potential and offered to coach her. Despite their concerns about her feet, they agreed to let her try.

Audain turned up to her first training session barefoot, in cut-off jeans and a sleeveless floral dress shirt. Once she'd complied with Pirie's first order—to 'dress correctly'—she discovered she loved the rhythm of good, hard running. 'I just wanted to run as hard and as fast as I could. I never liked to run slowly.'

In the next two years she refused to let her feet slow her down, biting back the pain to train and race. She began to win even against senior athletes. Though the surgery had been a success, her feet were crisscrossed with scars and remained fragile. 'My original doctors advised me not to continue running,' she said, later. 'They thought I was being too adventurous.' After training sessions, her father would bathe her feet in Epsom salts, and her mother would put her to bed with a shot of whisky and warm milk, to ease the pain. She was periodically forced to take time off to let her feet recover.

Her toes pushed constantly against the front of her flimsy canvas shoes, causing bruising and infections—a common ailment for runners, especially in the days before specialist running shoes. Her doctor would drill holes in her toenails to relieve the pressure, and she'd cut holes in her shoes to give her big toe more space. In cross-country races she'd shimmy through the mud under fences because she was too scared to climb over them and risk landing badly on her feet.

Pirie was another challenge. Though Audain grew physically stronger under his coaching and learned valuable lessons on pacing, rhythm and running her own race, the coach had a notoriously difficult personality. When she was sixteen and he was in his early forties he tried to bully her into sex. Too embarrassed to tell anyone, she remained under his tutelage. 'I was scared to death. His argument was that I was an attractive young girl and that he had been good to me, and that I basically owed him . . . I certainly rejected him, but from that moment on our personal relationship changed. He tried to make my life hell.'

Bureaucracy also frustrated her. As the 1972 Munich Olympics approached, Audain repeatedly ran the qualifying time for the new 1500 metres women's race. Each time, the New Zealand selectors would insist she run faster to earn her spot. One day the head selector told her he wanted her on the team, only to call her three weeks before the Olympics to say his colleagues had decreed she was too young, at a frail-looking sixteen. 'That's the sort of thing athletes had to deal with over and over again. We'd meet the Olympic standard—and in my case become the national champion—and then not get selected for the team. And it was always weighted in such a way as to allow more men to go, because women's sports were considered secondary.'

Money was a source of constant stress. The rules of amateurism forbade athletes from receiving prize money, so after high school Audain studied at teachers' college and became a primary school teacher, while trying to compete overseas. She'd wear her racing shoes until they fell apart. After one athletics meet in Germany, she sold her coveted black uniform to offset expenses. Looking back, Audain suspected that the stress of dealing with Pirie along with the other pressures manifested physically—she developed asthma-like symptoms, put on weight and suffered anxiety attacks.

In 1976, aged twenty, she made the Olympic team but finished last in her 800 metres heat and seventh in her 1500 metres heat—against some unusually masculine- and muscular-looking Russian and Eastern European athletes. Her consolation was that she'd broken a New Zealand record.

Disappointed, she returned home to discover her teaching career was on the rocks because she took so much time off. Finding the time and money to train and compete was a constant struggle, and her feet flared up. In the lead-up to the 1977 Athletics World Cup, she wrote in her diary, 'Rang [my friend] to see if they had sold my radio. Could only get $2.50 for it so didn't sell. That upset me no end as now I have no [spending] money to go to Europe with.'

Her trip to Europe was bleak—she was twice carried off the track on a stretcher, once for a stress attack and once with leg and back trouble. She believed she'd hit rock bottom. Upon returning home, she hooked up with a salesman she'd met, Steve Audain, and started going out more and drinking until late at night. The couple stretched their budget to buy an apartment in Auckland, and married in 1978. She was 22, he 27. Her running career continued to falter. She badly twisted an ankle when she leapt from the path of a car during a training run, had a disappointing yield on the track and succumbed to a succession of minor illnesses. One day she stole money from her father's dresser to pay for petrol. Food became a crutch, she put on more weight, and her relationship with Pirie deteriorated, but she couldn't see a way out. She abandoned her goal to reach the 1978 Commonwealth Games.

In early 1979 her situation began to improve. With her husband's help, she jumpstarted her training regime and began to find her way back to the winner's podium. In September she resigned from teaching to become a full-time athlete, supporting herself with a part-time job in an Auckland pancake cafe. Though Pirie was becoming ever more abusive and erratic, she began running her fastest times ever, so she stuck with him.

Over and over, she ran the international qualifying times for the 800, 1500 and new 3000 metres races for the 1980 Moscow Olympics, but the selectors refused to pick her. It became a moot point when New Zealand joined the United States' boycott of the Games.

In April 1980, during the European racing season, matters came to a head with Pirie. He had found a cabin for them to base themselves in while she hit the circuit, in a forest outside Norway. Not only was his coaching seemingly without purpose, but he hid her passport, forced her to dress as a man to work at the nearest wharves with him to fund the trip, and restricted her food and liquid intake. 'The threat of verbal and even physical abuse was ever present,' she recalled. 'One time he threw me in a sauna all day to make me lose weight, a ludicrous idea.'

After returning to New Zealand, Audain vowed never to speak to Pirie again, though he stalked her and verbally abused her for months. Exhausted, depressed and near penniless, she resolved to quit. 'I had a nervous breakdown,' she later said. 'I shook constantly. I couldn't even hold a knife and fork. I was an absolute mess. I couldn't find a job teaching and we needed the money. I lost confidence in myself. I was overweight, unfit, unhealthy, hated running.'

Her husband suggested she get in touch with coach John Davies, an Olympic and Commonwealth medallist who'd been trained by Arthur Lydiard. Davies had always been supportive and encouraging of Audain, and his gentle, stable personality was the opposite of Pirie's. It took her weeks to summon the courage to call him. Then he spent three days thinking it over before he agreed to take her on. 'I assessed her as a challenge,' he told journalist

Robyn Langwell. Audain turned up to their first training run wearing her husband's large football shorts and a baggy jersey, to hide her weight gain. 'It's not going to be easy,' Davies warned her. 'I'm going to have to take you completely apart and put you back together again.'

Shortly afterwards, she badly sprained her ankle. It took the rest of 1980 to heal. 'One might think that I would have been discouraged but, quite honestly, I had been through so much in the previous five years with Gordon that something like that didn't particularly get me down,' she wrote in her autobiography. 'In fact, considering that I'd been right up to the edge of my sanity, the fact that I survived left me so mentally tough that no challenge I ever faced again would seem so daunting.'

She was 167 centimetres tall and weighed 60 kilograms, about ten kilograms heavier than when at her peak condition. Though the weight began to come off, other runners and officials continued to make snide comments about it. 'At this point, such harassment had little effect on me,' she recalled. 'I'd been through a lot worse. All I cared about was running. It had become a protective barrier, a brick wall against a lot of things that might otherwise have hurt me.'

In April 1981 she competed in a ten-kilometre race in New Orleans. New Zealand athlete and friend Dick Quax had engineered the invitation, giving the organisers a false time for her in a distance she'd never raced. She fell at the start and was trampled by some of the other 8000 runners. Someone hauled her to her feet and got her moving. She'd lost her necklace and watch and skinned her knees and elbows. She ran the first part of the race on sheer anger. 'I was so mad to have started off so miserably I considered my options: I could have easily chosen to step off to the side of the road and called it a day, or I could pull myself together and start running down the people who had just run over me.' She chose the latter and came in third, behind two of the greatest American runners of the era.

She and Steve decided to give themselves two years to establish her career in the United States. If it didn't work out, they would move to London and settle into regular jobs. With the American running boom beginning, top runners were being courted and well treated with expenses and gifts from sponsors, and Audain began to win and place in road races. She'd found her niche and rediscovered her confidence. Then she made a decision that threatened to end her career.

The top American runners, fed up with being banned from officially earning prize or sponsorship money, banded together to race in the first event to offer prize money publicly, organised by Nike and held in Portland, Oregon. Audain desperately needed the money, but it was a safe bet that anyone who pocketed it could give up Olympic and Commonwealth dreams. 'I decided it was time to make a stand,' she told journalist and Commonwealth Games gold medallist Roy Williams. 'So I took the money. It was the biggest decision of my life.' She was hurled into the spotlight when she won the race, netting $10,000, with fellow New Zealand athletes Lorraine Moller and Allison Roe second and third respectively.

Shortly afterwards, Audain signed a sponsorship deal with Nike. Within hours she received two telegrams from the New Zealand Amateur Athletic Association advising she was banned from the sport for life. Though that would not prevent her running road races in the United States, she wouldn't be eligible for amateur races, including the Olympic or Commonwealth games. Shortly afterwards, she broke the world record for the 5000 metres, in Auckland. In shock, she cried. Administrators refused to accept the record because of the ban. 'She couldn't get past the male hierarchy ... people who all wore the same suits and ties,' Steve later told journalist Jane Phare. 'They were playing games with her head to feed their own egos and power.' He took up the battle with the New Zealand administrators, using a mixture of bluff and threats, suggesting he'd organise a media stunt and pointing out that they'd lose her for the 1982 Brisbane Commonwealth Games.

Undaunted, Audain returned to the United States for a dream season, winning twelve from twelve races and breaking course records in each of them. Davies continued coaching her from New Zealand, bringing her into the best shape of her life in time for the Commonwealth Games. He begged her to take time out from the lucrative American circuit for the Games, but she was scared to break her winning streak with a failure in Brisbane. Though she had become a changed athlete since Davies had begun coaching her, she was wary of attempting a track race when she'd grown accustomed to the road. Also, the 3000 metres distance she'd be running was an unfamiliar one, and her times weren't so hot.

'Do it for your parents, your country—you can get the gold,' Davies told her.

Feeling charged up by Davies's challenge, she relented. The ban was lifted just in time, she was reinstated as an amateur, and her world record was officially recognised.

In training at Brisbane, Audain—ranked ninth in the Common-wealth—marvelled at the fitness of the other runners in her race, among them some of the world's best athletes at their peak. She knew she wasn't expected to win—on paper, at least. 'But in my mind a thought began to take shape: I did not come this far not to win a medal. Thirteen years of my life had come to this. All the pre-dawn runs and the gut-wrenching intervals on the track, the miles of forest trails, Gordon's insane abuse, the maddening officials, the cross-country races in freezing rain. It had all come down to seven and a half laps.' She refused to let in negative thoughts. She pictured herself on the dais and her family celebrating at home in Otahuhu. 'Every time I went running in my build-up I used to pound along the road using images—seeing myself in my head crossing the line first, wearing my gold medal . . . mind over matter, psyching myself into it,' she told Langwell.

On the day of the race, the 26 year old crouched on the track and prayed for it to be over. It was the biggest contest of her life, and she felt sick with nerves. Davies had warned her not to lead the 24-strong pack early, to avoid tiring herself in the windy conditions, but the athlete who never liked running slowly had drawn the inside of the track and found herself in front by default. She looked across at the other runners and made a snap decision. She figured if she didn't start quickly and attack, she'd be caught up in a terrible mess. *To hell with them*, she thought. *I'm going to run hard.*

She took off like 'a scared rabbit', she later told the media, at a pace far quicker than she'd ever attempted in that distance. The BBC commentators mused about which runner from Great Britain was likely to overtake her for the win. As the field separated, it looked certain that race favourite Wendy Smith would prevail. For lap after lap she ran at Audain's shoulder, sheltering behind her on the blustery back straight while Audain did all of the harder running in front. Audain knew the smart money was on Smith. It was just a question of when she would pounce. She blocked out the lap times called by the officials, fearing they would have a negative effect on her.

By the last lap, Audain was still in front. She could hear Smith pounding away right behind and sensed her faltering slightly as they hit the wind. No way was Audain going to give up the lead now. Coming into the final curve, Smith surged. Anticipating it, Audain cranked her pace. 'This was a medal I really wanted for myself,' she later told Langwell. 'It was a goal that originally I thought was impossible—but I was determined to do it ... I battled for a lot of years, outclassed and outraged. I always believed I could be a world-class runner.'

Feeling exhilarated, Audain left Smith far behind and hit the tape first, in a Commonwealth Games and New Zealand record time. She became the first New Zealand woman to win a Games gold on the track.

'It seemed as if everything I had ever done had led me to that moment, and my life made perfect sense,' she wrote in her autobiography. 'All the solitary hours of my childhood, the taunting of other children, the endless pain of my feet, the training runs in the dark and the rain, the hills that demanded your dignity before they relented, the mean struggle to earn a living while trying to be an athlete, it had all been worth it. I had won.'

The win was the peak of a racing career from which Audain retired in 1991, aged 36. Many years later, she still ran more gracefully than she walked. 'I have a saying,' she once said, 'that if it's not life and death, everything can be overcome, and fixed.'

15

CHRIS LEWIS

'Hail Mr Nobody'

AS THE WIMBLEDON TENNIS TOURNAMENT began in 1983, few people noticed a mullet-haired, headband-wearing unseeded player from New Zealand. And for good reason. The 26-year-old Chris Lewis was in the worst form of his career. In the previous year he'd dropped 60 places in the world rankings, to 91, and he was rated a 500 to 1 outsider to claim the gentlemen's singles trophy. He'd come to London's hallowed All England Lawn Tennis Club courts fresh from bombing out at the French Open, where he'd contracted a virus. *The Times* of London, when it eventually noticed him, called him a 'scrappy retriever without much of a serve'.

All the attention for the men's tournament was on the world's top three players: defending Wimbledon champion Jimmy Connors, world number one John McEnroe and rising star Ivan Lendl. Even if by some disaster McEnroe and Connors didn't make the final two, another fourteen seeded players were on form to slip in.

When British newspaper *The Guardian* speculated on the most likely of the nine-dozen unseeded players to cause an upset, Lewis wasn't mentioned. If anyone was going to fly the underdog flag, it would probably be Pat Cash of Australia or Stefan Edberg of Sweden, both promising teenagers. But the discussions were hypothetical. Only seven unseeded players had reached a Wimbledon final since seeding began in 1927—the last in 1967—and none had won. It seemed Wimbledon was no longer a tournament in which an unknown could prevail.

Even Lewis didn't expect much from the tournament. If anything, he planned to use it as a warm-up to an upcoming Davis Cup tie with Sweden. With that in mind, he entered every category he could—the men's singles, the men's doubles and the mixed doubles.

Despite his lowly rating and poor form, Lewis had at least one advantage—he was reputed to be the fittest player in the world rankings, an obsessive exerciser who could outlast his opponents even if he couldn't always outclass them. As well as running long distances to build stamina, he regularly did sprint training to boost his speed on the court. And he was comfortable playing on a grass court, having launched his career by winning the junior Wimbledon singles in 1975, aged eighteen, though he'd never lived up to that early promise. After the knocks of the previous year, his confidence was recovering; the early exit from the French Open had prompted a round of bedridden soul searching that had motivated him to intensify his training.

'Every year I played Wimbledon I certainly had high hopes and there wasn't anything different about 1983 other than the fact I had probably been playing the worst tennis of my career in the first few months of that year,' he later told *The Dominion Post*. 'It had reached the stage where things weren't going that great and the bottom of the downward spiral was at the French [Open], which I shouldn't have played . . . I always felt as though I had the potential to do well at Wimbledon. I had the game to do it, whether I could was another matter.'

The smart money was on Lewis being eliminated from the singles in the first round, where he was drawn to meet ninth seed Steve Denton, an American hard-hitter with a big serve. Denton had won all three of their previous encounters, most recently in the Queen's tournament in London just weeks earlier. He'd eliminated Lewis from Wimbledon in the third round the year before. Denton's coach, Warren Jacques, figured Lewis's skill on grass might give them trouble but expected his man to prevail.

The match seesawed. Lewis won the first set, Denton the second. The third-set tiebreaker proved the turning point. 'I wasn't that confident going into the tiebreak,' Lewis told his biographer, Joseph Romanos. 'It's never nice having to play a big server in a tiebreak because the odds are that they can bang down some big ones and that you'll drop the odd point.'

Lewis won the set, which not only kept him in the match but boosted his confidence. Though Denton equalled the score by taking the fourth set, Lewis's optimism grew. With his superior fitness, a longer match would work in his favour. In the fifth set, he sensed the American fading. The legendary serve lost some of its sting and the rallies lengthened.

After three hours on court, the deciding set went comfortably to Lewis, 6–3. His fitness, speed and perseverance had launched him into Wimbledon's second round, despite being aced in the match 22 times and pinged for thirteen foot faults.

Next up against Lewis was another unknown, young Australian Broderick Dyke. The first set was tight and even, with the Kiwi winning, 7–6. After that, Lewis knew the match was his. 'I felt if I could just keep the pressure on I'd come out on top.' He won in straight sets, in a match on a distant court that barely rated a mention in the London newspapers.

Then came American Mike Bauer, who'd beaten Lewis in straight sets and number one seed Jimmy Connors in a tournament that year in Palm Springs. Lewis rated Bauer on par with Denton, with a tough serve and an aggressive game. The match shaped up much like the one against Denton, with Lewis winning the first set, losing the second, winning the third in a tiebreaker and losing the fourth in another tiebreaker. 'Next thing, I'm down 0–2 in the fifth with Mike playing really well and things looking grim,' Lewis recalled. 'I realised if something wasn't done soon the match would be over.' Desperate, Lewis raised his game, capitalising on his fitness to build up the intensity. He flew over the court, fighting back to overcome Bauer, 6–4. The match was his. Relief surged through him. He knew it could easily have gone the other way.

He was in the last sixteen. One more win and he'd be in the quarterfinals. Finally, fans and the media began to notice him. Far more of the world's attention, however, was focused on his next opponent, flamboyant Nigerian Nduka 'The Duke' Odizor, who had become the crowd favourite after unleashing the tournament's biggest upset so far, coming back from two sets down to eliminate fourth seed Guillermo Vilas in the opening round.

Lewis's nerves frayed. The night before the match, as good luck telegrams started arriving from New Zealand, he didn't sleep. 'I became conscious that this was a real opportunity to go all the way . . . the tantalising prospect of making the Wimbledon quarters and beyond was more than exciting.' In the morning he abandoned efforts to sleep and hauled himself to the courts for his usual pre-game training routine. After lunch he locked himself in a bathroom, made a bed beside the bath with a pile of towels, and slept. After 90 minutes, a friend woke him, and he dragged himself up to face Odizor in the 2 p.m. match, feeling like death.

Lewis served first. Odizor laid into him, clocking up a 0–40 lead before his opponent even properly woke up. *No,* Lewis told himself. *It's not going to be one of those nightmare matches.* He shook off his weariness and fought back to win the game. After that, he barely missed a ball. 'The rest of the match flowed through for me easier than I had dared hope,' he recalled. 'I think he felt a lot of pressure—maybe he felt he had let people down. I just made sure I never gave him any breathing room.' Lewis won convincingly, in straight sets.

Afterwards, on a television in the dressing room, he watched Connors' tournament implode at the hands of South African twelfth seed Kevin Curren, whose machine-gun serve aced Connors' 33 times in the five-set match. 'I'd seen a lot of Curren and felt he was the big danger in the top section of the draw, especially in a grass court tournament,' said Lewis, later. 'There wouldn't have been many players who would have relished being drawn to play him. He had a big serve and tons of flair.'

The New Zealander, however, always made a point of never thinking further than his next opponent. In the quarterfinals he was up against American Mel Purcell, whom he'd never played but knew to be a competitive man with a tricky, unpredictable game. It would be difficult to formulate a game plan and get into a rhythm. Before the match, he read dozens of telegrams wishing him luck, many from strangers. The support buoyed him.

The first set was fairly even. Lewis lost 6–7, kicking himself for failing to capitalise on the chances that had come his way. He came back with a nearly flawless second set and scraped through a tight third with a win. In the fourth he brought the game to match point but missed a straightforward volley. Purcell pushed him into a tiebreaker. Lewis won. The crowd rose to their feet, but the media remained unconvinced. 'The match will not go down in history as a classic,' claimed *The Times* tennis correspondent Rex Bellamy. 'Both players had their hair tucked into white bandannas and at times it seemed reasonable to speculate that Purcell was the less effective of the two because his bandanna was worn so low that it was almost a blindfold.'

More important than praise, though, Lewis had made the top four at Wimbledon. To the outsider it looked likely he'd have to be content with entering that result onto his résumé—his semifinal opponent was Connors' conqueror, Kevin Curren, on Centre Court. It was expected to be a predictable afterthought to the McEnroe–Lendl semifinal that preceded it. 'Curren must be the favourite to win,' wrote Bellamy.

Though Lewis greatly respected Curren, his confidence was at an all-time high. He'd played ten matches in the tournament, including two rounds of the men's doubles and three of the mixed doubles (before withdrawing when his partner suffered an injury), and his fitness was holding up. Curren was tired after playing eleven matches, including a doubles semifinal loss the previous day. Still, according to his coach, he was fairly confident he could overcome

Lewis without expending too much energy. The key would be to dispense of the New Zealander quickly, so the match didn't drag on into a battle of the fittest.

'It was one of those matches that both of us thought he could win,' Lewis recalled. 'In my own mind, I knew I had the game to beat him, especially on grass . . . I was ready. I was now two matches away from winning the greatest tournament in the world—the tournament that my brothers and I, when we were growing up, would play the imaginary final of in the backyard. It was the tournament that I would stay up all night to listen to on the radio when I was a kid in New Zealand.'

As he waited for the showdown, his nerves building, Lewis watched McEnroe take down Lendl in straight sets in the other semifinal. He and Curren prepared in the same dressing room, in silence. They walked out in front of an audience of 20,000, with millions more watching on television. British prime minister Margaret Thatcher had been expected to leave the courts after watching the McEnroe victory but stayed on to catch the Curren–Lewis opening.

In the first set, Lewis struggled to adjust to Curren's powerful, spinning serve. The South African won the set after a tiebreak. But Lewis had got a feel for his opponent's game and won the next set, 6–4. The third went to a tiebreaker and Lewis prevailed by a whisker. One more set, and he could be in the final. The crowd was delighted. For Lewis, the atmosphere became almost unbearable.

Curren, though tiring, came back strongly to win the fourth set, 7–6. As with the Bauer and Denton matches, it came down to a fifth-set decider. Curren quickly got up to 3–0. He was confident he had the win. Lewis knew that if he conceded another game he'd have a hard time getting back into the match psychologically. He drew on his reserves to fight back to 2–3. 'My serve followed and we had a very long service game where I struggled and struggled to hold,' he said. 'Finally I clinched it after five deuces.'

With the set tied, Curren was beginning to think the match would never end. Desperate to keep up his flagging stamina he drank Coke and ate chocolates in the breaks. 'I just couldn't break him,' he said, later. 'Most guys would have folded under the pressure but Chris seemed to get tougher as the match progressed.'

By this time, the men had been playing for three and a half hours, a vigorous, physical game that had left Lewis cut and bruised from diving for the ball and landing on his knees and even his elbows. He'd forced Curren into a physical game he lacked the energy for—at one point the South African had played a shot on his knees. 'Lewis clung to the match like a terrier,' declared American sportswriter Peter Bodo. '[It] was a slashing affair, full of diving volleys, impossible retrievals and shifting opportunities.'

The duel cranked up, point for point, until the set was poised at 6–6. Centre Court, according to *The New York Times* correspondent, 'quivered with tension'. Lewis felt stronger than he had at the start of the match. His momentum and athleticism—and several errors from Curren—brought him to match point. He looked up at his coach, Tony Roche, and training partner, Jeff Simpson, in the players' box, to acknowledge their contributions.

'When I stepped up for match point, there was a deadly silence,' he later told journalist Michael Brown. 'It was church-like. People wondered what was going to happen. It was so Wimbledon— there's nothing like it in tennis. He hit a return that floated out on my backhand side. That was it. I was in the final. It hit me then. That was the first time in my career when I lifted my hands above my head after I won. It was just wonderful.'

The crowd, which still included Thatcher, gave Lewis a standing ovation. He'd become the sensation of the tournament—the first New Zealander to win a final spot at Wimbledon since four-time champion Anthony Wilding in 1914, and the lowest ranked player ever to make it. Former Wimbledon champion Björn Borg noted that Lewis didn't even seem out of breath. 'There wasn't a trace of distress after nearly four hours of intense physical and mental anguish. We all thought Curren would win and I still rate the South African the better player. But he was broken by guts, nerve and incredible reflexes.'

Commentators decreed it the match of the tournament. London's *Daily Mail* declared, 'Hail Mr Nobody'. Lewis filled three lockers in the dressing room with thousands of telegrams and letters from wellwishers—he was told no player in Wimbledon history had received more. It was the pinnacle of his career; in the final he went down hard to the 24-year-old John McEnroe, in straight sets, 6–2, 6–2, 6–2. McEnroe, who also won the doubles title that year, was at the top of his game and returned to Wimbledon the next year to give Connors an even greater hiding in the final. Curren reckoned the only man who could have beaten McEnroe that day in 1983 was Borg, who'd retired months earlier.

Guardian journalist David Irvine said Lewis should be proud that he'd contributed to the greatest match of the championship (against Curren) and that it had taken the best player in the world to defeat him. 'Lewis, certainly, had no need to feel distressed at his loss, disappointing though it was. He praised McEnroe as "an artist with a racquet". His efforts were worth a title too; an artisan with the heart of a lion.'

Decades later, Lewis told an interviewer that the final was the greatest moment of his life. 'I was disappointed, but only to a point. In a deeper sense, I had the satisfaction of knowing that my preparation and my commitment were the maximum possible. I was able to look back on the tournament without a single regret. I felt I had extracted the maximum amount possible from my game and that I'd expended every last ounce of effort attempting to win the tournament. Thirty years later, if I had the opportunity to do the same thing all over again, attitudinally speaking, I wouldn't change a thing. Those two weeks were an unbelievable experience . . . I got within one match of the absolute ultimate in the game.'

16

JIM CASSIDY AND KIWI THE RACEHORSE

The horse that 'couldn't win'

ON THE EVE of the 1983 Melbourne Cup a little-known twenty-year-old New Zealand jockey left the sauna in his Melbourne hotel and headed to the bar. As Jim Cassidy ordered a beer, a bloke beside him said, 'You're riding in the Melbourne Cup tomorrow, aren't you?'

'Yep,' said the young jockey, 'and I'll win it too.' He promptly skolled the beer.

His ride, Kiwi, wasn't favoured for Australasia's most revered horse race. He was a farm-raised gelding from the tiny rural Taranaki settlement of Waverley. He'd been trained among sheep and cows, was occasionally put to work rounding them up and was sometimes taken hunting.

Trainer Snow Lupton and his wife, Anne, had bought the horse at a yearling auction in Te Rapa in 1978 for the reserve price of $1000, after only two bids. The placid colt with unusually small feet had passed largely unnoticed in the busy auction. For the Luptons, his colouring was a key motivation—Anne had a hankering for a chestnut horse—but his breeding was also important. He was the half-brother of a promising galloper and treasured pet the Luptons had been forced to put down after a fall in training.

Snow had been sceptical of Anne's instinct but agreed to inspect him. 'I said there would be something wrong with him, you only get one in a hundred that is right,' he later told a journalist. 'But I'm damned if I could see a lot wrong with him.'

Kiwi was their fourth-choice name—their preferred names were all taken. Snow wasn't impressed, as he mistakenly considered kiwis to be slow birds. He began trucking Kiwi to the local races in his old red Bedford. By age two, the horse was coming along nicely but showing no brilliance. In his first trial race, according to Snow, 'he didn't know his left from his right'. But he was unusually settled while racing—he seemed to enjoy it, like no other horse Snow had dealt with.

It took several seasons for Kiwi to find a consistent racing pattern. One day Cassidy, then an ambitious eighteen-year-old apprentice from Wellington, watched him race from the birdcage. Impressed, he approached Snow. 'If you ever need a rider give me a ring,' he said.

In early 1981, Cassidy got the call. He drove six hours to ride Kiwi to second place in a minor race at Stratford. 'I'd dreamed of winning a Melbourne Cup from a very young age and I knew straight off he was a Melbourne Cup horse,' he said, later. Still, even he had doubts. A year out from the Cup, he told Snow that Kiwi might not be as good as they'd thought. 'This horse thinks it's a joke. You might have to put him in blinkers.'

The breakthrough came when the Luptons and Cassidy realised Kiwi was stronger over longer rides than sprints. But though he and Cassidy won the Wellington Cup in early 1983, his form between that and Melbourne was patchy—two wins and a third from seven starts, mostly on small regional tracks in the lower North Island. He'd suffered from a reaction to oats in 1982 that had hampered his build-up. He'd never raced outside New Zealand. And no horse had won both the Wellington and the Melbourne cups—many said it couldn't be done because it would require peaking twice in one year.

Even so, once Kiwi arrived in Melbourne, his form and temperament began to turn the heads of keen punters, though some wondered at Snow's preparation strategy. Two days before the Cup, Snow was riding him up and down the hills of a Mornington farm, alongside sheep and cattle. Journalists were confounded that Snow didn't even take Kiwi for a practice run on the Melbourne Cup track.

'Are you going to take him up to Flemington for a look?' asked one reporter.

'No,' said the legendarily reticent Snow.

'Not even for a look at the track?'

'No.'

'You mean you're going to put him first up in a Melbourne Cup?'

'Yes. He knows his way around a racecourse.'

New Zealand journalist Chris Peters reported that Kiwi spent his time before the race relaxing. 'While his Melbourne Cup rivals have been driving the headline writers frantic with fast and slow training runs, experiments with blinkers and shadow rolls, and prophecies about who will have to do what to beat the ballot, Kiwi just wanders around his Mornington farm paddock. There are cattle and sheep in the pasture around him, and it's just like home.'

Snow told one reporter who went out to Mornington that Kiwi was 'lazy', and jockeys who weren't familiar with him could easily get the impression he was no good. 'You've got to understand him,' he said.

'He's dreadful to watch in a race, too—shocking,' said Anne.

'Jim knows him, and he's a patient rider, doesn't panic,' added Snow.

The Australians had to wait until race day to get a good look at Kiwi. He turned up to the track seeming hard, fit and calm. Later Cassidy said, 'There was a lot that said Kiwi couldn't win—his racing pattern and because he'd had a month between runs before the Melbourne Cup. But, you know, he was just about the only horse in the mounting yard that was relaxed, not sweating up. I remember Snowy was standing there, smoking a roll-your-own, absolutely no pressure.' By the final call, Kiwi's odds had shortened to third favourite. In New Zealand, by virtue of his name and provenance, he was the sentimental favourite.

Seconds after the 24 horses launched out of the cage for the 3200-metre race, any confidence in the horse appeared misplaced. Kiwi and Cassidy settled in at the very back of the pack. By the halfway mark, they remained there, barely acknowledged by the race callers. With 900 metres to go they'd overtaken one horse, but only because it was injured. As the field spaced out, they were a good 25 lengths behind the leaders, and fast running out of track. With less than 200 metres to race, they still hugged the back of the pack.

The commentary over the loudspeakers at the ground barely mentioned Kiwi until the last seconds of the race, except to say, twice, 'And Kiwi is last of all,' and 'A good long way back is Kiwi.'

Cassidy remained calm. At the top of the final straight, with all eyes on the fight between the leaders, Kiwi reached the tail of the bunch. Gaps began to appear, and Cassidy began zigzagging his relatively fresh ride through, their progress masked by a dozen horses' flanks, unnoticed by callers and missed by most of the television cameras.

'There was only another four or five in front of me,' recalled Cassidy. 'All I had to do was give Kiwi a clear passage, not run up one of their arses and get stopped. That was the thing with him, you just had to give him a clear crack at 'em.'

They reached the clock tower, a landmark on the famous Flemington course that signalled the finish was 150 metres away, and struck, ripping past the flagging competition to find space on the outside of the pack.

Still the callers didn't see them, figuring they had their final finishers in sight. Jockey Robert Heffernan, riding Noble Comment, thought the race was his. Noble Comment's trainer began mentally preparing his acceptance speech. Then Cassidy let loose. 'I noticed Kiwi out of the corner of my eye; a second later he was two lengths in front,' recalled Heffernan. 'He was flying.'

One television caller related those last seconds thus: 'Two hundred to go and Mr Jazz has stormed up on the outside to take the lead from Noble Comment and then Chiamare and No Peer. Noble Comment's fighting back. He's gone at Mr Jazz again. It's Mr Ja—. And here comes Kiwi, out of the blue.'

The caller at the ground was also taken by surprise: 'Two hundred and fifty metres left to go and Chiamare being tackled by Mr Jazz and Noble Comment. Mr Jazz on the outside, Noble Comment, Chiamare. No Peer running on. Noble Comment on the inside, and Mr Jazz. Noble Comment takes the lead—Kiwi!'

With Kiwi's ripping pace on the outside of the track, taking the lead with metres to spare, it was suddenly clear who would win. But where the hell had he come from? The loudspeakers blared, 'Kiwi will beat them all. It's come from last. Kiwi! Kiwi's won the Melbourne Cup. A blistering performance.'

Heffernan was stunned. He had to watch two video replays to figure out how his win had been stolen. 'I just can't believe it,' he told a reporter. 'We were flat out yet he went past us as though we were standing still . . . It all happened so quickly—I looked across and couldn't believe Kiwi had beaten me in one stride.'

One of the few people who didn't seem surprised was Cassidy. 'The horse was relaxed, I was relaxed, and 10 minutes later we won the Melbourne Cup. He give 'em all a start and just kicked their butts.'

Another man who wasn't surprised by the finish was veteran Australian jockey Roy Higgins, winner of three Melbourne Cups. Earlier that day, Cassidy had walked up to him in the Flemington birdcage and asked how to ride a Melbourne Cup. 'Are there any particular spots to look at?' he said.

'Make sure, when you are turning out of the straight, you remember it is very sharp,' replied Higgins. 'If you are three or four wide, it will be very detrimental.'

'Doesn't matter,' Cassidy said. 'I will be last.'

'When you get to the 1400 mark,' Higgins continued, 'you want to be looking at horses going forward, getting on their back, improving your position, because you don't want to be too far off on the home turn.'

'Doesn't matter,' Cassidy said. 'I'll be last there.'

'Let's talk about when you are in the straight,' Higgins went on, frowning. 'You don't want to be giving them four or five lengths.'

Cassidy replied, 'I'll still be last there, too.'

Higgins looked at Cassidy like he had two heads. 'You can't win a Melbourne Cup from being last into the straight!' The older man stormed off, muttering, 'Who is this little bastard?' Four hours later, as he watched Cassidy do exactly that, the penny dropped.

'Luck wasn't a factor on Kiwi,' Cassidy said, nearly thirty years later. 'To this day, I've never been so confident in winning a staying race as was the case with Kiwi. He was so relaxed. He rounded up sheep and cattle on Snowy's farm. He'd gone hunting, he was the ideal horse for the atmosphere on cup day. Plenty of horses will be wired up. Some will not cope with the crowd, the noise, and it can be detrimental to their chances. More so when asked to go 3200 metres. Conserving energy is paramount. Save the best until the final surge. Kiwi was an outstanding two-miler that didn't worry about anything. Knowing him so well, patience was the key. Hooked out at the clock tower, Kiwi rattled home from the tail. Mowed them down.'

Speaking to the 80,000-strong crowd after the race, Snow said, 'I hardly need to say it's the greatest thrill of our lives.' Then emotion overcame the usually stoic and attention-shy man. He muttered, 'Oh God,' and was momentarily lost for words.

Snow caused consternation when he arrived late at the lavish after-Cup function, having taken Kiwi back to his stables to feed and settle him. He was always adamant his horses should come first. 'Feed the animals before yourself,' he'd tell his daughters. As the television cameras rolled live, Anne assured the organisers he'd show, but she was thinking, *I hope he hasn't gone to bed*. When he finally arrived, some two hours later, the organisers made him stage a mock grand entrance for the benefit of the cameras. That night, he promised to pick up the $1000 bar tab at his local pub, the Clarendon Hotel in Waverley.

Kiwi returned to contest the 1984 Melbourne Cup in what the Luptons and Cassidy believed was the form of his life, but he was controversially scratched after the official veterinarian judged him to be lame. A conspiracy theory still circulates that the decision was made to prevent the horse taking two from two. To this day, Cassidy remains in no doubt that he was fit. 'He would've pissed in. He would've won by further that year,' he told a journalist in 2013.

Kiwi won only three more races after his Melbourne Cup success. He came eleventh in the Melbourne Cup in 1985 and a respectable fourth in 1986, as a nine year old. When he was retired, in early 1987, to work around the Lupton farm, he'd won thirteen races from 60 starts, for total stakes of $557,949. He died in 1995 and was buried on the farm.

Cassidy became one of the most successful and hardest working jockeys in Australasia. In 2013, aged 50 and with no plans to retire, he became only the third jockey in Australia to win 100 Group One races. They included a second Melbourne Cup win, in 1997. He still regarded Kiwi as 'the best two-miler' he'd ever seen. 'Especially when all the Aussies said kiwis couldn't fly—well, this one could. A New Zealander winning the Melbourne Cup on a horse called Kiwi—still the greatest thrill of my life. I reckoned back then if I never won another race I would have died happy.'

Jockey John Marshall, whose ride Mr Jazz came third in 1983, said Kiwi's story and the manner of his Melbourne Cup victory had ensured his memory lived on. 'It's the race where the underdog can win, not just the high-priced, big-stable horse.'

EWEN CHATFIELD

The day the rabbit roared

As Ewen Chatfield strode in to bat against Pakistan at Carisbrook in February 1985, his teammates began packing up and bringing their flights forward, figuring there wouldn't be a victory party. The final innings of the Third Test, which would decide the series, wasn't going the Kiwis' way. Lance Cairns had been helped from the field with a hairline skull fracture after being felled by a bouncer from eighteen-year-old sensation Wasim Akram that had earned him a warning for intimidatory bowling. Akram had demolished the New Zealand batting order. Jeff Crowe, John Reid and Cairns had all got out for ducks, while John Wright had managed just one run. Martin Crowe had propped up the innings with 84, and Jeremy Coney was sitting on 82, but it wasn't likely to be enough.

At the end of a dispiriting day, the last Kiwi to come in was Chatfield. To win the Test and the series, the Kiwis needed 50 more runs, after a draw in the First Test and a win in the Second. Pakistan were playing to restore their pride with a win that would tie the series.

'[We were] in really big trouble,' New Zealand wicketkeeper Ian Smith later recalled. 'The Pakistanis were looking very cocky. There was still more than two hours to play and the 50 runs we needed seemed far too many, especially with Akram bowling with such hostility and Chats not exactly known for his relish of the quick stuff.' Chatfield was becoming a New Zealand bowling stalwart, but his outings at the crease were legendarily barren. One of his many nicknames was 'Charlie', short for 'tail-end Charlie'. The previous year, London's *Observer* newspaper had named him 'the biggest rabbit in Test cricket'—the nickname for a hapless batsman. 'Chatfield looks a true tail-ender, as though he's been given somebody else's bat to hold while they pop down to the shops,' Australian cricket journalist Gideon Haigh once observed.

Chatfield's wariness of the crease was well founded. In his debut Test for New Zealand, at Eden Park in 1975, he was struck on his bare head by a short ball from an English bowler. He staggered, dropped to the ground and swallowed his tongue. His heart and breathing stopped. He began turning blue and frothing, and was eventually brought back to life by the opposition's physiotherapist. When he was raced to hospital, he was sitting on his highest first-class score, of thirteen runs—after scoring a duck in the first innings. Smith recalled, 'Though Chats seemed to recover from the incident well enough, his confidence against quick bowling—never high anyhow—took a jolt.'

Afterwards, Chatfield struggled to cement his position in the national team, securing a regular Test spot only in 1983, aged 33, eight years after his ill-fated debut. By the 1985 series against Pakistan, he still hadn't surpassed his thirteen-run record. 'I found all bowlers, especially quick bowlers, difficult to handle,' he said, later, 'and so Wasim Akram being both fast and a left-armer to boot made the angles all the more difficult.'

Coney, who played with Chatfield for Wellington, had more respect for his teammate's batting than the rest of the Kiwis, who were convinced they'd blown the Test, now that Cairns had gone off injured. 'It's not ideal when you come in to bat after the previous fellow has been carried off and then you take guard in a pool of blood,' Coney said, afterwards. 'I don't think anyone—the Pakistanis, Chatty, anyone—expected us to get the last 50 runs . . . The pessimists felt his Test average boded ill. Others using the same statistics quite rightly pointed out the large percentage of not outs. I wanted him to believe that anything was possible.'

Chatfield and Coney came up with a strategy. Coney would try to shelter his teammate from the bowlers he was least comfortable with—chiefly, Akram—and they'd break their required runs into small targets, just ten at a time. Coney would aim to take singles, resisting the temptation to risk boundaries, while Chatfield concentrated on defending the wicket. Chatfield privately set himself a goal of seeing Coney through to his second ever Test century, as compensation for the inevitable Test loss.

Pakistan sensed the opportunity to wrap up the Test. Chatfield heard a lot of sledging in a language he couldn't understand. 'The Pakistanis really got up my nose,' he told his biographer, Lynn McConnell. 'They made it plain they were after me and were not even interested in Jeremy.' They made a point of bowling singles to Coney at the beginning of an over, to put Chatfield on strike. To get Coney back on, he'd be forced to play the ball rather than just defend. After a while the pair decided to have a go at everything on offer, with Chatfield taking more of the strike rather than relying on Coney to shield him. There was still a chance Cairns would recover enough to return to the pitch should one of them get out. They chipped away—singles, doubles, leg byes. By the time they stopped for tea, they'd reached 25—halfway to their target.

'I was a nervous wreck,' Chatfield told McConnell. 'I had a cup of tea but I was shaking so much half of it ended up on the floor. The guys largely left me alone and didn't suggest what I should be doing. They were in no position to anyway, they had all been bloody out.'

Someone asked Cairns if he could bat. The injured man was lying on a table in the darkened changing room, still padded up. Coney recalled, 'He mumbled, "You hold 'em out and I'll knock off the runs tomorrow." As it was the last day of the Test we took that as an indication we'd have to do it by ourselves.'

Despite his nerves, Chatfield resumed batting feeling encouraged by the partnership's tally. Minutes later, Coney edged the ball straight to the wicketkeeper. He couldn't bear to look behind him. The wicketkeeper fumbled. Saved. The Pakistanis grew frustrated, breaking the gentleman's rule that tail-enders should be spared the short-pitched fast balls that had nearly killed Chatfield ten years before. The umpire gave Akram another warning, which prompted a row between the official and the Pakistani captain, Javed Miandad. Chatfield felt bad for Akram. 'It was not the bowler's fault that I couldn't handle his bowling,' he said, later. 'I've still got to be able to handle it, even if I don't like it.'

The Dunedin crowd sniffed the possibility of a thrilling victory. A train bound for Invercargill stopped on the tracks overlooking the ground and passengers hung out of the windows. The television coverage went into overtime, locals sneaked away early from work, and the stands filled. Coney reached his century, and still they played on.

Coney sensed Chatfield's growing tension. 'When the crowd began cheering every ball he faced, that was when the pressure began to tell,' he recalled. 'He didn't want to let any of them down . . . [He] began to realise the responsibility of the task now lying ahead and how much was resting on his performance. Fear began to lock him up, even shake him up a little. He began to play and miss, and occasionally a ball lobbed off his bat just out of reach of a fieldsman . . . It was a tribute to Chats' phlegmatic nature that he continued to soldier on. After all, the man had died on the field . . . Suddenly facing Wasim in those circumstances was not easy.'

After striking his only four of the innings, through midwicket, leaving eight runs to victory, Chatfield nearly cracked. *Oh Jesus, here we go*, he said to himself. *I'll stuff it up now.* Exhausted, he walked down the pitch and told Coney, 'Jerry, I'm a bowler. I'm picked to bowl in this team. You're the bloody batsman. I've been out here shielding you from the strike for the last two and a half hours. I can't do it anymore. You'll have to do it.'

Despite their game plan to put Coney in the bowlers' sights, Chatfield had faced two-thirds of the deliveries, taking hits to the helmet and body. 'And really he literally couldn't do it anymore,' Coney later told journalist Joseph Romanos. 'He was white. He'd given so much. He realised we were on the point of pulling off a miraculous victory. I admired him so much that day.'

Chatfield was buoyed by Coney's conviction that if they just stayed alive, they'd win. They worked down the remaining runs single by single. Finally, just two runs remained. Coney played a ball down to backward square leg. The two Kiwis sprinted. They scored one run and came back for a second as a fielder gathered the ball. He threw. The Kiwis made it to the crease. It was over. They'd won. Coney had reached 111 and Chatfield 21, finally beating his debut tally.

With the crowd rushing the field, Chatfield didn't stop running until he made it to the pavilion, shaking, and with tears in his eyes. In the changing rooms he sat next to Smith, too wound up to drink a beer or even take off his pads. Other players cried, too. It was only New Zealand's second ever series win over Pakistan. 'It was the most emotional moment in my career,' Smith said, years later. 'It did so much for the other guys in the side, and it showed those cricketers around the world who apparently couldn't hold a bat, that they could contribute. The victory was as good as any we have ever had.'

It quickly became obvious to Chatfield that the team hadn't expected to win. 'They all thought the game was going to finish earlier and had packed their bags and booked flights home. So within minutes of the game finishing, the dressing room was empty and I was left to celebrate on my own.'

With that Test, Chatfield finally felt he'd made it as a fully fledged member of the national team, ten years after his disastrous debut. He played in 43 Tests in total, scoring a modest 180 runs while taking 123 wickets, but he always rated that innings as his career highlight, 'because I helped win a Test doing something I wasn't recognised for'.

The innings, as well as his legendary precision and reliability as a bowler, made Chatfield a folk hero. 'I think I was a player that everyone could relate to—the good old Kiwi battler,' he once said.

'I didn't have as much talent as a lot of the others on the team, but I worked pretty hard on my game.'

Smith wrote in a 2003 memoir that Chatfield never gave up trying, whether he was batting or bowling. He rated his teammate's innings in that Test as the bravest he'd ever seen. 'His 21 not out said everything about guts and determination ... It's more often than not the unlikely happening in sport, the underdog getting up against all odds, which results in tears being shed. There were more than a few seeping from the eyes of big tough grown men in the old Carisbrook dressing room that afternoon.'

GREG COOPER

'I'm not going to die. I'm going to be an All Black'

FIFTEEN-YEAR-OLD aspiring fullback Greg Cooper bent his knees, gripped the barbell and hoisted it to chest height. It was December 1980. Four months earlier, the skinny fourth former had made his debut for the first XV rugby team at St John's College, Hastings. He was determined to bulk up over the summer and prove he deserved his place with the 'big boys'.

But something wasn't right. As he lifted the weight, the bar slipped from his right hand. It felt as if his hand was losing strength. Shortly afterwards, he started having trouble with tennis, breaking two racquets as they flew out of his hand. When his sister beat him at indoor bowls because he kept dropping the ball, he knew he was in trouble.

He began having shoulder pain. It felt as if he'd pulled a muscle, and he was constantly asking his mother, Tricia, to rub the back of his shoulders. His parents took him to Auckland to see a specialist. The diagnosis was devastating. Cooper had Ewing's sarcoma, a rare form of cancer that grows in soft tissue or bone. A huge tumour over his top right rib was pressing on a nerve centre, causing a loss of feeling in his right arm and turning his rib to mush.

Cooper's parents were told that the condition had an eight per cent survival rate, with recovery usually occurring only if an affected limb could be amputated. His tumour was inoperable. Any attempt to remove it would damage nerves and cause paralysis in his right side. The specialists told his parents to 'take him home and love him', because in six months he'd be desperately ill. They gave him no chance of survival.

When Cooper's parents gave him the news, he cried for a few minutes. Then he snapped out of it, looked at them and said, 'I'm not going to die. I'm going to be an All Black.'

For Cooper, the prospect of paralysis was more frightening than death. To his mind, paralysis was permanent, while cancer was something he could fight. And fight he did. Although doctors believed treatment would be futile, they proceeded anyway, trying everything they possibly could. Cooper would have six weeks of radiotherapy to destroy the tumour, followed by two years of chemotherapy to tackle any cancer that had spread elsewhere.

For the first six months after the radiotherapy, Cooper had chemotherapy once a week in hospital at Palmerston North. He reacted badly to it, vomiting every twenty minutes for twelve to fourteen hours. Sometimes he retched for three minutes at a time, gagging so hard he burst blood vessels in his eyes. His parents sat up with him through the nights in four-hour shifts.

He shed weight and lost his hair. He watched another boy die from the same condition. But he never missed a treatment and never doubted he'd get better. One day he lay in his hospital bed, his face drawn and pale, his once-strong limbs like twigs, watching children playing rugby in a park across the street. He turned to his father, Pat. 'I'm going to play for New Zealand Schools,' he said.

By 1982, his chemotherapy treatments had been reduced to one a month. Although the effects were still brutal, he could at least resume normal life in between. School became a welcome distraction.

At the beginning of each month he'd walk into hospital weighing 76 kilograms, knowing that within a few hours he'd be violently ill. Sometimes the anticipation of the horrors ahead was so strong that he'd be sick before the treatment started. Within a few days, his weight would drop to 64 kilograms. He'd be weak and gaunt. But it never occurred to him that he wouldn't get well again. 'I tried to turn it into something positive,' he later told writer Joseph Romanos. 'I'd think that if [the chemotherapy] was doing that to me, it must be really doing something to the tumour.'

Two or three days after finishing treatment, he'd be out running, pounding his stick-thin legs along the pavement. He could still taste the toxic chemotherapy in his mouth, but no matter how bad he felt, he never stopped his running regime. That would be giving up. As his lungs burned, he'd imagine the oxygen circulating in his body, renewing the blood cells fighting the cancer. When he got home to the family farm, he'd head out to the barn to lift weights. Each time he lifted the bar, he closed his eyes, visualising himself standing on the rugby pitch wearing the All Blacks jersey. He could feel the nervous anticipation of his first Test match. As he began his squats, he could hear the national anthem and feel the tears streaming down his cheeks. The words of 'God Defend New Zealand' would carry him through to his tenth repetition. He'd pump weights twice a day, eat well and drink milk with added meal supplements, determined to regain his strength and his weight before the next cycle of treatment. He wanted to give his body the best chance of fighting the illness.

There were dark times, when he drew on his Catholic faith for strength. For him, a strong mind was the most important thing of all. 'I never doubted that I would live.'

Once back with his classmates, Cooper was desperate to get out on the rugby field. After a year's break from the game, in 1982 he was reselected for the school's first XV. He asked his doctors to schedule his chemotherapy treatments early in the week, so he'd be ready to play rugby by Saturday. They agreed. Although his body needed energy to fight the cancer, they could see rugby helped him to thrive, mentally and physically.

In his first match, Cooper was determined to prove himself, throwing himself at the opposition and splitting his eye open within ten minutes. In his second match, he tore his shoulder and had to have reconstructive surgery. Still he visualised himself wearing the black jersey and played accordingly. Towards the end of the year, while still undergoing monthly chemotherapy, he was named in the New Zealand Schools team for a match against their Australian counterparts.

In February 1983, Cooper's doctors decided his body had had enough chemotherapy. He needed a break. It was time to stop the treatments and see how his body reacted. His parents feared the cancer would return and hoped desperately for some evidence of healing. When an X-ray showed his rib bone had started to regrow and harden up, the doctors were astonished. To his family, it felt like a miracle. For the first time in two years, Cooper was able to live beyond the constraints of his treatment cycle. He had almost no muscle in his right shoulder, and reduced capacity in one lung as a consequence of the radiotherapy, but he was more determined than ever to make his dream a reality—and fast.

He left school at the end of 1983 and made the Hawke's Bay squad the following year. After the first game the selectors told him that no matter how well he played he was too young to cement a place in the side. He grew impatient. He was no regular eighteen year old, and after three gruelling years he was eager to make his dreams reality. Halfway through the season, he was selected by John Hart to play for the New Zealand Barbarians against Otago, on the strength of his performance for New Zealand Schools. The Otago coaching staff were impressed, and Cooper moved south to join the team. His consistent form for Otago brought further recognition. In 1986 he moved to Auckland and was soon a regular starter in a stellar side that included Sean Fitzpatrick, John Kirwan, Michael Jones, and Gary and Alan Whetton.

It was a controversial year for New Zealand rugby. After the New Zealand Rugby Football Union cancelled an All Blacks tour of apartheid-era South Africa, 30 team members formed a rebel squad, known as the Cavaliers, and went ahead with the tour. The union banned them from the next two All Blacks Tests.

Cooper was standing in Wellington airport when he got a call from a journalist. It was the first he knew of his selection to play for the All Blacks against France at Lancaster Park, in Christchurch. His knees shook as he dialled his parents' number, fighting back tears as he told them his dream had finally come true. 'It was almost like me paying them back,' he later told writer Gregor Paul. 'It was my way of saying thanks for all the help they had given me.'

The Wednesday before the game, Cooper reported for All Blacks training. Coach Brian Lochore had just three days to develop a game plan and create a convincing international side from a squad of newcomers, including future All Blacks greats Frano Botica, Joe Stanley and Sean Fitzpatrick, and the two current All Blacks who had refused to go on the rebel tour, David Kirk and John Kirwan. The team became known as the Baby Blacks.

Though defeat seemed inevitable, the men's pride in donning the black jersey was palpable. While they prepared for the match in the dressing room at Lancaster Park, one of the players shouted out, 'New Zealand!'

As an emotional Cooper ran onto the pitch, the experience seemed so familiar, the images so vivid, it was as if he'd been there before. For his parents and siblings, watching from the stands, it was impossible to believe this was the same boy they'd been told to take home to die. But few in the crowd or the media box knew anything about his battle. Cooper wanted to be known for his rugby, not for the illness he'd overcome.

Cooper played the game of his life. He leapt high to capture a punt from the French first five-eighth, Jean-Patrick Lescarboura, outwitting three opposition players. He was the first to score, taking one of the best drop kicks of his life to put the New Zealanders up 3–0. In all, he kicked three goals from four attempts, caught seemingly every ball and repeatedly frustrated the French with his long touch kicks. He played with a deep sense of composure, convinced the game would go his way. In *The New Zealand Herald*, D.J. Cameron described his performance as 'quite marvellous . . . almost without flaw'.

The Baby Blacks gave it their all, determined to prove they deserved their black jerseys. They defended hard, took every opportunity to score points, and won twice as many lineouts as the French in the first half.

The French were clearly rattled by the spirited onslaught. They failed to adjust their predetermined game plan and missed six relatively easy penalty goals. When the final whistle blew, the Baby Blacks had defeated them, 18–9. The crowd of 20,000 could scarcely believe what they'd witnessed. 'In the cold callous realities of sport this amazing All Blacks triumph should never have happened,' wrote Cameron. 'From the first minute to the last, these All Blacks, these heroes, fashioned for themselves a tribute of determination and skill and unyielding fortitude that should never be forgotten. The fledglings played like eagles ... This was a day when 15 raw, brave, young New Zealanders put on the All Blacks' jersey—and played like All Blacks.'

For one of those brave players, the fight of his life was finally won. Cooper had played for the All Blacks, and in his mind that was the final proof he had triumphed over the cancer. He returned to Otago in 1988 and went on to forge a stellar rugby career as a stalwart of the Otago side and as a National Provincial Championship, Super Rugby and age-group coach. He played six more Tests for the All Blacks, but none could match the triumph of his extraordinary debut. 'If somebody had said to me that is the only Test you will ever play,' he told Paul, 'I would have been a very happy man.'

ROSS NORMAN

To conquer the Conqueror

ON AN EARLY SUMMER DAY in 1983, Ross Norman leapt from a plane over rural England, relishing the surge of adrenalin. The 24-year-old professional squash player had an adventurous spirit. He enjoyed skiing and scuba diving during breaks from squash and had always loved flying. His father was a commercial pilot and had sometimes flown his teenage son from their hometown of Whitianga, on the Coromandel Peninsula, to squash championships in Auckland.

Norman pulled the cord and felt the silky chute ripple out over his head, rapidly slowing his descent. For a few minutes, the world number eight squash player drifted happily over the patchwork fields and pretty hedgerows of the Hampshire Downs. As he approached the landing site, a sudden gust caught his parachute. He overshot the field, pounded awkwardly into a concrete runway and smashed his left knee.

He soon found himself lying in the Royal London Hospital. As he watched his damaged leg waste away to skin and bone, the doctors talked about attempting to rebuild the knee in the hope he might walk with only a minor limp. No one discussed the possibility of a return to squash.

Day after day, as he watched broken motorcyclists being wheeled onto the ward, Norman felt he'd let his country down. He realised he'd attained his world ranking relatively easily. If he wanted to be a true professional, he'd need a more serious approach. He vowed that if the surgeons managed to put his leg back together he'd fight his way up to a fourth ranking or better.

After a successful surgery, Norman worked hard at his rehabilitation. It was four months before he'd built up enough muscle strength to walk again, and eight before he picked up a racquet. He couldn't afford to pay his mortgage and had to survive on a state benefit.

Within a year of the accident he was back on court, more driven and determined than ever. At the 1984 New Zealand Open, in just 48 hours he defeated three players ranked in the world's top ten. Still he dug deeper, working hard on fitness, game strategy and perfecting his shots. He was strong willed and flexible, able to adjust his play to best test his opponent. He also concentrated on his mental preparation, developing a reputation as a player with single-minded focus. No matter how physically tired he got, he never lost his nerve.

By October 1985 he'd clawed his way to number two in the world. But there was one player against whom victory remained elusive—Jahangir Khan. The 22-year-old Pakistani had won more than 550 matches straight, a winning streak of five and a half years seldom rivalled in any sport. Known within squash circles simply as Jahangir, he came from a great squash dynasty, with his father, brother and cousin all international players. He had burst onto the scene in 1979, when he took the world amateur title at the age of fifteen. He almost gave the game up later that year when his 29-year-old brother and coach, Torsam Khan, died of a heart attack while playing in the Australian Open.

But Torsam had always wanted to see his younger brother become senior world champion, and a devastated Khan, whose first name means 'world conqueror', vowed to fulfil his brother's dream. He threw himself into training, performing rigorous daily aerobic drills and dedicating long hours to practising. Within two years he had achieved his goal. At seventeen, he became the youngest ever World Open champion, and he held the title year after year. On the rare occasion he lost a single game within a match, it made the headlines.

Khan was renowned for fast footwork, power, speed and stamina. He'd draw out each game, exhausting his opponent's physical and mental reserves, and then deliver a devastating blow, often a drop shot from the back of the court. Many considered him the best player squash had ever known. Some said he was unbeatable. Squash players joked that the way to beat him was not through superior racquet skills but by making the match as long as possible—surely Khan had forgotten how to play a fifth game?

The relentless pursuit of Khan was said to have broken other players, but Norman quietly bided his time. Whenever he lost to Khan, it only made him more determined to win. He told his parents, Geoff and Mollie, that if he ever got two games up on Khan, he'd win the match.

In 1985, Norman entered every major tournament in the world, winning almost every competition when Khan was absent, and losing the rest to Khan. 'Those who face [Norman] in combat learn to fear his phenomenal athletic strength and his implacable dedication to victory. Apart, that is, from Khan,' wrote squash reporter Colin McQuillan in *The Times*. 'Norman has pursued Jahangir doggedly around the world this season, constantly raising his game beyond the rest of the professional pack but hardly disturbing the winning rhythm of the Pakistani maestro.'

At the World Open in Cairo in 1985, Norman pushed Khan to extraordinary levels of concentration, prising away a single game before the Pakistani took the match, 3–1. 'One day he will be off his game and I will beat him,' Norman declared afterwards. Few believed him, but Norman never lost faith. 'I knew I had to keep improving, keep working away at it, and be ready so that when my day came I was able to take advantage,' he later recalled. 'The person who beats Khan will be the person who out-Jahangirs Jahangir,' he said to *International Squash Player* in early 1986. 'Be fitter than him, be more accurate than him and be more aware on court than him . . . I always feel I am in with a chance—you have to feel you have a chance or you feel disheartened.'

In November 1986, Norman faced Khan once again, in the World Open final, in Toulouse, France. By then, they'd played each other 30 times, including in 21 major finals, and Khan had won every match.

The reigning champion, aged 23, was in brilliant form and had disposed of his semifinal opponent relatively quickly, despite losing a game. Norman, aged 27, had beaten an unseeded Australian in a hard-fought semifinal that dragged on for one hour and 51 minutes. Both Khan and Norman had had trouble with the new 'television ball'. Designed for greater visibility for television audiences, it glowed like 'a space-invader blimp', according to commentators, but was inconsistent and tended to skid off the side walls of the court. Norman was fitter and faster than ever, but the tough, drawn-out semifinal had tired him. He knew he'd have to stay on court for almost two hours to seriously challenge Khan, and the Pakistani had always been comfortable playing for that long. 'I won't change my style and am just hoping for the best,' he told the press the night before the match.

As the two men stood before a crowd of 2900 at the Palais des Sports, Khan was widely predicted to come out with his sixth consecutive world title. Despite his weariness, Norman felt good. He told his brother David, a professional squash coach living in France, that he just hoped he could get into the game properly.

Norman took the first point in the opening game, but Khan responded. The advantage switched back and forth until the score evened at 5–5. Norman hit the ball sharp and low, taking the next four points, as Khan made two unforced errors. 'That's not something we see a lot of,' the commentator remarked. The New Zealander took the first game, 9–5. The crowd muttered in amazement. It was unheard of for Khan to lose two games within two days.

The reigning champion looked uneasy, and Norman got the second game off to a fiery start, taking the lead, 3–2. Khan came back to win three points in five rallies, with Norman questioning some of the referee's decisions. He managed to maintain his composure to pull back the score to 7–7. By this point in a match, Khan would usually have a comfortable lead. But he was scrambling and looking frustrated, repeatedly wiping his sweaty hands against the court's acrylic walls. The pressure seemed to be getting to him.

Norman took the score to 8–7, where it remained for several prolonged rallies. Both men appeared to tire. Khan made another unforced error, handing Norman the second game. It was 2–0. The crowd's cheers threatened to lift the roof.

In New Zealand, the phone rang at Geoff and Mollie Norman's home at 6.02 a.m. Their son David was on the line, breathless with the news that his brother was two games up on Khan. One more successful game and he'd take the match and the world title.

At the Palais des Sports, the delighted crowd clapped rhythmically. Norman held his nerve, refusing to get excited or nervous. The first two points of the third game went his way, but Khan retaliated, taking five in a row. The game evened out at 7–7 and then Norman made a critical mistake, giving Khan the lead at 8–7. 'You can never write this great champion off,' said the commentator. '[Khan] will surely have something in reserve. One suspects this is going to go the full distance to five games.'

Khan took the final serve in a high-energy rally that had the two men bouncing all over the court, before Norman tapped the ball into the 'tin' at the base of the front wall. Game to Khan. It had taken 90 minutes for the two men to play just three games. In top-level squash, a five-game match would usually be over in that time. 'It was a gruelling match,' Norman recalled. 'I was 2–0 up and then he came back to snatch the third and I wondered what might happen.'

In the fourth game, Khan quickly grabbed the first point, but Norman responded with a brilliant drop shot to even the score. He was gaining confidence, pushing Khan harder than he'd ever been pushed, dragging out the rallies, zigging and zagging all over the court and dropping the ball just out of Khan's reach.

Khan showed flashes of brilliance, but he also made mistakes, often trying to end rallies too quickly. Norman was playing Khan at his own game with brilliant drop shots. He'd draw Khan to the front of the court and thrash the ball right past him.

Sweating profusely, Khan released a wild out-of-court shot that prompted a groan from the crowd. Norman maintained control, driving the ball hard. When Khan failed to lift a shot and then didn't even run for a drop shot from Norman, it was clear that the unprecedented had happened: Khan was tired.

The score was 8–1. It was match point. Norman took a moment to collect himself. 'You got here playing sensible squash,' he told himself. 'All you have to do is play more sensible squash to take out the leader of the pack.'

He took a drop shot followed by a killer cross-court forehand. Khan scrambled to the back of the court, scraping the wall with his racquet as he tried—and failed—to return the ball.

Norman leapt up, punching the air. 'It was absolute elation, a moment of triumph,' he said, later. 'I could just let go and shout for joy. I thought of all the people who had helped me along the way and of all the work I'd done and all the times Khan had beaten me. It felt great.'

After an intense one hour and 39 minutes, Norman had beaten a man widely regarded as the best player in the history of the game. The final score was 9–5, 9–7, 7–9, 9–1. The last, match-winning game had taken less than ten minutes. Norman was the first New Zealander to win the men's world championship. With Susan Devoy the reigning women's champion, it gave New Zealand a rare double title.

It took a few moments for the news to filter down the phone line to Norman's anxious parents. David was so excited he could hardly talk. 'He couldn't even remember what the score was, he was in such a state,' recalled Geoff.

A stunned Khan told the press he'd had great difficulty seeing the ball. 'But Ross played very well. I made many mistakes on important points.'

'The feeling is unbelievable, it's just fantastic,' Norman told reporters. 'To beat Jahangir would have to be the highlight of any squash player's career—especially in the world final—and it certainly is for me.'

'With a forehand drop shot on a squash court in Toulouse, Ross Norman's life took on a new dimension,' said Squash New Zealand's chief executive and former professional player Robin Espie. 'No longer would he be just a highly respected, brilliant international squash player. He had now become one of a tiny elite group of people—a world champion.'

STEVE GURNEY

The multisport masochist's toughest
endurance test

WHEN THE PHONE RANG at his cliff-top home in Christchurch in October 1994, Steve Gurney wasn't even thinking about another adventure race. The 31-year-old multisport and adventure athlete had just returned from the mountain biking world championships in Vail, Colorado. He had his sights set on making the New Zealand mountain biking team for the 1996 Olympic Games in Atlanta, Georgia. After a decade of tackling events involving various combinations of kayaking, road and mountain biking, and running, Gurney wanted to see how far he could go if he dedicated himself to a single sport.

But his fellow adventure racing mate John Howard was on the line. He needed a ring-in team member for the Raid Gauloises, a multiday adventure race in Borneo. With no set course, teams of five would have to navigate their way through the jungle to specific checkpoints by mountain biking, canoeing, climbing, trekking, canyoning and caving. The race was predicted to take at least ten days, pushing each team to their physical and mental limits in intense heat and humidity.

Gurney had been mad about multisport since his early twenties, when he met Robin Judkins, founder of the world's first multisport race, the Coast to Coast. This gruelling 243-kilometre event begins at Kumara Beach on the West Coast and traverses the Southern Alps via a combination of cycling, kayaking and running, to finish at Sumner Beach, Christchurch. Gurney had first taken part in the Coast to Coast in 1986 and soon became a self-styled 'multisport masochist'. He had no coach but followed Arthur Lydiard's principle of endurance building and trained in off-road running, cycling, mountain biking, orienteering and rock climbing. He loved the challenge of pushing himself beyond his limits, making the most of what he had and never giving up.

In 1989 he had teamed up with Howard and three other experienced racers to win the inaugural Raid Gauloises, a 400-kilometre, five-day multisport race across Fiordland from Lake Ohau to Lake Manapouri. The team navigated by map and compass, surviving on little sleep. The Raid Gauloises was the first example of what became known as adventure racing, and Gurney was hooked. 'Risk is what makes [adventure racing] the wild child of sport,' he told journalist Margot Butcher in 2001. 'The feeling you get when you beat the odds, cheat the avalanche of danger. Swimming through swamps, scraping through caves, over mountains through foul or freezing or lip blistering weather, across the paths of lethal snakes and spiders, crocodiles, bears and through the domain of diseases.'

Gurney had won the Coast to Coast on his fifth attempt, in 1990. When he retained his title in 1991, he did so as the world's first professional multisport and adventure racing athlete. He was determined to make a living from the sport he loved, notwithstanding the absence of development funding, the high costs of participation and a shortage of lucrative races.

So when Howard phoned in 1994, it didn't take much to persuade Gurney to join the team. For a professional athlete, the possibility of winning what could be the world's toughest adventure race was irresistible, especially with a team prize of $55,000 up for grabs. Gurney felt certain they were in with a chance.

Within a week of Howard's phone call, Gurney was on the plane to Sarawak, in remote north-west Borneo. There, he and Howard hooked up with their three tough but inexperienced Malaysian teammates, all of whom had just learned to ride a bike. Together they battled through the jungle, leaving higher ranked teams in their wake, surviving on just 90 minutes' sleep per night and, in Gurney's case, overcoming severe heat stroke—after he insisted on mountain biking up a steep hill in extreme humidity. Still, the bruised and scraped team pushed on, entering the world's biggest cave system, the Mulu Caves, parts of which are still unexplored. Hundreds of bats hung from the roof as the team waded through an underground river, finding their way in the pitch black for eight hours.

Howard, Gurney and the team shocked officials by winning the race in just five days. They now had a week to wait for the prize giving. They were all exhausted, and Gurney had sore joints. When he began to feel feverish in the tropical heat, the race doctor prescribed aspirin and malaria pills.

On the day of the prize giving, Gurney still felt rough. He was so cold he had a hot bath despite the humidity. He took a couple of aspirin and rallied enough to enjoy the afterparty, even enticing a female competitor named Karen back to his hotel room. But he soon became delirious and began hallucinating. Karen found him teetering on the edge of the balcony railing and had to drag him back to safety.

Unbeknown to Gurney, for a week his body had incubated a deadly infection, leptospirosis. The *Leptospira* bacteria is spread by bats, rats and other vermin, and thrives in water and caves. Although the river in the Mulu Caves looked clean, it was full of bat guano, and the bacteria had entered Gurney's system through a cut on his shin. In the initial phase, leptospirosis is easily treated with antibiotics. But once the disease takes hold it rapidly progresses, shutting down vital organs.

The following day, Gurney continued to deteriorate. His joints were excruciatingly sore and he spent the entire day in a hot bath. His friends realised he needed to get to hospital—and fast—but the nearest was in Kuching, a 90-minute plane ride away, and all the day's flights were fully booked.

By the time they negotiated him a seat, Gurney was entering the second stage of the disease. He was jaundiced, the whites of his eyes were turning red, he was suffering severe abdominal pain, and he could no longer walk. On arrival in Kuching, he crawled off the plane, passing the homeward-bound race officials, and collapsed on the air bridge. Howard was there to meet him, along with another New Zealand competitor, Vivienne Prince, and an ambulance. The pair had flown out to Kuching the previous day but had cancelled their onward connection when they heard of Gurney's deterioration. Their faces were the last lucid things he'd discern for ten days.

When he arrived at the hospital, he asked the doctor if he would die. The doctor didn't say yes but refused to say no. Within seven hours, Gurney had suffered a circulatory collapse and his lungs had filled with fluid. He was put on a ventilator. Next, his kidneys failed. Doctors began dialysis. He was terrified that he'd die in his sleep, so he willed himself to stay awake for three days and nights, but he was delirious and lashing out. In the end, Howard had to help pin him down so the hospital's sole doctor could induce a coma.

After five days, he was transferred by chartered Lear jet to the intensive care unit of a larger hospital, in Singapore, with his life support machine in tow. Howard and Prince sat by his side throughout the flight, taking turns to squeeze the ventilation bag keeping him alive. When the plane landed at a Singapore military base, officials didn't believe Gurney was the man in his passport photograph. His bones stuck out and his eyes were a deep red. He looked nothing like an endurance athlete.

It took two days to stabilise him. When his father arrived from New Zealand, he was told that his son might have brain damage. The antibiotics were kicking in, but when Gurney awoke he hallucinated and felt that the ventilator was suffocating him. He pulled it out, then turned blue and lapsed in and out of consciousness. He had to be sedated again, and this time his limbs were tied down.

He spent ten days in intensive care and another week in the general ward before his father delivered another devastating blow. The Raid Gauloises' insurance policy would not cover his $92,000 medical bill. With hospital care costing $5500 per day, it was imperative he get back to Christchurch as soon as possible. His kidneys were still not working, and he'd be travelling against doctors' wishes, but it was agreed he could go if he went straight to Christchurch Hospital for dialysis.

Lying flat out in first class with a drip suspended from the overhead locker, Gurney felt tears stream down his face when he saw the Southern Alps through the window. He was home. He felt a weight lift, and for the first time dared to think he might survive.

After ten days in Christchurch Hospital, his kidneys began working and he was allowed to go home. He'd left New Zealand a little over a month earlier, and 30 kilograms heavier, as a supremely fit endurance athlete. Now his muscles had atrophied and his eyes were still a brilliant red. He was so weak he couldn't manage the steep gradients to his cliff-top home and had to move in with his father. He was warned not to overdo it, lest he prompt a recurrence. He concentrated on eating well and set himself small goals—first walking to the letterbox, then to a lamppost, then to the end of the street, with rest days in between. Before long he gained weight and was able to cycle for an hour or so at a time.

He was desperately worried about his financial and medical situation. He had no idea how he would pay his medical bill or how he'd live. His eyes, now yellow, had a haunted look, and he woke most nights from anxiety. Even worse, the doctors had told him there must be no more endurance racing. The extreme stress and dehydration would place his recovering organs under too much strain. 'I thought I would be glad that I survived,' Gurney told journalist Gregor Paul, 'but coming out of it and reassessing what I would do without my sport . . . that was so hard.'

Still, he fast regained his strength. In February 1995, just four months after becoming ill, he completed the kayak leg of the Coast to Coast as part of a celebrity team entered by a local radio station. It should have been a time for celebration, but he was frustrated by his greatly diminished speed and yearned for the satisfaction of crossing the finish line. He was severely depressed and worried that there would always be a deep void if he remained without the ability to race and win. 'The black dog has got him,' Judkins told journalist Bruce Ansley.

On one black night, Gurney found himself standing on the flat roof of his house, looking down at the power lines. He wanted to jump. 'I wanted to commit suicide, which was something I never thought I would feel,' he told Butcher. 'My sport was everything to me. I liked winning races, because it made me feel good about myself.' But while standing on that roof, he felt a tiny spark of hope, a realisation that his recovery was the ultimate endurance test. He was an expert at endurance. All he had to do was find a way to hang on.

Among his get well cards was a copy of a poem written by a woman on her deathbed, cataloguing the things she regretted not doing in life. Gurney vowed that the next time he was on his deathbed, his wish list would be empty—a blank sheet of paper. 'I wanted to die with a smile on my face, nothing left to do, no regrets, with my body suitably worn out,' he wrote in his 2008 autobiography.

He made a list of the things that were important to him and set about achieving them. He wanted to know he'd done all he could to get back to adventure racing. 'I always picture myself as the older, wiser me, and looking back, [I think], as the older, wiser me what advice would I give myself today?' he told journalist Marc Hinton in 1995. 'I'm sure it would be give it my best shot.'

He declined antidepressants, concentrating instead on positive thinking and employing the Neuro-Linguistic Programming techniques he'd used to win races to drive a change in mindset. He put a piece of paper on his bedroom ceiling reminding him to think three positive thoughts before sleep and upon rising. 'I learned I had to pick up the pieces that were left and make do,' wrote Gurney.

'I can either get back on, bruised and battered, and do my best to finish the race, or I can be a wimp and use the excuse to not even try. I'd had a second chance at life and now I wanted to give it an even better shot than I did before.'

In the meantime, there were insurers to battle. Gurney was terrified by the thought of losing his heavily mortgaged dream home. It had taken him two years to persuade the previous owner to sell it to him, and convincing the bank to give a loan to a professional multisport and adventure athlete had been no easy feat. Now he had no sponsors and no income, and all his race winnings had gone on expenses.

Eventually the insurers agreed to cover half the bill. The Malaysian government chipped in $8000, and a public appeal raised $15,000, leaving Gurney with a bill for around $25,000. It was a huge relief, although paying it off would still be a struggle. While continuing to build up his training, he took on personal training clients and picked up design work, drawing on his mechanical engineering background.

Overwhelming public interest in his illness added to the pressure, as he suddenly found himself described as an inspirational role model. He decided he had no choice but to go with it. Within eight months he ran the Peak to Peak, a 45-kilometre mountain run from the top of The Remarkables to Coronet Peak. 'I'm a really impatient person,' he said after the race. 'Most people would have sat back and waited a couple of years to get over an illness like that . . . but hey, life's short and I've busted a gut to come back.'

By the end of the year, he was badgering Howard to include him in a team for an overseas adventure race. But he was still underweight, lacked stamina and hadn't yet rebuilt all of his wasted muscle. 'I didn't think he was ready then but I always knew he would make it back,' Howard told Paul. 'Steve never gives up. If we were out on our mountain bikes and we came to a particularly steep section that Steve couldn't cycle [all the way] up, he would go back down and keep trying until he was able to do it. Most other people would just walk up.'

Gurney was disappointed to miss out on the race. Life felt empty without competitions. But he kept his focus, trained ever harder and with each week grew stronger and more confident in his body's resilience. The fear that he'd never race again made him more determined than ever to win.

In February 1996, he raced the full Coast to Coast, placing seventeenth. With new-found confidence in his body, he threw himself into other multisport events around the world. By the end of the year he'd chalked up some impressive results, but the title he coveted most was that of the Coast to Coast, his signature race. No longer worried about what might go wrong with his body, he began thinking about what he needed to do to win it the following year. Without the luxury of working at it full-time, he focused his twenty weekly training hours on sessions that would give the best return. He reduced his running to allow a suspected fracture of his foot to heal, and concentrated instead on improving his performance in cycling and kayaking. He made sure he got plenty of sleep and tapered off his training two weeks before the event to give his body time to rest. Lining up with the other competitors on Kumara Beach in February 1997, he looked like an athlete again. He was still unsure how far he could push his organs but was determined to give the race his best shot.

As he paddled down the Waimakariri River into the lead, tears began to flow. *Yeah, no one is going to catch me now*, he thought. He was soon well in front, completing the kayak leg in record time.

He reached Sumner with a nineteen-minute lead. As he crossed the finish line into the arms of emotional friends and supporters, it felt like a new beginning. A little over two years after facing death, he kissed the Coast to Coast trophy again. He considered it his best win—evidence he was himself once more. 'I was back,' he wrote in his autobiography. 'It proved that if you are determined enough you can do anything. Never, never give up. Adversity causes some people to break, and others to break records.'

Gurney went on to win seven Coast to Coast titles in a row, for a total of nine wins. Seven years after his battle with leptospirosis, he told Butcher it was one of the best things that had ever happened to him. 'The appreciation of being alive and making the most of what you've got that I now have absolutely outweighs the horror I went through. Everything in my life now is about my passions, about doing and achieving what I really want to do.'

21

THE 2002
TALL BLACKS

'We can take these guys'

TALL BLACKS POINT GUARD Mark Dickel had one message for his team as they prepared to face Australia in the deciding match of the 2001 Oceania World Championship qualifying series: 'We can take these guys.'

The New Zealand basketball team had begun the series with a surprising 85–78 victory in Wellington, their second ever win over Australia. In the second match, in Hamilton, the Boomers had hit back, taking the Tall Blacks to extra time to win, 81–79. The tiebreaker, at the North Shore Events Centre, was do or die. The winner would go to the 2002 International Basketball Federation World Championship in Indianapolis. The loser would stay home.

Dickel's confidence reflected a radical attitude change for his team. At their first Olympic Games, in Sydney the previous year, they'd tried merely not to lose by too much. After coach Thomas 'Tab' Baldwin took charge, in April 2001, the Tall Blacks no longer just competed; they played to win. Florida-born Baldwin concentrated on creating chemistry among the team members and fostering a culture of trust and individual accountability. He looked for players who were not only skilful but committed, enthusiastic and willing to sacrifice themselves for the good of the team.

The Australian Boomers had dominated Oceania basketball for decades and were clear favourites to win the decider. While the Tall Blacks had prepared for the series on a Hillary Commission grant of $20,000, the Boomers had a budget of $1.2 million to take them right through to Indianapolis. The Australians had the advantage in height, power and experience, especially with Tall Blacks stars Sean Marks and Kirk Penney unavailable for the series. But the New Zealanders believed that what they lacked in size they could make up in fast footwork. They knew their best chance of winning was to run the ball, hold possession and focus on smart play. After two strong performances, they'd tasted the possibility of the world championship. All they had to do was win this last match.

It didn't start well. The Boomers took early control and towards the end of the first quarter they led, 29–18. As Tall Blacks guard Paul Henare ran at full speed down the court, he looked at the clock and saw one second remaining. He lifted the ball and fired a three-pointer from halfway, sending his team into quarter-time with a psychological boost.

In the second quarter, the Tall Blacks began to close the gap. The Boomers' top scorer slipped at the hoop, missing a sure slam-dunk. They were feeling the pressure as the Tall Blacks kicked into gear. By half-time, the Boomers' lead had narrowed, to 51–45.

Tall Blacks captain Pero Cameron came into his own in the third quarter, shooting consecutive goals and a three-pointer to even the score. As the New Zealanders cranked up their defence, the Boomers grew frustrated, missing free throws, giving the ball away and questioning the referee. They finished the quarter just three points up.

In the final quarter, the Tall Blacks quickly took the lead. With five minutes left on the clock, Dickel sunk a three-pointer, bringing the score to 80–69. The New Zealand bench were on their feet, cheering and lifting their arms to amp up the crowd. With thirteen seconds to go, their 89–78 lead was unassailable. A smiling Baldwin called time-out. He told his players to savour the moment and enjoy the drama and noise. The crowd clapped down the remaining seconds. The buzzer sounded. New Zealand had taken its first series victory against Australia and booked a place in Indianapolis. Supporters and autograph hunters rushed onto the court, thrusting T-shirts, posters and pens into the hands of their heroes.

Across the Tasman, the loss became known as the blackest day in Australian basketball. For the first time since 1970, Australia would sit out a world championship. Coach Phil Smyth resigned, eight months into a four-year contract. Baldwin was insulted by the reaction. 'When we got beaten by Australia we saw it as a learning curve. They see it as a loss of face, which is not very complimentary,' he told journalists. 'You don't think like that if you have respect for your opposition.'

With less than twelve months to prepare for the world championship, Baldwin had new challenges on his hands. The first was securing enough funding for an effective campaign. 'I'm not going over there to come home with respectable score lines,' he told journalist Peter Jessup. 'I only know one way and that's to win.

I'll be shooting to win every single game between now and the end of that tournament.' The second challenge was arranging enough international competition to prepare his side to meet the world's best. New Zealand coaches had long struggled to convince overseas teams to make the trek down under. European and North American sides had plenty of quality competition a short flight or drive away, and the few that ventured into the South Pacific visited only Australia. Even the Australians had rejected the idea of an annual trans-Tasman series, believing New Zealand wasn't competitive enough.

With additional funding from the Sports Foundation, Baldwin arranged a flurry of international fixtures including games against leading American university teams and a European tour. The Tall Blacks chalked up significant wins against Hungary, China and Canada, and creditable performances against Lithuania and Germany. As their skills grew, their confidence soared.

In August 2002, a few weeks out from Indianapolis, they met reigning world champions Yugoslavia at the Super Cup in Braunschweig, Germany. Yugoslavia had suffered three consecutive losses. Baldwin's game plan was to keep them under pressure by constantly changing the defence and trying to block out the sharpshooters.

The Tall Blacks charged confidently onto the court and never let the Yugoslavs get comfortable. Marks shot 27 points, while Cameron scored a series of long-range goals and took seven rebounds, despite being much shorter than his opponents.

With two minutes and 26 seconds left before full-time, Baldwin called time-out. The Tall Blacks were three points down, with a score of 73–76. In two recent games against France, he'd watched his players give their all only to let the match slip away in the dying minutes. As his men huddled, Baldwin had no magic match-winning suggestions. He simply asked, 'When would close enough not be good enough?'

Almost in unison, they replied, 'Now!'

Infused with a fresh dose of self-belief, the Tall Blacks fired back onto the court. Penney quickly evened the score, but Yugoslavia immediately took another three-pointer. Then Marks sunk a pass from Dickel, bringing the score to 78–79. The crowd leapt to their feet. With 15.6 seconds on the clock, Cameron launched a three-pointer and the Tall Blacks pulled ahead by two.

The buzzer sounded. The Tall Blacks had beaten the world champions. Baldwin later told journalist Gilbert Wong they'd 'shouldered the burden of failure and shed the burden of the expectations of success'.

If the victory had heightened expectations, the Tall Blacks were unconcerned. 'We were like virgins when we went to Indianapolis, so we didn't feel the pressure,' Baldwin told writer Joseph Romanos. 'Pressure stems from expectation. We were massive underdogs and rightly so.'

The Tall Blacks arrived in the United States ranked 23rd out of 24 teams. Only one of their players—Marks, of Miami Heat—played in the National Basketball Association. Half of them were semi-professional, taking time off work to travel to Indianapolis, and their tallest player, 2.13-metre forward Tony Rampton, had been ruled out of the competition after a slow recovery from ankle surgery. This gave the Tall Blacks the distinction of being the third-shortest team at the championship, after Algeria and Lebanon.

Although Baldwin told his players to take it one match at a time, winning the tournament was firmly on their minds. 'We didn't come to the world champs to lose,' Marks said. 'We're just going to see how far we can go. Who knows?'

They made a strong start to the tournament, causing a major upset when they fought back from seventeen points down in the second half to beat silver medal holders Russia, 90–81. Next to fall was Venezuela, 98–85. But trouble struck in the third pool game, against Argentina, when Marks was poked in the eye during the third quarter. The Tall Blacks lost, 85–112, and Marks was ruled out of the tournament with a scratched and bleeding iris.

The Tall Blacks looked more like the Small Blacks, with a huge gap in their front line and no remaining players over two metres tall. But they'd qualified for the second round, and Baldwin had convinced his men that no team was unbeatable. He knew they weren't as talented as other teams, but they had guts, determination and a team spirit that would drive them to push their limits in the toughest of matches.

In the second round they lost to Germany (64–84) and the star-studded United States (62–110) but rallied with a stunning come-from-behind victory over China (94–88) to make the quarterfinals. For the first time, Baldwin felt the weight of his adoptive nation, pressure 'born of a country that is desperate to believe in their sportsmen and women'.

The tough Puerto Ricans were next. Athletic and strong, they'd had a stellar run at the championship, winning five of six matches. As with any pitting against a superstar team, Baldwin believed it was simply a matter of breaking the game down. 'Will they score every time they get the ball? No. And will we sometimes score when we have the ball? Yes,' he told Romanos. 'Each of those occasions is a mini-victory. So you break the game down to the fundamentals as much as possible, rather than setting one goal of winning.'

The night before the match, Baldwin and his assistant coach and video analyst holed up in a hotel room and pored over videos and statistics, as they'd done every night of the tournament. They looked for weaknesses and favoured ploys or habits in the Puerto Rican game, and deconstructed the Tall Blacks' latest game. They worked until three or four in the morning, preparing a report on each member of the Puerto Rican side with suggestions for exploiting their weaknesses. As they presented their findings to the players over breakfast, a wave of confidence washed through the Tall Blacks. 'We watched the video of Puerto Rico and thought, "Man, we can beat these guys,"' Dickel recalled.

That afternoon, as the crowds gathered at the RCA Dome, Baldwin called the team members together for his pre-match speech. He read aloud an email from some of New Zealand's longshot sporting heroes, like Wynton Rufer, Brian Turner and their teammates who took New Zealand to its first soccer World Cup, in 1982, as well as members of the men's hockey team that won gold at the Montreal Olympics, in 1976. 'And now,' the email read, 'names like Penney, Dickel, [Dillon] Boucher, and [Phill] Jones will become part of New Zealand folklore.'

From the opening moments of the game, the advantage switched back and forth. The Tall Blacks remained composed, leading the score at every quarter. It was the toughest game Baldwin had ever coached. He racked his mental playbook, looking for opportunities to execute any of the hundreds of complicated sequences his team knew by heart. He switched players and tactics to keep the Puerto Ricans on their toes but never felt the Tall Blacks were in control.

As the clock hit zero at the end of the third quarter, Jones sunk a stunning three-pointer to take the Tall Blacks' lead to 48–44. In the final four minutes, the score tied three times. With 23 seconds left on the clock, Cameron snatched the lead and the Tall Blacks maintained a tight defence to deny Puerto Rico a shot in the final seconds of the game. The Tall Blacks won, 65–63.

It was their fourth win in eight days. They'd secured not only a place in the semifinals and a chance at a medal, but a guaranteed spot at the 2004 Olympics, in Athens. They were overwhelmed. 'We, from little New Zealand, have gone and made it into the top four in the world and made it to the Olympics,' said Penney.

Baldwin was ecstatic. 'I feel so good I could explode,' he said. 'The impact of our success on the world basketball stage is gigantic ... I wish I spoke other languages because the English language just seems inadequate to me. Words like rapture, thrilled, unbelievable and awesome—you should be able to grab them all and mash together to come out with a new word ... It's amazing to know that something you have been a part of will live beyond you.'

After a day's rest the Tall Blacks faced Yugoslavia, a team stepping up for their tenth consecutive semifinal, with five NBA players in their ranks. After a strong beginning, the Tall Blacks stalled in the second half, struggling to find momentum as Yugoslavia stepped up their defence. The New Zealanders missed vital rebounds and were unable to make enough scoring opportunities. The final score was 81–78 to Yugoslavia.

For the exhausted Tall Blacks, their bodies wrecked after eight games in ten days, the defeat was gut wrenching; but Baldwin was proud. 'When there's a small band of guys who believe, and a small country who believes, it is very satisfying to get this far,' he said. 'What our team have done so far is still pretty superhuman.'

At the bronze medal play-off, the visibly tired New Zealand side was defeated by Germany. They finished the world championship in fourth place, higher than any other Oceania team in history, in a sport with 450 million players in 212 accredited countries. Rugby, by comparison, had just two million players worldwide. The Tall Blacks finished ahead of many superstar teams. The United States came sixth—its worst ever result—and Russia finished tenth, out of the medals for the first time in a decade. Cameron was the only player not in the NBA to be named in an all-tournament team chosen by media covering the championship. 'These guys never quit, they gave it their all,' Baldwin said of his players after their final game. 'They're a special group and we as a team have accomplished something special, but let's put the credit squarely on the shoulders of the guys that went out and played their hearts out.'

Former Tall Blacks captain John Saker wrote that the team's performance was like the miracle of the planet itself. 'It seemed to demand a metaphysical explanation. I luxuriated with the rest of the country in every Tall Black victory. I revelled especially in the beautiful way they did what they did . . . So many times, when they had to for their team, they managed to create something out of nothing. It was an unadorned, truthful kind of beauty. The Tall Blacks pulled together in harmony and showed the world that the game can be won at the highest level with skill and togetherness and simplicity and intelligence.'

MICHAEL CAMPBELL

'Coming back from the dead'

NOBODY PAID MUCH ATTENTION to the lone golfer checking in to the Pine Needles Lodge on a Sunday evening in June 2005. The small settlement of Pinehurst, tucked away in the sandhills of North Carolina, was about to host the 105th US Open. The field was the strongest in years, and commentators speculated about which of the 'Fab Five of the Fairways' would take the title. Would it be Tiger Woods, gunning for his second major title of the year? Vijay Singh, ranked number two in the world? Ernie Els, two-time winner of the Open? Phil Mickelson, winner of the 2004 Masters Tournament? Or reigning Open champion Retief Goosen?

The US Open is considered the toughest of the four major golf championships. The Pinehurst No. 2 course demands respect, with its narrow fairways and undulating greens complex enough to intimidate the world's finest golfers.

Hawera-born Michael Campbell, 36, was ranked 80th in the world. He hadn't even planned to enter, having experienced a bad eighteen months. That year he'd already missed the cut in five tournaments, including the New Zealand Open, and he'd never had much luck on American soil. From 63 starts, he'd won not a single tournament. He'd entered the US Open at the last minute and only because the United States Golf Association had held a qualifying event in the United Kingdom for the first time that year. Even so, his wife, Julie, had to convince him to show up on the day, and he had just scraped in to the last of nine qualifying spots.

Campbell arrived at the Pine Needles Lodge a week later, with no professional support crew and no entourage. Julie and their two young sons had stayed home in Brighton, England, while his caddy, Michael Waite, was sharing accommodation nearby. Campbell didn't mind the solitude. He'd learned from bitter experience that too much fuss drained his energy and distracted him from his golf.

The following morning, he went out for a practice round with two old friends, Singh, and Irish golfer Paul McGinley. As Campbell struggled with a tough bunker shot, Singh noted that the way he cut across the ball gave it too much spin. He demonstrated a different approach, flopping the ball up high and letting it roll out with less spin.

Later that day, Campbell's coach, Jonathan Yarwood, arrived on a flying visit from Florida. The two men spent the next day working on technique at the Pine Needles course, well away from the media spotlight. Campbell practised putting, concentrating on feel and speed, and worked with his eyes closed for better long-distance speed control.

On the Wednesday, Campbell did a practice round in 40-degree heat at Pinehurst No. 2, working out his game plan with Yarwood. With the exception of the fourth hole, every putting green on the par-70 course had a low mound-like shape. Golfers had compared trying to land a ball on the rounded putting surfaces to aiming for an upside-down salad bowl, or a Volkswagen Beetle. With only 28 per cent of the green deemed 'safe', just keeping the ball on it was considered an achievement. Some players predicted that a score as high as seven or eight over par might take the tournament.

Campbell wasn't thinking about taking the tournament. He was a player better known for his potential than for his achievements. He'd first picked up his father's left-handed clubs at the age of five, waiting four years for his parents to buy him a set of right-handers. At thirteen he stood in front of his class at Mana College in Porirua and announced his ambition to be a professional golfer. 'Everyone started laughing,' he told journalist John Huggan. 'In those days golf just wasn't played by people with my background. It was a rich man's sport. And I wasn't rich.'

By sixteen, he had a handicap of six and was champion of the Titahi Golf Club. He burst onto the international scene in 1992, initially as the winner of the Australian Amateur Championships and then as part of the first New Zealand team to win the World Team Amateur Championship (Eisenhower Trophy) in Vancouver. In 1993 he was named Rookie of the Year on the Australasian tour and was hailed by former world number ones Greg Norman and Nick Faldo as the next big thing.

It didn't work out like that. By 2005 he'd competed in 24 majors and made just nine cuts. His best result came at the age of 26 in the 1995 British Open, when he led the play by two strokes going into the final round, but choked under pressure and fell back to equal third. At one low point in 1997, he threw his bags and clubs across his hotel room in despair. He considered taking an axe to the clubs and either going back to his previous job as a telephone technician or pursuing a career selling golf balls.

But after his first son, Thomas, was born in 1998, Campbell switched focus. It was no longer just about trying to make the perfect stroke; he needed to provide for his family. With Yarwood's help, he clawed his way up from number 371 in the world, a recovery Yarwood compared to 'coming back from the dead'. Still, commentators had good reason to describe him as hot and cold. After winning six tournaments in Europe between 2000 and 2003, he made a disappointing foray into the US PGA Tour, missing the cut in all eight tournaments.

By 2005, Campbell knew he had to make changes. He began working full-time with Yarwood, took on a new sports psychologist and switched management teams. He saw a posture specialist, who prescribed eye exercises to align his vision and make it easier to judge putts. He was making steady progress by June, with several top ten finishes in European tournaments. When he arrived at Pinehurst, he was feeling good, but happy to be flying under the radar—so far under that Tiger Woods' Kiwi caddy, Steve Williams, saw Waite and did a double take. 'I wondered what [Campbell's caddy] was doing here,' said Williams. 'I didn't realise he'd qualified.'

Nor was Campbell's bid garnering much attention back home in New Zealand. The build-up to the US Open was being eclipsed by coverage of the first Lions rugby tour since 1993. The TAB offered Campbell odds of 100 to 1.

Teeing off for the first round on the Thursday, Campbell was calm and at ease. The course felt similar to some he'd played in Australia and Europe. He pretended he was just doing a round with a mate, reminding himself to 'swing it like you can, hit the fairways, hit the greens, make some putts'. By the end of the first round he had a score of one over par, four shots behind leaders Olin Browne and Rocco Mediate.

In the second round Campbell maintained his calmness, shooting one under par for a score of 69, including six birdies. For the first time since 2000, he'd made the cut in the US Open. He was now in sixth place, two shots behind leaders Browne, Goosen and Jason Gore. His was one of only two sub-par rounds on the day. Still the television cameras paid him no attention.

As Campbell ascended the leader board, Yarwood kept in touch by phone, trying to simultaneously deflect the fear of failure and fire up the New Zealander. 'No matter what, it is great experience,' he'd say. 'No one is watching you as they think you do not have a chance.'

Campbell teed off for the third round in scorching mid-afternoon sun. After a brilliant start on the difficult second hole, he faltered, dropping back to two over par by the sixth. Maintaining par was critical, and it was imperative for him to stay focused. He regrouped and kept a steady hand through to Hole 17, where he overplayed his shot into a bunker.

With the green sloping away, it looked as if he wouldn't make the par-three hole. Recalling Singh's demonstration, he tried the 'Vijay shot'. The ball flopped up high and sank into the hole. The crowd went wild, and a triumphant Campbell turned to an impassive Waite. 'Good shot,' said Waite. 'But you've got the last hole to play so hit your tee shot.'

Campbell ended the round one over par to put himself in the top four, with Goosen four shots ahead at three under par. Woods was two shots behind, tied for seventh place.

On the Sunday morning Campbell relaxed over a late breakfast and a telephone chat with Julie. He went out on the green for some stretching and had lunch with Goosen. Later, he donned a white shirt from his Cambo golf clothing line. The Maori design between his shoulderblades was a nod to his Ngāti Ruanui and Ngā Rauru origins, and symbolised *kia kaha*, meaning 'stay strong'.

Many of the players and commentators thought Goosen had it in the bag with his three-stroke lead. But he dropped six shots in the first nine holes, missing five putts from a distance of about two metres. Suddenly the competition was wide open.

Meanwhile, Campbell made a strong beginning. Most of the crowd was following Goosen or Woods, so only a handful of spectators saw Campbell hit a birdie followed by pars on the next six holes. He was leading the US Open. 'I couldn't believe it,' he told New Zealand cricketer Martin Crowe, who was watching from the sidelines and later wrote a book about the tournament. 'I was playing for second. Goose had won the US Open twice before and all of a sudden he's off to a bad start . . . Then I'm leading and I quickly got used to the feeling.'

Woods, playing one group ahead, began the round with two bogeys but rapidly climbed to second place with birdies on Holes 4, 7, 10 and 11. He was just two strokes behind Campbell and hungry for his first come-from-behind victory in a major.

Goosen, Gore and Browne were struggling. Then Campbell missed a downhill one-metre putt for par on the eighth hole, and it looked to the crowd as if he might join the others on the backward slide. In the past he'd struggled to shrug off bad shots and had carried his frustrations on to the next green. This time, he held it together. 'I was cool,' he told Crowe. 'Just move onto the next one, simple as that. I got rid of that shot very, very quickly.'

On the ninth he played a poor shot but recovered with an unlikely up and down strike from behind the green for a birdie. It was a shot he later described as 'unbelievable'.

Campbell began the final nine holes with a one-stroke lead over Goosen and two over Woods. The pressure was intense, with every shot a test of nerve as well as skill. After a birdie on Hole 10, he made a mistake on 11, swinging too hard and sending the ball into the trap. But he remained calm and centred, once again using the 'Vijay shot' to flop the ball out of the sand.

Woods, meanwhile, was gunning for victory, with back-to-back birdies on Holes 10 and 11, then par on 12 to 14. Things had got so bad for Goosen that he was just trying to finish up and go home. As lightning threatened, the grandstands emptied. An eerie hush descended as Campbell and Woods battled through the final holes.

Just before his last stroke on the twelfth hole, Campbell disappeared into a portaloo. He needed to refocus. 'I could feel my body getting tired, my legs were aching, my eyes were sore, and I could sense tiredness creeping in,' he recalled. He picked up a tee and began eye exercises, moving it in a circular motion while keeping his eyes on the tip. The muscles around his eyes began to strain and realign.

He returned to the green and sank a perfect putt. The lightning threat had disappeared, and the crowds returned. Woods took par at Hole 14 and Campbell at 13, the Kiwi staying ahead by two shots.

As Campbell stepped up for his second shot on the fourteenth green, he heard the crowd at the fifteenth hole cheer. Woods had just shot a birdie. Campbell nodded, stepped up swiftly, swung his seven iron hard and dropped the ball within 1.5 metres of the hole. He turned towards the fifteenth and doffed his cap, before sinking a birdie.

At Hole 15, he slipped the ball into the bunker. Once again, he drew on Singh's advice to recover. 'You have no idea how difficult that bunker shot on 15 was,' Campbell told Crowe. 'If I went back there and played 10 shots from the same place I wouldn't get close to that hole.'

While Campbell calmly carried on, Woods struggled with his putt, scoring bogeys on Holes 16 and 17. The New Zealander also bogeyed the sixteenth, but as he stepped up to Hole 17 he felt he was in the zone. 'As he hit that 8 iron, I honestly thought I had never seen a more beautiful thing in sport,' wrote Crowe, who was watching from behind the tee. 'The sound off the club was pure magic. The hush around the entire hole was eerie and surreal. It was a moment I will never forget. The way the ball floated and hung in the air, and then landed sweetly on the front of the green and rolled serenely to within 20 feet of the hole, was like it was all in slow motion. I shook my head in disbelief that I was being privileged to watch this moment.'

To the bewilderment of the commentators, Campbell immediately dropped his club, dipped under the barrier and pushed through the crowd to the portaloo. As he ran through his eye exercises one last time, Woods lined up the eighteenth hole. He sank the birdie and the crowd erupted. Woods had finished the final round one under par, with a score of 69.

Returning to the green with renewed focus, Campbell sank a beautiful six-metre uphill shot. 'The 17th hole will be in my mind forever,' he said afterwards. 'If I ever design a golf course, [that] 17 will be in it: same distance, same dimensions of the green.'

Campbell had a three-stroke lead. If he sank his next ball in four strokes or fewer he'd win the US Open. He knew he could win, but his thoughts turned to French golfer Jean Van de Velde, who had lost a similar lead on the last hole of the 1999 British Open. As he walked to the eighteenth tee he kept repeating to himself, *Keep your focus. Keep your focus.*

He stepped up and looked down the fairway to the Pinehurst clubhouse at the far end of the green. He was almost home. He struck the ball powerfully, but his shot ran out of fairway on the left and dropped into the rough. He chopped it onto the green, landing it 70 metres from the flag. With a crisp stroke, he lifted the ball and at the last second it sloped away to the right, settling just over 30 centimetres from the hole. This was it. If he got the shot, he'd win.

He clipped a short uphill putt, and the ball dropped into the hole. He'd won the US Open.

Campbell looked skywards, his thoughts turning to his late grandmother, who'd once told him he would change people's lives. Then he buried his face in his cap, tears of joy coursing down his face. After an emotional hug with Waite, he walked off the green to find Williams waiting to embrace him. 'That was the single greatest moment in New Zealand sport,' Williams said.

Campbell had finished the competition on even par and with a two-stroke lead over Woods, becoming the first Kiwi to win a major title in the sport since Bob Charles took the British Open, 42 years earlier. As he held the silver trophy in disbelief, he said that Charles's 1963 win had been in the back of his mind all day. 'I stayed patient for 10 years and went through ups and downs and injuries, but deep down inside I knew that I had something in me to do something special. And today I did . . . I won this for the people back home.'

In Wellington, where the final round had held up the day's parliamentary proceedings, Prime Minister Helen Clark described

Campbell's performance as one of New Zealand's greatest sporting achievements. 'His win is a triumph of immense skill, determination and perseverance, along with great modesty and humility,' she said.

It was 11 p.m. by the time Campbell finished the press interviews and climbed into his rental car. He placed the silver trophy on the passenger seat beside him and looped the seat belt through the handles. As he drove back to the Pine Needles Resort alone, he laughed, screamed and cried, all at once.

23

THE 2008 KIWIS

'Go out there to die for your brothers'

IF ANY TEAM could do the impossible and defeat Australia to win the Rugby League World Cup, it wasn't likely to be the Kiwis squad of 2008. After a series of injuries, retirements and defections, the New Zealand team consisted mostly of unknown and inexperienced newcomers. They were led by a relatively young and untested coach, Steve Kearney, assisted by legendary former Kangaroos and National Rugby League coach Wayne Bennett. Kearney had taken over after a disastrous tour of Britain the previous year, which had left the Kiwis administration broke and the team defeated by the Lions in all three Tests. Their star playmaker, 23-year-old Whakatane-born Benji Marshall, had been dogged by injuries, a lack of confidence, poor form and heavy criticism. He'd played in just three international Tests and had never won against the world champion Kangaroos.

Even if the Kiwis could nudge out England to make the top two, their record against favourites Australia was pitiful, with seven straight losses over three years, including a 58–0 slaughtering the year before—their biggest ever defeat.

The Australian side had remained relatively constant for two years and were being talked up as the greatest league side in history. Australia had won nine of the twelve World Cups since the first one, in 1954, and hadn't lost the title since 1975, while New Zealand had never won the Cup. And with the 2008 tournament being held in Australia, the Kangaroos had the home advantage. Australia were such favourites it was hardly worth betting on them—prior to the opening game the TAB offered $1.20 odds on an Australian win, $5.50 on second favourites New Zealand and $8 on England, the only other big-name team in a tournament otherwise populated by minnows.

Sportswriters lamented the prospect of another Australian whitewash. 'It's not about who wins the tournament,' wrote former NRL player and coach Phil Gould in *The Sydney Morning Herald*. 'There is only one winner. Australia win the cup. Do as much spin-doctoring as you like. Talk up as many of the other teams as you like. No other nation can get near Australia in this competition.' Gould said there was enough Australian talent in the NRL that they could pick five teams capable of winning. 'We could even pick a team made up of former NRL players currently playing in the English Super League and still win the World Cup.'

Australian captain Darren Lockyer made a point of publicly talking down his team's chances, saying they were 'rusty', while

New Zealand runner Anne Audain, who was born with deformed feet and endured decades of pain and frustration, wins the 3000 metres at the 1982 Brisbane Commonwealth Games. Race favourite Wendy Smith, from Great Britain, can only watch. (*The New Zealand Herald*)

In 1983, lowly ranked New Zealander Chris Lewis rose out of nowhere to reach the pinnacle of world tennis: a Wimbledon final, against American legend John McEnroe at the height of his playing career. (Getty Images)

In 1983, young New Zealand jockey Jim Cassidy took his ride, Kiwi, from dead last to first to win one of the most thrilling Melbourne Cup races of all time. (Newspix)

Thanks to doggedly reliable bowling, Wellingtonian Ewen Chatfield (drinking) became a stalwart of the New Zealand cricket team in the 1980s. However, it was an unexpected turn with the bat in 1985 that made him a national hero. Pictured here in 1984 with teammates Stephen Boock, Geoff Howarth and Ian Smith (at rear) and Jeff Crowe and Derek Stirling (at front). (*The New Zealand Herald*)

Diagnosed with cancer at the age of fifteen and given no chance of survival, Greg Cooper never doubted he would live to don the coveted black jersey. Cooper, seen here in 2006, went on to forge a stellar rugby career as a player and coach, scoring a record 1520 points for Otago (1988–1996). (Linda Robertson/*The New Zealand Herald*)

'If I ever get two games up on Jahangir I will win.' With grit and determination, Ross Norman pursued world champion Jahangir Khan, finally bringing the Pakistani's five-and-a-half-year, 550-match winning streak to an end at the World Open squash final in Toulouse, France, in November 1986.

(Stephen Line/SquashPics.com)

Steve Gurney crosses the finish line of the 1998 Coast to Coast to take his fourth title. A little over three years earlier, the multisport and adventure athlete lay in an induced coma in a Singapore hospital after contracting a deadly infection during a race in Borneo. (John McCombe/Getty Images)

The Tall Blacks perform the haka ahead of their second-round match against Germany at the World Championships in Indianapolis, 2002. (Andreas Rentz/ Getty Images)

Michael Campbell walks up the eighteenth fairway in the final round of the 2005 US Open, at Pinehurst No. 2, North Carolina. (S. Badz/Getty Images)

Kiwis fullback Lance Hohaia (number 1) is congratulated after scoring a game-changing try against Australia during the final of the 2008 Rugby League World Cup. New Zealand were widely expected to lose to their dominant trans-Tasman rivals. (Greg Wood/Getty Images)

Shane Smeltz celebrates his goal in the seventh minute of the All Whites' second pool game at the 2010 World Cup, as Azzuri goalkeeper Federico Marchetti looks on in disbelief. (Martin Bernetti/Getty Images)

Stephen Donald, an unpopular last-minute ring-in for the All Blacks in the 2011 Rugby World Cup, watches his penalty kick squeak through the posts in the tournament final, against France at Eden Park. The kick would win the All Blacks the game, and the cup that had eluded them for decades. (*The New Zealand Herald*)

coach Ricky Stuart told a reporter that being the 'best team in the world' and the tournament favourites added pressure.

Marshall figured the lack of expectation could work to the Kiwis' advantage. 'We don't mind it,' he told the media. 'It's not always the worst thing going in as underdogs. I can tell you we're certainly not. We'll be out there firing. If anyone's written us off already I think we'll be showing them. Everyone here seems to think this will be a walkover for Australia. The press guys are saying, "You've been thrashed the last few times, how will it be any different this time?" That's fine. We just don't believe that sort of rubbish. There's more pressure on them than us and we're happy with that.'

Any hopes of a Kiwi upset were dashed in the opening pool game at the Sydney Football Stadium, when Australia caned them, 30–6. Before play had even finished, New Zealand fans began leaving the ground. Sydney's *Daily Telegraph* said the Kiwis were undisciplined and had shown less animation than shop mannequins. 'Overall it was what it was. A mismatch, between a potentially slick and stylish side running out the kinks while desperately playing down its chances of winning this series easily—and a team desperately trying to improve its status without having the talent or the motivation.' Then England struggled to overcome minnows Papua New Guinea. 'The World Cup is already over as a contest,' bemoaned *The Sydney Morning Herald*. 'Anything can happen, but the Kiwis haven't got it in them to win this event and they were always a more likely threat than the Poms.'

Australia proceeded to demolish England and Papua New Guinea in the pool round and Fiji in their semifinal to secure a final spot. They'd scored 180 points in the tournament and conceded sixteen, letting through just three tries. Publicly, Lockyer tried to keep the hopes of the other teams alive. 'We were favourites at the start but now we're unbeaten favourites,' he said. 'There's a lot of pressure on us. But the other countries will get better each week. You've got to encourage them not to believe what they read. Anyone on their day can test us.'

New Zealand, meanwhile, solidly beat Papua New Guinea and were lucky to come away with a pool match victory over England, after trailing by sixteen points. They met England again in the semifinals and limped to another win in an error-ridden match.

Marshall, who made several major clangers before scoring the match-clinching try, told a reporter the team was happy simply to make the top two. 'I'm just going to have to pick myself up for next week. It may not have been the greatest game, but we're in the World Cup final. Everything in the past doesn't matter anymore. We just have to look to the future and improve.'

A journalist asked Kearney what the team needed to work on. 'How big's your pad?' replied the coach. 'I'm still disappointed with a few aspects of our game. You've got to get a lot of things right on the day to be competitive against Australia.'

As the final approached, Kangaroos players generously talked up the Kiwis' chances, pointing out that the team had improved immensely during the tournament. But the odds on an Australian win shortened to $1.11. One Australian punter wagered A$220,000 on it.

Reports circulated that the Kangaroos had devised a 'Bash Benji' campaign, figuring Marshall was scared, vulnerable to injuries and a soft target—prompting an urgent phone call from his worried mother. Bennett asked Marshall how he felt about the reports. 'It makes me angry, but they can bash me if they want,' he said.

Bennett replied, 'They've got to catch you first.'

On both sides of the Tasman, journalists, pundits and fans declared it impossible for the Kiwis to win. In *The New Zealand Herald*, former league star Dean Lonergan wrote that the lack of faith was the only thing the team had going for them. 'Every time New Zealand have beaten Australia it has been when all interested parties completely write off their chances. But when you look at the two teams you see that the upset victory that every New Zealand league fan yearns for is very unlikely. This Australian team, without a doubt, is one of their best ever.' Kiwis trainer and former playmaker Stacey Jones tried to look on the bright side: 'The other thing the Kiwis have is that the Australian team has been absolutely on fire. Maybe they might be due to play not quite as well. Maybe they'll be off their game just a little bit.'

In the Kiwis camp, the talk was about pulling together and standing up to Australia, not letting them be the bigger brother. 'No one gave us a chance but, within ourselves, we knew if we just stuck together and did what we did, it would give ourselves every opportunity,' forward-turned-centre Simon Mannering later told a journalist. Kearney said the team were well aware of the enormous task in front of them. 'But that doesn't frighten us. It doesn't deter us from doing our very best.'

The game plan was to come out strong at the beginning of both halves, to tackle the Kangaroos out of the contest, keep the pressure on and shut down the Australian halves, including Lockyer. One day, each player found a photo of himself taped to the front of his locker, emblazoned with the message 'No regrets'. The idea came from Bennett, a taciturn man with a reputation for getting players to believe in themselves.

'Everything seems like it's coming together,' Marshall told a reporter. 'We've got a lot of self-belief. It's a different team.

We've grown a lot, and we've formed a few more combinations. Everyone's keen, everyone's ready to play. It's one of the greatest Australian teams in a while but we've got the belief that we can beat them.'

Kiwis legend Mark Graham handed out the Test jerseys before the game and gave a pre-match speech in which he told the players, 'Go out there to die for your brothers.' As they made last-minute preparations in the dressing room at Suncorp Stadium, in Brisbane, Bennett ordered that their booming music be switched off. 'Just let the music be in your head,' he said.

Marshall felt relaxed, knowing the team had done the necessary work, had prepared well and had everything in place. He asked himself, *What do I want to be after the game? How do I want to feel?* He reflected that it wasn't just about not getting beaten by the Kangaroos, 'but not letting us beat ourselves'.

They ran out in front of a capacity crowd of more than fifty thousand, many of them vocal English supporters who'd stayed on to cheer for their fellow underdogs. The first opportunity in the game came the Kiwis' way. Halfback Nathan Fien launched a perfectly timed kick over the tryline, but Marshall, with no opposition players in sight, fumbled as he tried to land the try.

The Kangaroos got stuck in to Marshall's confidence, sledging and taunting him. They'd point at him, saying, 'Run at Marshall' and 'There he is.' Marshall knew he had no choice but to handle the pressure.

Eight minutes after Marshall's attempt, Kangaroos superstar Billy Slater skipped through two defenders and, with men to spare, passed to Lockyer for a try that went unconverted. Their teammate David Williams followed with a 50-metre breakaway try, duly converted. A fumble on the tryline denied Lockyer a third. After twenty minutes, the match was proceeding just as everyone had predicted. So much for the game plan.

At one point, Kiwis reserve Sam Rapira found himself blocked by Kangaroos prop Petero Civoniceva. Rapira had long looked up to the big front rower and decided to test himself. 'I gave it my all, ran as hard as I could. It felt like I hit a brick wall and I ended up on the ground. That sparked my game: it made me go a bit harder the next time.'

The Kiwis launched a sustained attack. They pounded the Kangaroos' line, and eventually lock Jeremy Smith ran through three green-clad men to score under the posts. The Kiwis converted and capitalised on the momentum six minutes later when centre Jerome Ropati scored under the posts, after a controversial call that an apparent fumble by Marshall had a Kangaroos' hand on it. The score evened up. Reserve Issac Luke potted the conversion, putting the Kiwis in front, 12–10. The lead lasted all of six minutes before Lockyer stole it back with another try. With the conversion, the Kangaroos took the game to half-time leading 16–12.

Adhering to the game plan, the Kiwis came back out fighting. Winger Manu Vatuvei was unlucky to miss a try in the corner in the first two minutes, but fullback Lance Hohaia made up for it eight minutes later, with a try after a sustained period of attack from the Kiwis. Luke converted to retake the lead. 'It was real gritty,' said Kearney, later. 'We dragged them into an arm wrestle and things just flowed on from that.'

The Australians scrambled, but a try attempt on the line by their centre was held up. A few minutes later, Marshall kicked downfield. Slater caught it for the Kangaroos, ran it up, sidestepped a tackler and overbalanced. As he drifted over the sideline, he blindly flung the ball back into the field of play—and Marshall picked it up and carried it over the tryline. He failed to convert, but his quick hands and feet gave his team a 22–16 lead with less than twenty minutes to go.

Marshall sensed the Australians had cracked, but they rallied, with a try in the corner. It wasn't converted, but it chewed the Kiwis' lead back to two points. New Zealand refused to let up. Minutes later, Hohaia chipped a kick over the tryline. As he chased it down, he was clotheslined with a neck-high tackle. The referees controversially awarded a penalty try. Marshall converted. Even the Kiwis looked stunned. They were ahead by eight points in a World Cup final, with nine minutes to play. The chant of 'Kiwi, Kiwi' rose from the crowd.

A dangerous, desperate run by the Kangaroos' halfback was brought down by a feather-light ankle tap from Smith. A minute later, Smith intercepted a Kangaroos pass to set up a dogged team assault that ended with Marshall lobbing the ball across the posts. After a pinball-like scramble from both sides, Kiwis prop Adam Blair casually picked up the ball one-handed and planted it. Marshall converted, making it 34–20. With four minutes to go, the lead was unassailable. The Kiwis had defied logic to win the World Cup.

The players began celebrating even before the whistle sounded. Kearney felt numb. Marshall burst into tears. The win blindsided the Kangaroos and tournament officials. Lockyer was inexplicably awarded man of the match—the decision had been made before the outcome was determined. *New Zealand Herald* league writer Peter Jessup remarked that Lockyer looked like he was 'chewing on tinfoil' when he accepted it. 'I'd swap this medal any day for a win, but not to be,' the captain told the crowd. The player of the tournament award went to Billy Slater, the Kangaroo who had handed the Kiwis the game-changing try—another decision made before the tournament ended. 'To see the look on the faces of the

Australian players . . . I knew it well,' Marshall later reflected in his autobiography. 'It was the look we were used to.'

The Kiwis did a lap of honour and an impromptu haka, and shed tears in their dressing room. Rapira told a reporter he could have played better, 'but I came off the field feeling like my whole body was broken, and that's good enough for me'. Later, in the pub, Civoniceva congratulated the Kiwis. 'I thought during the game you guys were going to give up, but you took it to another level,' he told them.

Media reports claimed that the Kangaroos refused to accept their runners-up medals at the stadium, shunned interviews, left the ground early and snubbed the after-match function, forcing the Australian Rugby League administration to issue a statement denying the early exit and claiming that officials had made the decisions about the function and medals before the game. Kangaroos coach Ricky Stuart was initially magnanimous: 'Please don't make this too much about Australia,' he told media. '[The Kiwis] were better than us tonight. They've got their trophy in their shed. It's not in ours.' That night at the stadium, however, Stuart reportedly launched a tirade against ARL chief executive Geoff Carr, suggesting the Kangaroos were victims of a conspiracy. Witnesses told *The Sydney Morning Herald* that Stuart had blamed match officials and accused them of stitching up his team, making defeat almost inevitable. The following morning, Stuart reportedly bailed up match referee Ashley Klein in a hotel foyer, accusing him of being a cheat and the 'c— who cost us the World Cup', and shoulder-charged another official when he tried to intervene. After an inquiry, the coach apologised and resigned.

Former Kangaroo Mark Geyer defended Stuart but was philosophical about the game's result. 'Questions will be asked, but

I don't think that's his fault,' he told a reporter. 'It was the game of the year. I hate seeing Australia get beaten, but sometimes the greats have got to be sacrificed for a bigger view. It was one of the biggest upsets in sporting history.'

Even the Australian media and pundits seemed to get a ghoulish satisfaction out of the upset, commending the Kiwis' tactics, commitment and ferocity. Gould called it 'a great result for the game'. *The Sydney Morning Herald* claimed, 'It was meant to be predictable, but the finish was irresistible. A joke became a choke.' The league correspondent of London's *Sunday Times* wrote, 'New Zealand tore away the mask of invincibility that Australia have worn for the past 20 years with a magnificent display packed full of panache, power and polish.'

Marshall felt the young team had proven themselves. 'Before the game it wasn't who was going to win, it was a matter of Australia by how much. Now, we're the world champs. No one can take that away from us.'

THE 2010 ALL WHITES

'A few seconds to etch your name in history'

JUST AFTER 6 A.M. on a chilly November morning in 2009, All Whites striker Rory Fallon slipped out of his hotel room on the second floor of Wellington's Copthorne Hotel. As his roommate, goalkeeper Mark Paston, slept, the 27-year-old Fallon walked along the city's waterfront. That day, the All Whites would play Bahrain in their final World Cup qualifying match. Win, and they'd be heading to South Africa in 2010, the first New Zealand team to compete at the World Cup since 1982. Lose or draw, and Bahrain would go instead.

As the nation's excitement grew, Fallon had felt self-doubt creep in—fear of losing the game and forever being known as the team that choked at the last hurdle. He needed to clear his head and get in the zone. He walked until he found a concrete step at the harbour's edge looking across to the Westpac 'Cake Tin' Stadium, where the afternoon's game would take place. There was no one else around. In the stillness and quiet he sat and prayed, as he'd prayed all week, that he'd get a chance to score the goal that would take the All Whites to the World Cup.

The game would be just the third All Whites appearance for New Zealand–born Fallon. He'd represented England as a teenager and had only recently become eligible to play for his birth country after a FIFA rule change.

Fallon had Kiwi football pedigree. Nearly 30 years earlier his father, Kevin, had been the assistant coach of the legendary 1982 All Whites. That year, 22 young men—including Ricki Herbert and Brian Turner—took leave from their full-time jobs to become the first team to represent New Zealand at the World Cup in Spain. Despite losing all three games, scoring two goals and conceding twelve, the All Whites' achievement remained the highlight of New Zealand football history.

Come 2009, Herbert was the All Whites' coach, and Turner his assistant. They were hoping to join an elite group of 46 men worldwide who had both played and coached at the finals of a World Cup tournament, including Argentina's Diego Maradona, England's Bobby Robson and Germany's Franz Beckenbauer. Herbert had taken charge of the All Whites in 2005, inheriting a team riddled with self-doubt and devoid of passion. He was determined to bring pride back to the white shirt. He began rebuilding team spirit and introducing the relatively inexperienced players to top-level opposition. From the outset, he told Turner they were going to the World Cup. If Turner expressed doubts, Herbert would say, 'It's written in the stars.'

In late 2007 the rejuvenated All Whites had embarked on the Oceania World Cup qualifying series, which was without the Australian Socceroos, as they had switched to the Asian Football Confederation. Over the next year they chalked up five wins from six games, against Fiji, Vanuatu and New Caledonia, to become Oceania champions. The final hurdle between them and the World Cup was a two-match play-off against Bahrain, the fifth-placed team in Asia. Bahrain was a big step up from the Pacific nations. Many in the football world believed the All Whites would falter.

With Kiwi goalkeeper Glen Moss suspended for four World Cup matches after swearing at a referee, captain Ryan Nelsen was worried that second-string keeper Paston wasn't up to the job. Nelsen had just rejoined the All Whites after four years with English Premier League side Blackburn Rovers and was concerned about the national team's lack of a world-class goalkeeper. Paston had spent a lot of time on the All Whites' bench. But Paston would prove himself in the first game against Bahrain, held in the Bahraini capital, Manama, in October 2009. He made two world-class saves and played a crucial role in the nil-all draw.

The result left them one shot from glory. It was imperative they won the second match. If they drew, Bahrain would advance to the World Cup on overall points. Ahead of the decider, Nelsen joked with the press that he hoped for a 'good dirty southerly, some beautiful Wellington wind and maybe some sleet'. The Bahrainis had come from the desert via Sydney and were used to a dry ball and pitch.

As the two sides warmed up at Westpac Stadium, the 1982 All Whites did a lap of the field to a rapturous reception from the capacity crowd of 36,500. 'The whole place was as white as the Southern Alps in mid-winter,' Nelsen recalled. 'The crowd started singing long before the game and they never stopped throughout the 90 minutes. It was noisier than playing Man U at Old Trafford.' When the national anthem played, Nelsen placed his hand over the silver fern on his heart, then raised it to his lips and kissed it. Pride had returned to the white shirt.

The All Whites took a while to settle into their play. Herbert stood on the sidelines, mentally kicking every ball. Midway through the first half, All Whites striker Chris Killen took a long-range shot, but it bounced off the crossbar. Just on half-time, the All Whites were awarded a corner. Leo Bertos lifted the ball across to Fallon, who blasted it into the back of the net with a powerful header. The score was 1–0. The All Whites and their fans were ecstatic.

Five minutes into the second half, Bahrain were awarded a penalty kick. Nelsen was anxious. Bahraini striker Sayed Adnan had been nominated as Asian player of the year. It was highly unlikely he would miss. As Adnan stepped up for the kick, the All Whites coaching staff frantically tried to tell Paston that he usually kicked to the keeper's right. Paston couldn't hear. He was in the zone. As Adnan kicked, Paston took a guess and dived to the right. He grabbed the ball and held it tight. The crowd leapt into a standing ovation.

It seemed as if the fight had gone out of the Bahrain team. Through the rest of the game the All Whites held tight on defence, Paston making another brilliant save. When the final whistle blew, the stadium erupted. All Whites players, coaches and staff surged onto the field, laughing, shouting, crying and huddling together. Fallon's prayer had been answered. The All Whites were going to the World Cup. The following day's *Sunday Star Times* declared it 'one of the most momentous results in New Zealand sports history'. Herbert later described it as 'the proudest moment of my life'.

When the World Cup pools were announced, the All Whites drew Group F. They would play Slovakia, ranked 34th in the world, and Paraguay, ranked 30th and fresh from beating football heavyweights Brazil in a qualifying match. The All Whites were ranked 77th in the world, behind Montenegro, Macedonia, Uganda, Panama and Wales.

But their toughest match was expected to come from defending world champions Italy, a country with 3541 professional footballers to New Zealand's 25. The Italian team, known as the Azzurri, included players from football giants AC Milan and Inter Milan. Their goalkeeper, Gianluigi Buffon, was paid more in a year by his club, Juventus, than all of the All Whites' earnings put together. Italian coach Marcello Lippi was said to earn $5.3 million a year, while Ricki Herbert received $50,000, less than the minimum wage for an A-League player, and juggled the part-time role with his job as coach of New Zealand's only professional club, the Wellington Phoenix. 'From outside the group there were no expectations from anyone ... the New Zealand media, the public, certainly other countries,' striker Shane Smeltz recalled. 'If you spoke to anyone before the World Cup, we were written off a long time before it kicked off.'

The French sports daily *L'Equipe* said, 'If the All Whites score a goal, the whole country will be satisfied. If they take a point they will be received as heroes on their return. If they progress beyond the pool stage you will see a statue erected in Wellington. Unfortunately it is possible that not even the first will happen.' But within the All Whites camp the self-belief was unstoppable. They were not going to South Africa simply to make up the numbers; they were going to achieve a result that would prove they deserved a place on the international stage. 'We will be making sure we make every New Zealander proud,' Nelsen told the press ahead of their opening match, with Slovakia in June 2010. 'That is one of our number one goals.'

As his men lined up for the game at the Royal Bafokeng Stadium, Nelsen reminded them that although the game was 90 minutes long, 'all it takes is a few seconds to etch your name in history'. For Herbert, it was a defining moment. The white shirt was finally back at the World Cup.

Slovakia had run an impressive qualifying campaign, topping their European group and winning every match in their Cup build-up. The All Whites got off to a promising start before the crowd of almost forty thousand, with Killen taking a shot at goal after just three minutes. But Slovakia were fast and skilful, and their superior ball handling soon came to the fore.

The All Whites created chances but couldn't see them through. A few minutes into the second half, Slovak Róbert Vittek slipped ahead of 21-year-old fullback Winston Reid, picked up a cross from the right and scored, despite being technically offside.

The pressure was on. The All Whites fought hard, keeping up a strong defence, including a brilliant tackle and goal deflection by Reid. Two minutes from full-time Smeltz had an opportunity to score. In clear sight of the goal, he took a header. It went wide. The All Whites were heading for a 0–1 loss.

As the game went into injury time, Nelsen knew they had to take a chance if they were to score. Figuring a younger player was more likely to take a match-winning risk, he pushed Reid forwards. Reid, who was used to spending his time at the back of the field, puffed his way towards the goal. He was exhausted but determined to give everything he had. Nelsen stayed back, reorganising the defenders and concentrating on keeping Slovakia from scoring again.

In the 93rd minute, Smeltz neatly turned on the ball, blocked his opponent and lifted a deep cross over the box. Reid waited, unmarked, right in front of the goal. He didn't see the ball until it was almost too late. He leapt and awkwardly twisted his neck to give a light header, knowing anything harder would spell disaster. It went in, hitting the bottom-right corner of the net.

The score was tied. Reid ripped off his shirt in elation and sprinted to the corner flag with his celebrating teammates, earning a yellow card for his bare-chested display. The crowd roared, drowning out the ever-present buzz of the vuvuzelas, the monotone plastic horn that became a symbol of the tournament.

Minutes later, the game was over. The All Whites had earned their first ever match point on a World Cup table. Reid, who had joined the All Whites only three months earlier after playing for Denmark's under-21 side, became a New Zealand hero.

'The tournament has been startled,' declared London's *Guardian* newspaper. 'Nobody supposed this would be the fixture to set the World Cup alight.' Still, the newspaper warned, the All Whites would find it 'extremely taxing to repeat this feat of resilience' in their next game, against Italy, who had won four World Cup titles, a record second only to Brazil's. The All Whites had played in just four World Cup matches. For many in the team, merely lining up against the world champions was an achievement. 'You grow up as a lad, and you watch the Italians, the Brazilians, and want to . . . test yourselves against them,' said twenty-year-old defender Tommy Smith, who had also made his All Whites debut just three months earlier. 'It's a dream come true for me, as it is for all the lads . . . We've got nothing to lose. Nobody is expecting anything from us. We're just going out there to prove to ourselves that we can cope against the top level teams.'

To the Italian team and the world's press, the result seemed a foregone conclusion. Italian midfielder Daniele De Rossi told journalists that if Italy didn't make it to the second round, it would be as serious as New Zealand getting knocked out at the pool stage of the Rugby World Cup. 'We're Italy and we should win.' His teammate Giorgio Chiellini agreed, though he noted New Zealand could be very physical, and dangerous in the air and in set pieces. 'It won't be easy but with all the respect we owe our opponents, we should win. We will be in trouble if we don't. I don't even want to think about the possibility of a draw or something else.'

The Azzurri were known for making a slow start in World Cup tournaments and building momentum with each game. They'd drawn their first game, 1–1, against Paraguay, and needed to beat the All Whites to have a chance to top the group. They were also known for their superb ball handling and expressive play, while the All Whites had a more aggressive aerial style and relied heavily on tight defence.

The All Whites were optimistic, their confidence riding high after their comeback against Slovakia. They also had what 36-year-old midfielder Simon Elliott called 'the X-factor'—an enviable group dynamic and team spirit, without the petty rivalries and egos prevalent in professional teams. Smeltz told journalists, 'The environment here is fantastic. You hear of other teams in the World Cup with issues or problems in the camp. We go out there and play for one another. As soon as we cross that line, we'd die for our teammates.'

The All Whites were convinced they had a chance, and the press conceded that an upset wouldn't be without precedent. 'Italy may traditionally be the suave sophisticates of world football ... yet when it comes to the World Cup they have a peculiar habit of creating a huge wet patch around the business area of their £4000 cotton slacks,' wrote *The Guardian*'s Rob Smyth. 'Of all the superpowers, Italy have suffered the greatest humiliations against the minnows of world football ... [But] you wouldn't expect them to mess up against New Zealand, this is surely the biggest mismatch of the tournament: the world champions against the 2000–1 outsiders.'

Just seven minutes after kick-off at Mbombela Stadium, things were looking dicey for those expensive cotton slacks. Elliott took a free kick, delivering an expert cross. Italian defender Fabio Cannavaro flicked the ball with his hand and it ricocheted off another Italian player. Smeltz strode forwards and pounded the ball past the goalkeeper into the net. Ecstatic, he sprinted to the corner and leapt high in the air, as the New Zealand supporters roared louder than even the vuvuzelas. Some commentators questioned whether the ball had grazed Reid's head on its way to Cannavaro, rendering Smeltz offside, but replays were inconclusive. The score was 1–0.

A wounded Italy charged into action, dominating possession and attacking the goal. Paston batted away one free kick only to watch in horror as a shot by Italian midfielder Riccardo Montolivo rocketed past him. It deflected off the goalpost. Saved. The All Whites fought back with an aerial assault. At fourteen minutes, Fallon got a yellow card for elbowing an Italian defender in the air.

With the pressure mounting, the Azzurri brought out their famous Hollywood-style appeals. At twenty minutes, Cannavaro fell to the field grabbing his chest after contact with Killen. Four minutes later, Chiellini rolled around pounding the pitch after Fallon's elbow accidentally connected with his face. 'The Italians were diving around like little girls,' Fallon told journalists after the game. 'You can't really do much about it. If someone's going to ruin the game then so be it but we kept fighting.'

In the 29th minute, De Rossi went for the ball and Smith grabbed his shirt, giving a small tug backwards. The 85-kilogram Italian tumbled forwards and flopped onto the field. *The New Zealand Herald*'s Michael Brown said it looked as if he'd been tackled by All Black Ma'a Nonu, not the 82-kilogram Smith. 'He was clearly looking for a penalty and the referee duly obliged.' Juventus's Vincenzo Iaquinta lined up the penalty kick, blasting it into the right side of the net as Paston dived to the left. Italy had equalised.

The All Whites appeared unfazed. They got straight back into the match, with some brilliant midfield play from Elliott and stunning defence by Nelsen. The Azzurri continued their dramatic appeals, falling to the ground clutching their bodies whenever they encountered Fallon. At 62 minutes, Herbert pulled Fallon from the field, substituting eighteen-year-old striker Chris Wood. Fallon was clearly a target. Though Herbert thought he'd been harshly treated, he couldn't risk a second yellow card that would automatically send him off the field with a one-match ban.

In the 70th minute, Montolivo launched another rocket, from 25 metres out. Paston dived left with his arm extended and deflected the ball with his right glove. It would rank as one of the finest saves of the tournament. Thirteen minutes later, Wood outwitted Cannavaro for a shot at goal. He narrowly missed, the ball shaving the post as it flew clear.

An exhausted Nelsen lay down on the field, as every muscle in his legs cramped. The referee gave him a yellow card for delaying play. He forced himself to his feet. After working so hard for 85 minutes, there was no way he was giving up.

The atmosphere was electric as the All Whites hung on, fuelled by self-belief. Another superb aerial save from Paston in the 88th minute buoyed the team. They fought hard through four minutes of injury time, pushed to the limit.

As the final whistle blew, an emotional Herbert pumped both fists. A 1–1 draw was an incredible result in a game where Italy had taken 23 shots at goal and New Zealand had managed just three. Around the stadium, bare-chested New Zealand fans twirled their white shirts in delight. 'New Zealand have made the impossible possible,' declared a television commentator. 'It would have been unthinkable even a matter of weeks ago.'

Herbert told journalists the result was far above anything else New Zealand had achieved in the history of the game. 'We're doing okay for a team that supposedly has some amateurs in it and wasn't good enough. A lot of people thought we shouldn't be part of the World Cup . . . that the way we qualified was easy. Well, you can go and write your own stories now.'

The match fired journalists' imaginations around the world. They applauded the All Whites' guts and determination, and criticised the Italians' theatrics and the referee. They declared it 'the feel good hit of the summer' (*The Guardian*) and 'the most heart-warming and unforeseen development at the World Cup' (*Daily Mail*). They noted that the All Whites had arrived as 'cannon fodder . . . the team from the ultimate backwater, the proverbial team of part-timers and no-hopers' (*The Telegraph*) and were now 'only behind Italy on alphabetical order' (*The Guardian*).

The All Whites couldn't afford to get carried away. They had four days' rest before facing Paraguay, who were top of the group. Win, and they'd not only secure a ticket to the second round but would top the group, a result no one would have predicted when they left New Zealand. Lose, and they'd be going home. Draw, and they could only qualify if Italy also drew with Slovakia, and New Zealand surpassed Italy on goal count.

They were buzzing with the possibilities. Their hearts and minds were set on advancing to Round 2. Then Nelsen fell ill. Vomiting, suffering from diarrhoea and unable to eat, he couldn't even make it to training.

On game day, as the All Whites lined up in their black strip at Peter Mokaba Stadium in Polokwane, Nelsen still felt dreadful, rating himself just 40 per cent fit. Meanwhile, at Ellis Park Stadium in Johannesburg, Italy prepared to face off against Slovakia. Both games started at 3 p.m. Only two of the four teams would advance to the next round.

The All Whites went out hard. Paston, Nelsen, Reid and Smith held strong on defence, but the team struggled to find attacking opportunities. Paraguay concentrated on containing the All Whites' aerial game, descending as a pack of two or three any time a New Zealander got the ball. They blocked the Kiwis' attempts to send the ball long to their strikers. Fouls and free kicks interrupted the flow, and much of the play was confined to the middle of the field.

At 24 minutes, word came that Slovakia had scored against Italy. The All Whites now had to score against Paraguay if they wanted to progress to the next round—a nil-all draw wouldn't be enough.

Early in the second half, Elliott took a shot at goal, but it flew just wide and high. At 56 minutes, Nelsen received a yellow card for fouling his former Blackburn teammate Roque Santa Cruz.

The Paraguayans struggled to penetrate the New Zealand defence, and Paston made several shoulder-crunching saves. Then it was the All Whites strikers' turn for disappointment, when an offside Wood just missed getting his toe on a cross from Smeltz in front of the goal.

The All Whites took just four shots at goal, while Paraguay made seventeen attempts. When the final whistle blew, the score was nil-all. Two minutes later, the whistle sounded on injury time in the Slovakia–Italy game. Slovakia won, 3–2, sending the defending champions home at the bottom of Group F.

The undefeated All Whites were also going home. It was only the fourth time an unbeaten side had been eliminated in the group round of a Cup. They ended up in 22nd place in the tournament—ahead of big guns Italy (26th) and France (29th)—and remained the only undefeated team. Even that year's eventual winner, Spain, lost a pool game.

It was a monumental achievement, but for the shattered All Whites that night in Polokwane, it still felt like defeat. A pale Nelsen said, 'Just to play in the World Cup—I would have given my left arm for that. It is a pretty amazing achievement, really. But I feel really gutted, disappointed, because I know the whole country had got behind us. I just want to say sorry . . . we were so close but we just didn't get there.' Nelsen was later named in a World Cup Best XI chosen by American sports channel ESPN for 'defending defiantly throughout the tournament and heroically against Italy'.

For fifteen minutes after the game the All Whites and their coaching staff stood on the pitch, acknowledging and applauding their fans. Herbert told the media it had been an emotional game, and he was both proud and disappointed. 'It was incredible tonight. We were resolute and tough against a team that is right up there again and they really struggled to penetrate. I'm disappointed, but no one is prouder than me of what this team has achieved. Can you get any closer?'

25

STEPHEN DONALD

From 'zero to hero'

ON A SPRING DAY IN 2011, rugby player Stephen Donald was whitebaiting on the Waikato River near his hometown of Waiuku when his mobile phone rang. He didn't recognise the number, and didn't answer.

The man widely known by his nickname of 'Beaver'—because, he said, he was an ugly child with protruding teeth—was a few weeks away from taking up a contract with English premiership side Bath. He was enjoying a bit of down time, fishing, whitebaiting and following the Rugby World Cup over a few beers. The specialist goal kicker hadn't lined up a ball in six weeks.

He and his mate were having a good day, having hauled in kilogram after kilogram of the tiny fish. The phone rang again. Same number. Still he didn't answer.

Watching the All Blacks blaze through their pool matches in the four-yearly tournament had been bitter-sweet. Like every New Zealander, Donald desperately wanted his team to win the Cup for the first time in 24 years—especially as New Zealand was hosting it. But he hadn't been selected in the Cup squad after serving three years with the All Blacks. Though he'd just retired from the Waikato Chiefs, after 85 games over seven years, and had earned 22 Test caps, he was set to go down in history as one of the most vilified men ever to have worn the black jersey.

Donald's patchy All Blacks career had ended miserably the previous year, after a horror performance against Australia in Hong Kong. Among other mistakes, he had failed to kick a ball into touch about ten minutes from the final whistle. Australia had capitalised with a try to win the match and end a record All Blacks winning streak.

In another year it might not have mattered. With the Rugby World Cup approaching, the nerves of rugby writers and fans were raw. An unprecedented outpouring of vitriol flooded the internet and talkback radio. Cruel jokes and jibes went viral, and anti-Donald Facebook pages sprouted like mushrooms. People shouted abuse during his practice runs. His parents cowered in the stands, holding their tongues as insults flew around them. He became the personification of a choker, the scapegoat for the collective fear that once again New Zealand would fail to win the World Cup, rugby's ultimate prize. One blogger remarked that it had become fashionable to hate Donald.

The media joined the flogging. An Australian reporter named him one of Australia's best players, and former All Blacks Inga Tuigamala, Richard Loe and Sean Fitzpatrick called for his axing. When he remained in the team for a further two Tests that year, the *Herald on Sunday*'s sports editor, Paul Lewis, wrote, 'Donald's return to the All Blacks was the most unwelcome comeback since Jimi Hendrix's vomit.'

Donald's family and friends became drawn into arguments in pubs when they tried to defend him, but the man himself gamely brushed off the criticism. 'I would be pretty suicidal if I took too much notice of what's going on out there,' he told Richard Knowler of *The Press*. 'You've just got to keep boxing on and have faith in yourself.' The All Blacks and their coaches refused to say a bad word about Donald publicly. Assistant coach Wayne Smith told the media he believed in the boy from Waiuku. 'It's not easy at a time like this—you go to a dark place. I've been there myself. That's the accountability of the All Blacks jersey. He'll get another opportunity.'

In May 2011, it became evident to Donald that he wouldn't, when he was left out of an All Blacks training camp—effectively a short list for the World Cup squad. Disappointed that he was never again likely to play for his country, he signed with Bath. Sure enough, when the New Zealand squad was announced, his name was missing. His Waikato teammate Richard Kahui, who'd made the cut, urged him to keep the faith. 'You stay fit, Beaver, because you'll kick the winning goal in the World Cup final.'

Donald replied, 'Gee, you talk crap.'

The selection omission didn't immediately blunt the knives. *Sunday Star Times* rugby writer Marc Hinton claimed, 'Donald, for all his bright moments for the Chiefs and Waikato, is simply not good enough to play Test rugby at the level the All Blacks require of him. And well done to [All Blacks coach Graham] Henry for sticking to his guns, trusting his intuition and adhering to the formula that says if something looks like a dog and smells like a dog and barks like a dog, then it pretty much always is a dog.'

As Donald dragged the river for whitebait that spring day, Graham Henry tried calling him for the third time, without success. Henry's squad was in crisis. He'd lost his star first five-eighth, Daniel Carter, to a groin injury. Carter's replacement, Colin Slade, had gone down with the same injury, leaving just a single first five-eighth in the team—inexperienced ring-in Aaron Cruden. Henry badly needed a backup in the key position.

Though Henry had been publicly supportive of Donald after his poor performance against Australia, he'd appeared dismissive just two weeks earlier at a press conference confirming Carter was out of the Cup. *New Zealand Herald* rugby writer Wynne Gray noted a telling moment during the conference. 'An inquiry came from the floor about the replacement choices. Was Stephen Donald considered for the job? Henry looked down his nose and batted away the inquiry with a curt negative. To those of us in the room the response carried a scornful tone in its solitary word.'

Henry was down to his fourth-choice first five-eighth. When he couldn't get hold of Donald, Mils Muliaina, Donald's Chiefs teammate, tried calling. 'Start answering your phone, you idiot,' he said.

Finally, as Henry later recorded in his autobiography, Donald picked up the phone. Henry said, 'Beaver, it's Graham Henry here. What are you up to?'

'I'm whitebaiting, Graham.'

'Have you caught any?'

'Yeah, I've got about three kilograms so far.'

'Well if you bring it to my room in the Heritage Hotel in Auckland, you'll be in the All Blacks.'

Donald arrived in Auckland with the requisite seafood. Several hours later, he fronted a press conference, looking as if he hadn't showered since leaving the river, with unkempt hair and an unshaven jaw. He answered questions with trademark calm confidence. 'I never gave up the dream, but I was fairly surprised considering what's happened. I've had a good month off and like everyone else have enjoyed watching the World Cup. Obviously I watched it thinking, "Jeez I'd love to be a part of it," and now that opportunity potentially is here.' When asked about his match fitness, he said, 'I'm pretty confident, very confident.' Later, he confessed that his preparation hadn't been ideal. 'When you go whitebaiting you take a few beers with you, so the fitness probably wasn't what it could be.'

Internet chatrooms and social media sites exploded, Donald's few supporters going head-to-head with his many detractors. A media website poll asked, 'Will you be concerned if Stephen Donald takes to the field in the Rugby World Cup semi-final?' More than two-thirds of respondents ticked the box that said, 'Yes, he's a choker.'

Richard Loe, who'd criticised Donald's performance the previous year, was philosophical: 'I know a lot of people are sounding off about Stephen Donald being there but it's time to get over all that now. I haven't been Donald's greatest fan either but, come on—who else is there? We have broken two top first fives; there's no one else left.'

Donald sat on the reserves bench in the semifinal, watching Cruden help the team to a 20–6 victory that set them up to meet France in the final, at Eden Park, on 23 October. It would be a rematch of the first—and last—World Cup final New Zealand had won, in 1987. Same teams, same stadium.

Again, Donald was named as a reserve. 'I never ruled out the dream of being part of it,' he told Hinton. 'You pride yourself on fronting up. After all that Hong Kong criticism, I didn't want that to be what people remembered me for, and with this potentially being my last game, I wanted to go out and prove I'm a genuine All Black.' As a crowd waited outside the home team's hotel to watch the players board their bus for Eden Park, a man shouted, 'Stephen Donald, stay at home. Everyone else, on the bus.'

The game was one of the tensest and closest matches in All Blacks history, with a strong French side pummelling the New Zealand line. Halfback Piri Weepu, on goal kicking duties instead of the less experienced Cruden and troubled by a groin strain, missed three from three attempts. In the 34th minute, with the score 5–0 to the All Blacks, Henry's worst-case scenario eventuated. Cruden was taken out in a tackle and stayed down, clutching his knee and grimacing. 'He looked in a bad way,' Donald later told Fox Sport, 'and the reports coming back from the field to me, from the medicos, were to get warm and get warm quickly. The shock of reality was, right you're going to be out there. But I felt pretty confident. I craved to be out there, craved to get the opportunity.'

Donald ran out onto the field, tugging down a jersey that was evidently too small. Henry later revealed that because Donald was such a late arrival, he'd had to wear another player's backup jersey, which was two sizes shy.

'You could feel the nation suck in its cheeks,' wrote Gray. In the stands, packed to capacity with 61,079 fans, the cheers outweighed the boos, perhaps thanks to Weepu's poor kicking performance. Despite his errors against Australia, Donald was one of the leading point scorers in the Super Rugby competition, with most of those coming from goal kicking. 'Maybe they sensed he needed a lift,' wrote Hinton, later. 'This is a bloke who's copped more flak than anybody in New Zealand rugby for the odd hiccup in the black jersey.'

In London, Nick Pearce, *The Telegraph* website's World Cup live blogger, hurriedly typed, 'Stephen Donald at 10 in a World Cup final is Graham Henry's worst nightmare. Yup, Cruden's gone. Stephen Donald is on and Graham Henry has just gone pale. This could be a game changer, people.' A minute later, he added, 'The Donald curse strikes immediately as New Zealand are pinged at the scrum.' Donald was nowhere near the scrum.

Half-time came and went, with no change to the score. Several minutes into the second half, the All Blacks were awarded a penalty kick. The country held its breath to see who would take the kick— Weepu or Donald.

'Who's this striding forward?' wrote Stuff.co.nz's live blogger, Dan Gilhooly. 'Stephen Donald of course. He's taken the kicking duties from Weepu. Cometh the hour.'

Donald felt remarkably calm as he lined up the ball on its tee and stood over it. The kick wasn't a difficult one, certainly the kind a man of his experience had made hundreds of times in high-pressure games. He'd been kicking well in the week he'd been in the squad. He felt ready, focused, determined. 'There was nowhere to hide,' he said, afterwards. 'It was the World Cup final—time to front.' As soon as he kicked it, he knew it was good. It soared into the air and sneaked inside the goalposts, adding three points to the All Blacks' tally.

The kick's significance became evident only at full-time. Not long after Donald struck it, France scored and converted a try, knocking back the All Blacks' lead to one point. The New Zealanders held off the French attack for the rest of the tense game. Donald played a solid match—kicking, tackling and running with the confidence of a man with a nation behind him, though he had a sick feeling in his gut and his lungs were bursting. Captain Richie McCaw felt reassured by his assertive presence, which allowed the team to get on with the business at hand.

When the final whistle went, the All Blacks won the Cup and Donald went from 'zero to hero', according to a television report. Henry, interviewed over the loudspeakers after the game, said, 'Didn't he do well, Steve Donald? Superb.' The crowd screamed their agreement. Later, the coach told a press conference, 'I had a long talk to him after the game and he had a huge smile on his face to be part of this because you people have given him a bit of stick at times—and perhaps he deserved it occasionally—but he has got great character.'

Donald was mobbed outside the team hotel. Columnists and radio jocks publicly apologised. Journalists from around the world clamoured for interviews. Fans called for him to become prime minister in the upcoming general election. His local rugby field in Waiuku was renamed 'Beaver Park', and his street unofficially became 'Beaver Boulevard'. A Facebook page called 'Sorry Stephen Donald. We Were Wrong' collected thousands of likes. The national film funding body, NZ on Air, allocated $2.7 million to a telemovie about his story. For several years, whenever a New Zealand team was losing in any sport, from cricket to America's Cup racing, the call would go up: 'Bring on the Beaver.'

Donald accepted the public adulation with the same good-humoured confidence he had used to handle the vitriol. 'For someone who doesn't really crave the limelight it was certainly hard case for a few days there,' he told the *Waikato Times*. 'I'm no hero, it's still old, plain me, to be fair.'

He never played again for the All Blacks.

ACKNOWLEDGEMENTS

We couldn't have brought these stories to life without the dedication and passion of the dozens of New Zealand sports journalists, authors, documentary makers and athletes who have collectively chronicled the history of sport in this country in the last hundred years or more. And we couldn't have accessed their articles, books and other materials without the tireless efforts of librarians and archivists in cataloguing, scanning, digitising and conserving them. In the References section you'll find extensive lists of the sources we've used, in case you feel inspired to find out more about the underdogs we've featured.

Thanks to the team at Allen & Unwin, in Sydney and Auckland, for their enthusiasm and expertise—including Melanie Laville-Moore, Angela Handley, Clare James, Nicola McCloy, Abba Renshaw and copyeditor Penny Mansley. And thanks to Ron Palenski at the New Zealand Sports Hall of Fame in Dunedin for his assistance with sourcing some hard to find photographs.

We'd also like to acknowledge the support of our families—especially Simon and Brad—as we've written this book. Liliane, Tom and Louis, and Oscar and Leo: we hope you learn from these stories that if you believe in yourself, you work hard and you never give up, the impossible can become the possible.

REFERENCES

Introduction

Allison, Scott T., & George R. Goethals, *Heroes: What they do and why we need them*, New York: Oxford University Press, 2011

Smith, Ian, with Joseph Romanos, *Outrageous Cricket Moments*, Auckland: Hodder Moa Beckett, 2003

1 Harry Watson

'1928 Tour de France', BikeRaceInfo, <bikeraceinfo.com>, n.d.

'Arrangements criticised, Australian team too small', *The Argus* (Melbourne), 8 June 1928

'Australian cyclists: Engagements for Opperman', *The Argus* (Melbourne), 18 July 1928

'Begins on Sunday', *The Argus* (Melbourne), 14 June 1928

'Details of 1928 race', *The Murray Pioneer and Australian River Record*, 23 March 1928

'Further misfortunes', *The Argus* (Melbourne), 9 July 1928

'Interesting impressions of Harry Watson—riders must know the course', *The Referee* (Sydney), 10 October 1928

Kennett, Jonathan, Bronwen Hall & Ian Gray, *Harry Watson: The mile eater*, Wellington: Kennett Brothers, 2006

Le Tour de France, <www.letour.com>

Opperman, Hubert, *Pedals, Politics and People*, Sydney: Haldane Publishing, 1977

'Opperman's misfortune', *The Argus* (Melbourne), 4 July 1928

Palenski, Ron, 'Tour de France not elementary for this Watson', *The Dominion*, 18 January 1997

'Perfectly hopeless! Tour de France manager guided team into Queer
    Street', *NZ Truth*, 11 October 1928
Ramsay, Isabel, 'Amazing disclosures about our Tour de France team',
    The Referee (Sydney), 1 August 1928
'The third lap', *Auckland Star*, 20 June 1928
'Tour de France begins: Australians competing', *The Argus* (Melbourne),
    18 June 1928
'Tour de France team: Best wishes for H. Watson', *Auckland Star*,
    16 June 1928

2 The 1929 Southland rugby team
'The big test', *The Evening Post*, 14 September 1929
Carman, A.H., *Ranfurly Shield Rugby*, Auckland: A.H. & A.W. Reed, 1960
'Comfortable win', *The Evening Post*, 29 August 1929
'The impossible happened', *NZ Truth*, 5 September 1929
'Impressive form', *The Evening Post*, 31 August 1929
Knight, Lindsay, *Shield Fever: The complete Ranfurly Shield story*,
    Auckland: Rugby Press, 1986
'The lost shield', *The Evening Post*, 3 September 1929
McConnell, Lynn, *Something to Crow about: The centennial history of
    the Southland Rugby Football Union*, Invercargill: Craig Printing,
    1986
'Near the century', *The Evening Post*, 27 August 1929
Palenski, Ron, *NZ Rugby: Stories of heroism and valour*, Auckland:
    Cumulus for Whitcoulls, 2002
'Ranfurly Shield: Southland tourists win', *Auckland Star*, 2 September
    1929
Smith, Max, *Champion Blokes: 44 great New Zealand sportsmen then
    and now*, Christchurch: Whitcombe and Tombs, 1965
'There is many a slip', *NZ Truth*, 5 September 1929
'Wairarapa beaten', *The Evening Post*, 2 September 1929

3 Billy Savidan
'Appeal to Aucklanders', *Auckland Star*, 17 June 1930
de Quetteville Cabot, Phillipe Sidney, 'At Empire Games', *Auckland Star*,
    15 October 1930

'Empire Games', *Auckland Star*, 26 March 1930

'Empire Games', *Auckland Star*, 30 May 1930

'Empire Games', *Auckland Star*, 28 June 1930

'Empire Games funds', *Auckland Star*, 12 June 1930

'Financing Savidan's trip', *The Evening Post*, 30 June 1930

'Funds for athletics', *Auckland Star*, 7 June 1930

'Good luck', *Auckland Star*, 1 July 1930

'A happy family', *The Evening Post*, 16 July 1930

Harris, Norman, *Lap of Honour*, Wellington: A.H. & A.W. Reed, 1963

McKinnon, Murray, 'Athletics: Moon beats 70-year-old record for most
    times', *The New Zealand Herald*, 12 August 2002

McMillan, Neville, *New Zealand Sporting Legends: 27 pre-war sporting
    heroes*, Auckland: Moa Beckett, 1993

'Olympic nominees', *Auckland Star*, 25 February 1928

Romanos, Joseph, *Our Olympic Century*, Wellington: Trio Books, 2008

'Savidan's position', *The Evening Post*, 28 June 1930

'Savidan's selection', *Auckland Star*, 30 June 1930

'Savidan wins', *Auckland Star*, 4 July 1927

Smith, Max, *Champion Blokes: 44 great New Zealand sportsmen then
    and now*, Christchurch: Whitcombe and Tombs, 1965

4 Norman Read

'100 medals: Five Olympic medallists you've never heard of (but
    probably should)', *The New Zealand Herald*, 9 August 2012

The Glow of Gold, short film (producer John O'Shea), Pacific Films,
    <www.nzonscreen.com>, 1968

Lawrence, Richard, *Triumph and Tears*, Napier: Richard Lawrence,
    2006

McConnell, Lynn, '"Grinning New Zealander" demolishes Olympic field',
    The Evening Post, 19 November 1999

New Zealand Olympics team, <www.olympic.org.nz>

Palenski, Ron, & Joseph Romanos, *Champions: New Zealand's sports
    greats of the 20th century*, Auckland: Hodder Moa Beckett, 2000

Peters, Paul, 'Our global sporting stars', *North Taranaki Midweek*,
    6 January 2014

Taylor, Mark, *High Flying Kiwis: 100 heroes of New Zealand sport*, Auckland: Sporting Press, 1988

Te Ara, <www.teara.govt.nz>

The Victorian Race Walking Club, <www.vrwc.org.au>

Winder, Virginia, 'Read walks into NZ hearts', Puke Ariki, <www.pukeariki.com>, first published 18 August 2004

5 Peter Snell

Corrigan, Robert J., *Tracking Heroes: 13 track and field champions*, Nashville, TN: Winston-Derek Publishing, 1990

Gilmour, Garth, *Arthur Lydiard: Master coach*, Auckland: Exisle Publishing, 2004

——*A Clean Pair of Heels: The Murray Halberg story*, Wellington: A.H. & A.W. Reed, 1963

The Golden Hour, television documentary (producer Steven O'Meagher), Desert Road, 2012, accessed at <www.nzonscreen.com>

Hobbs, Leslie, 'Meet the world's best runner', *Sports Illustrated*, 12 February 1962

Leggat, David, 'Athletics: Snell relives New Zealand's golden hour 50 years on', *The New Zealand Herald*, 28 August 2010

'Lydiard ranks Snell the best,' NZPA/*The New Zealand Herald*, 27 January 1990

McLean, T.P., *Silver Fern: 150 years of New Zealand sport*, Auckland: Moa Publications, 1990

Maddaford, Terry, & Ron Palenski, *The Games*, Auckland: Moa Publications in association with Dominion Breweries, 1983

Romanos, Joseph, *Arthur's Boys: The golden era of New Zealand athletics*, Auckland: Moa Beckett, 1994

——*Makers of Champions: Great NZ coaches*, Lower Hutt: Mills Publications, 1987

——*Our Olympic Century*, Wellington: Trio Books, 2008

Snell, Peter, & Garth Gilmour, *No Bugles, No Drums*, Auckland: Minerva Limited, 1965

This is Your Life, television special feature screened on TVNZ (producer Julie Christie), Eyeworks, 2000 <www.nzonscreen.com>

6 Burt Munro

AMA Motorcycle Hall of Fame, <www.motorcyclemuseum.org/
halloffame>

Begg, George, *Burt Munro: Indian legend of speed*, Christchurch: Begg
& Allen, 2002

Donaldson, Roger, *The World's Fastest Indian: Burt Munro—a
scrapbook of his life*, Auckland: Random House, 2009

——(producer), *Burt Munro: Offerings to the God of Speed*, television
documentary screened on New Zealand Television One, Aardvark
Films, 1971

Hanna, Tim, with David Larsen, *Legend of Speed: The Burt Munro story*,
Auckland: Penguin, 2007

——*One Good Run: The legend of Burt Munro*, Auckland: Penguin, 2005

7 The 1968 New Zealand coxed four

Anderson, Ian, 'Cole finds perfect mix for a golden time', *Waikato Times*,
10 December 2013

Bidwell, Peter, *Reflections of Gold: A celebration of New Zealand rowing*,
Auckland: HarperCollins, 2010

——'Stroke of success', *The Dominion Post*, 16 July 2004

'Big boats still hold major appeal', *Waikato Times*, 10 December 2013

'Celebrating New Zealand: New Zealand's top 10 sporting teams', *The
Press*, 1 January 2008

'Life service to rowing', *The Press*, 26 October 2000

McConnell, Lynn, 'Following a fine tradition', *The Evening Post*,
3 September 1999

Mallory, Peter, *The Sport of Rowing: Two centuries of competition*,
London: River and Rowing Museum, 2011

Mirams, Chris, 'Player power pays for 1968 coxed four', *The Evening
Post*, 15 September 2000

Romanos, Joseph, *Makers of Champions: Great NZ coaches*, Lower Hutt:
Mills Publications, 1987

——*Our Olympic Century*, Wellington: Trio Books, 2008

8 Denny Hulme

'Australians out of car rally', *The Canberra Times*, 14 May 1970

Becht, Richard, *Champions of Speed: A celebration of Bruce McLaren, Denny Hulme and Chris Amon*, Auckland: Moa Beckett, 1993

Friedman, Dave, *McLaren Sports Racing Cars*, Osceola, WI: MBI Publishing, 2000

Kerr, Phil, *To Finish First: My years inside Formula One, Can-Am and Indy 500*, Auckland: Random House, 2007

Ludvigsen, Karl, *Bruce McLaren: Life and legacy of excellence*, Sparkford: Haynes Publishing, 2001

Young, Eoin, *Memories of the Bear: A biography of Denny Hulme*, Auckland: HarperCollins, 2007

9 Jaynie Parkhouse

'Coach predicts 16 gold medals for swimmers', *The Canberra Times*, 16 January 1974

'Coach's dismay at draw', *The Canberra Times*, 19 July 1976

Commonwealth Games commentary, Sound Archives, <www.soundarchives.co.nz/audiolibrary>, 1974

'Commonwealth Games results on the first day', *The Times* (London), 26 January 1974

Hudgell, Jaynie [Jaynie Parkhouse], interview, Radio Live, <www.radiolive.co.nz>, 26 January 2014

'Jaynie Parkhouse wins gold for New Zealand: Women's 800m freestyle—1974', video, Commonwealth Games Federation, <thecgf.com>, n.d.

Maddaford, Terry, & Ron Palenski, *The Games*, Auckland: Moa Publications in association with Dominion Breweries, 1983

Parkhouse, Jaynie, interview, Radio New Zealand National, <www.radionz.co.nz>, 31 December 2007

Romanos, Joseph, 'Magic memories: Savouring the moment—Jaynie Parkhouse', *Listener & TV Times*, 22 January 1990

Sounds Historical, part 1, Radio New Zealand, <www.radionz.co.nz>, 20 May 2012

10 Peter Petherick

Edwards, Brent, 'Greatest moments in Otago sport: Number 54', *Otago Daily Times*, 12 September 2011

Graham, Alan, 'Petherick now hero', *The New Zealand Herald*,
    12 October 1976
Neely, Don, & Francis Payne, *Men in White: The history of New Zealand*
    Test cricket, Auckland: Hodder Moa, 2008
Robson, Toby, 'Tale of hat-trick ball', *The Dominion Post*, 2 January 2004
Romanos, Joseph, *A Century of New Zealand Cricketers*, Auckland:
    David Bateman, 1993
Smith, Ian, with Joseph Romanos, *Outrageous Cricket Moments*,
    Auckland: Hodder Moa Beckett, 2003
Williams, Tony, *Great Moments in New Zealand Cricket*, Auckland:
    David Ling Publishing, 1999

11 The 1976 New Zealand men's hockey team

'1976 New Zealand men's hockey Olympic final', video, YouTube,
    <www.youtube.com>, uploaded 28 November 2013
Agnew, Ivan, *Aim High: Ivan Agnew's Olympic report*, Auckland: Agnew
    Enterprises, 1976
Alexander, John, 'Golden days in Montreal', *Marlborough Express*,
    18 July 2012
Bruce, David, 'Chase your dreams, says Olympian', *Taranaki Daily News*,
    28 May 2003
Gray, Kent, 'The day we beat the odds', *The Dominion Post*, 9 July 2004
Jackman, Amy, 'The Wellingtonian interview: Trevor Manning', *The*
    Wellingtonian, 21 September 2012
Knox, Malcolm, 'Warning to Kiwis: If we can't beat you, we'll steal you',
    The Sydney Morning Herald, 28 June 1997
McMurran, Alistair, 'Hockey: Hills of Dunedin played part in securing
    gold', *Otago Daily Times*, 11 May 2010
Maddaford, Terry, 'Hockey gold at Montreal', in Don Cameron (ed.),
    Memorable Moments in NZ Sport, Auckland: Moa Publications, 1979
——'Olympics: Golden Kiwis vividly recall glory days', *The New Zealand*
    Herald, 28 July 2001
——& Ron Palenski, *The Games*, Auckland: Moa Publications in
    association with Dominion Breweries, 1983
Mangan, Patrick, *So Close: Bravest, craziest, unluckiest defeats in Aussie*
    sport, Sydney: Hachette, 2013

'NZ hockey's finest hour', NZPA/*Waikato Times*, 29 December 1997
'NZ team "should have been withdrawn"', *The Canberra Times*, 7 August 1976
Patel, Ramesh, interview with Kent Johns, *Legend's Hour*, Radio Sport, <www.radiosport.co.nz>, 22 November 2013
Robson, Tony, 'Goalie's grinding ordeal at an end', *The Dominion Post*, 20 July 2013
Romanos, Joseph, *Our Olympic Century*, Wellington: Trio Books, 2008

12 Linda Jones

Costello, John, *The Linda Jones Story*, Auckland: Moa Publications, 1979
Flynn, Greg, 'Linda Jones: Making Australian racing history', *The Australian Women's Weekly*, 25 April 1979
Hawkes, Jennifer, 'First among equals: Women pioneers back on racetrack', *Waikato Times*, 2 January 2001
'Jones rolls retired rivals in Australia', *The Press*, 31 March 1998
Mountier, Mary, *Racing Women*, Wellington: Daphne Brasell Associates Press, 1993
New Zealand Racing Hall of Fame, <www.racinghalloffame.co.nz>
Petley, Jack, 'Payne honours pioneer women', *The Daily Telegraph* (Sydney), 27 December 2003
Quay, Phillip, 'Keeping up with Jones', *Waikato Times*, 23 March 1998
Simons, Dorothy, *New Zealand's Champion Sportswomen*, Auckland: Moa Publications, 1982
Te Ara, <www.teara.govt.nz>

13 Digby Taylor

Becht, Richard, *Champions under Sail: 25 years of New Zealand yachting greats*, Auckland: Hodder Moa Beckett, 1995
Gifford, Phil, 'Ceramco New Zealand: Blake's dream', *New Zealand Listener*, 29 August 1981
——'Never the underdog', *Listener & TV Times*, 10 July 1982
'Hitch delays NZ race yacht', *The New Zealand Herald*, 2 November 1981
Parker, Alan, & Digby Taylor, *Digby Taylor's Outward Bound: One man's dream*, Auckland: D. Taylor, distributed by Lindon Publishing, 1982

Pickthall, Barry, 'Jail force winds delay the Outward Bound crewman', *The Times* (London), 2 November 1981

——'Outward Bound comes home to a welcome', *The Times* (London), 10 December 1981

The Sir Peter Blake Trust, <www.sirpeterblaketrust.org>

Taylor, Digby, *Digby Taylor's NZI Enterprise Story*, Auckland: D. Taylor, distributed by Lyndon Distribution, 1986

'Taylor offered maxi yacht for next race', NZPA/*The New Zealand Herald*, 10 April 1982

Te Ara, <www.teara.govt.nz>

Toogood, Chas, 'Outward Bound: Will to win', *Listener & TV Times*, 29 August 1981

Volvo Ocean Race, <www.volvooceanrace.com>

14 Anne Audain

'Anne Audain: Running Her Way', <www.anneaudain.com>

Audain, Anne, with John L. Parker, *Uncommon Heart*, Tallahassee, FL: Cedarwinds Publishing, 2000

Gifford, Phil, 'The third woman', *Listener & TV Times*, 17 April 1982

'Halberg Hall of Fame: Anne Audain', Audain's acceptance speech screened on TVNZ, <tvnz.co.nz>, 4 February 2009

Langwell, Robyn, 'They moved mountains to get their golds', *New Zealand Woman's Weekly*, 25 October 1982

Lundy, Lesley, 'Anne Audain not afraid of failure', *The New Zealand Herald*, 27 November 1982

Maddaford, Terry, 'Off like scared rabbit', *The New Zealand Herald*, 5 October 1982

Moran, Malcolm, 'Players', *The New York Times*, 1 June 1985

Myers, Virginia, *Head & Shoulders: Successful New Zealand women talk to Virginia Myers*, Auckland: Penguin, 1986

Perrott, Alan, 'Spurned coach made life hell for teen Audain', *The New Zealand Herald*, 25 August 2000

Phare, Jane, 'The business of winning', *The New Zealand Herald*, 8 January 1992

Rattue, Chris, 'Run-down running in need of heroes for the kids, says Olympic legend', *The New Zealand Herald*, 2 June 2012

Ray, Pauline, 'Anne Audain: Running her life', *Listener & TV Times*,
    15 January 1983
Roger, Warwick, 'The ego and Anne Audain', *Metro*, May 1986
Romanos, Joseph, 'Front runner', *Listener & TV Times*, 15 January 1990
Wheeler, Jenny, 'Anne Audain: This is the real me', *New Zealand Woman's*
    Weekly, 18 January 1982
Williams, Roy, 'Courage nothing new for Anne', *Auckland Star*, 5 October
    1982
——'South Island lure just too much', *New Zealand Woman's Weekly*,
    27 January 1992

15 Chris Lewis
Amdur, Neil, 'McEnroe and Lewis reach final', *The New York Times*,
    2 July 1983
——'McEnroe captures Wimbledon final', *The New York Times*, 4 July
    1983
Atkin, Ronald, 'Lewis, the rising star with a big-hearted racquet',
    The Observer (London), 3 July 1983
Barrett, John, *Wimbledon: The official history*, London: Vision Sports
    Publishing, 2013
Bellamy, Rex, 'Kiwi flies headlong into final with McEnroe', *The Times*
    (London), 2 July 1983
——'Mrs King's head falls after she is let down by the court', *The Times*
    (London), 1 July 1983
——'Whiff of madness in the air and Lewis catches the mood', *The*
    Times (London), 29 June 1983
Berkow, Ira, 'Sports of the Times: The Wimbledon finalist', *The New York*
    Times, 27 August 1983
Brown, Michael, 'The day the dream came true', *Herald on Sunday*,
    22 June 2008
Burgess, Michael, 'Wimbledon memories: Chris Lewis—part 1', TVNZ,
    <tvnz.co.nz>, 22 June 2009
——'Wimbledon memories: Chris Lewis—part 2', TVNZ, <tvnz.co.nz>,
    29 June 2009
Irvine, David, 'McEnroe's tide swamps Lewis', *The Guardian* (London),
    4 July 1983

——'Viewing the outsiders looking in', *The Guardian* (London), 18 June 1983

Kirkpatrick, Curry, 'A giant stride ahead of the field', *Sports Illustrated*, 11 July 1983

Morris, Rupert, 'Unseeded Lewis to play McEnroe in final', *The Times* (London), 2 July 1983

Romanos, Joseph, *Chris Lewis: All the way to Wimbledon*, Auckland: Rugby Press, 1984

Vecsey, George, 'Lewis relies on fitness in final', *The New York Times*, 3 July 1983

——'Round 12 goes to McEnroe', *The New York Times*, 2 July 1983

——'A stranger on the court', *The New York Times*, 4 July 1983

Woodcock, Fred, 'Ace face of 1983', *The Dominion Post*, 21 June 2008

16 Jim Cassidy and Kiwi the racehorse

'1983 Melbourne Cup—Kiwi', video, TAB NZ/YouTube, <www.youtube.com>, uploaded 22 October 2013

'1983 Melbourne Cup—Kiwi', video, TVN Racing Network/YouTube, <www.youtube.com>, uploaded 1 July 2013

'1983 Melbourne Cup', video, YouTube, <www.youtube.com>, uploaded 27 October 2006

Cassidy, Jim, 'When the chips are down, I'll be counting potatoes', *The Sydney Morning Herald*, 1 November 2011

Dillon, Mike, 'Cassidy brings up his ton', *The New Zealand Herald*, 4 November 2013

Hilton, Tony, *Kiwi*, Fielding: Dunmore Press for Graeme Lupton, 2004

Hinds, Richard, 'Cassidy back on prowl on biggest stage of them all', *The Age* (Melbourne), 1 November 2010

Hourigan, John, 'Kiwi's Cup with best finish in years', *The Canberra Times*, 2 November 1983

Jones, Kristine, 'Anniversary of Kiwi legend', *New Zealand Thoroughbred Magazine*, accessed online at <www.nztmag.co.nz> on 6 January 2014

'Kiwi's dash to front the stuff of legends', NZPA/*The New Zealand Herald*, 3 November 2008

Lambert, Max, *November Gold: New Zealand's quest for the Melbourne Cup*, Auckland: Moa Publications, 1986

'Melbourne Cup inspires', <www.stuff.co.nz>, 8 October 2011

'Snow Lupton: Obituary', NZPA/*The New Zealand Herald*, 18 December 2004

'Strange Kiwi methods have worked before', *The Canberra Times*, 31 October 1983

Walsh, Scott, 'The secrets behind a "clipped" Kiwi flyer—and why he should have won another Melbourne Cup', *Sunday Mail* (SA), 2 November 2013

Webster, Andrew, 'The hundred club', *The Sydney Morning Herald*, 19 October 2013

17 Ewen Chatfield

Berry, Scyld, 'Spinning the wrong line', *The Observer* (London), 29 January 1984

Chatfield, Ewen, interview with Bryan Crump, *Nights*, Radio New Zealand National, <www.radionz.co.nz>, 14 June 2013

——& Jeremy Coney, interview with Jonathan Agnew, *Test Match Special*, BBC Radio, 18 March 2013

Coney, Jeremy, *The Playing Mantis: An autobiography*, Auckland: Moa Publications, 1985

Haigh, Gideon, 'The art of Ewen Chatfield', *The Australian*, 31 October 2012

McConnell, Lynn, *Chats: Ewen Chatfield's life in cricket*, Auckland: Moa Publications, 1988

——*The First Fifty: New Zealand cricket Test victories*, Auckland: HarperSports, 2002

Neely, Don, & Francis Payne, *Men in White: The history of New Zealand Test cricket*, Auckland: Hodder Moa, 2008

Romanos, Joseph, *Cricket Confidential*, Wellington: Trio Books, 2005

Seconi, Adrian, 'Greatest moments in Otago sport: Number 22', *Otago Daily Times*, 19 October 2011

Smith, Ian, with Joseph Romanos, *Outrageous Cricket Moments*, Auckland: Hodder Moa Beckett, 2003

18 Greg Cooper

Cameron, D.J., 'The most marvellous All Blacks', *The New Zealand Herald*, 30 November 1986

——'Young All Blacks rise to occasion', *The New Zealand Herald*, 30 November 1986

Evans, Jane, 'Beating the big C', *North & South*, September 1989

Paterson, Kimberley, *The X Factor: Finding inner courage when life goes terribly wrong*, Auckland: Penguin, 1997

Paul, Gregor, *Hard Men Fight Back*, Auckland: Exisle Publishing, 2006

Romanos, Joseph, 'The big comeback', *Listener & TV Times*, 25 May 1992

19 Ross Norman

Beyond Sport, <www.beyondsport.org>

Humberstone, Brian, 'Skinny boy turns squash sensation', *The New Zealand Herald*, 13 November 1986

McLean, Terry, 'Why no Norman conquest?' *Listener & TV Times*, 7 November 1987

McQuillan, Colin, 'Conquest Norman is hoping to achieve', *The Times* (London), 22 April 1986

——'Jahangir takes fifth world title but Norman takes a game', *The Times* (London), 26 November 1985

——'Norman conquest of the world', *The Times* (London), 12 November 1986

——'Norman's irrepressible ambition', *The Times* (London), 13 November 1986

——'Rivals hope Jahangir will lose his memory', *The Times* (London), 14 April 1986

——'Robertson holds the stage', *The Times* (London), 10 November 1986

'Norman: It's fantastic', NZPA/*The New Zealand Herald*, 13 November 1986

'Old rivals in squash final', NZPA/*The New Zealand Herald*, 12 November 1986

'Parents knew victory on way', *The New Zealand Herald*, 13 November 1986

'Patience proves a virtue for Norman', *The Times* (London), 12 March
    1986
'Personality of the week program: Jahangir Khan', Kalpoint, <education.
    kalpoint.com>, 10 December (year unknown)
Romanos, Joseph, *Long or Short? The story of New Zealand squash*,
    Waitakere: New Zealand Squash Hall of Fame, 2010
Squash New Zealand, <www.nzsquash.co.nz>
'Squash: Ross Norman v Jahangir Khan 1986 Squash World Open final',
    video, YouTube, <www.youtube.com>, uploaded 1 December 2011
Sullivan, Bob, 'Khan the Conqueror', *Sports Illustrated*, 6 May 1985
Taylor, Mark, *High Flying Kiwis: 100 heroes of New Zealand sport*,
    Auckland: Sporting Press, 1988

20 Steve Gurney
Ansley, Bruce, 'A test of endurance', *New Zealand Listener*, 11 February
    1995
Butcher, Margot, 'Is Steve Gurney mad?', *North & South*, July 2001
Forsyth, Jenny, 'Against the odds', *The New Zealand Herald*, 13 February
    2000
Gurney, Steve, with Robin Major, *Lucky Legs*, Auckland: Random House,
    2008
'Gurney's win dramatic return to form', *The New Zealand Herald*,
    10 February 1997
Hinton, Marc, 'Gutsy Gurney shows his fighting qualities', *Sunday Star
    Times*, 23 July 1995
Paul, Gregor, *Hard Men Fight Back*, Auckland: Exisle Publishing, 2006
'A sadist's choice: Selecting the location for the Raid Gauloises', Action
    Asia, <actionasia.com>, first published October–November 1994
Speight's Coast to Coast, <www.coasttocoast.co.nz>
'Steve Gurney: The king of adventure', Intrepid Adventure,
    <www.intrepidadventure.co.nz>, n.d.

21 The 2002 Tall Blacks
'Captain among the big names', NZPA/*The New Zealand Herald*,
    10 September 2002
'Classy Cameron in nick of time', NZPA/*The New Zealand Herald*,
    17 August 2002

Cleave, Louisa, 'Basketball: Tall Blacks drag 800,000 out of bed',
    The New Zealand Herald, 10 September 2002

'Eye injury sidelines Marks for rest of world champs', NZPA/*The New
    Zealand Herald*, 2 September 2002

'Heavy schedule saps spring out of Tall Black', NZPA/*The New Zealand
    Herald*, 19 August 2002

'Injury hits Tall Blacks' hopes', NZPA/*The New Zealand Herald*,
    3 September 2002

Jessup, Peter, 'Baldwin opens books as Tall Blacks' hone plans', *The New
    Zealand Herald*, 7 February 2002

——'A basketball dream team we should treasure', *The New Zealand
    Herald*, 9 September 2002

——'Best of the rest press claims for Tall Blacks', *The New Zealand
    Herald*, 11 April 2001

——'Coach puts head down for march to world champs', *The New
    Zealand Herald*, 5 September 2001

——'Coach ready to take on the world', *The New Zealand Herald*,
    26 September 2001

——'Cull hardens resolve for 2004 qualifier', *The New Zealand Herald*,
    1 September 2003

——'Double change on the bench', *The New Zealand Herald*, 9 February
    2001

——'Injuries limit Baldwin's options', *The New Zealand Herald*, 15 July
    2002

——'New Zealand are minnows in a very big pool', *The New Zealand
    Herald*, 14 September 2000

——'Tall Blacks classy in 14-point win', *The New Zealand Herald*, 9 July
    2002

——'Tall order to scale the "Great Wall"', *The New Zealand Herald*,
    28 May 2002

——'Walk tall, think tall . . . and win', *The New Zealand Herald*,
    24 August 2002

Rattue, Chris, 'All fun and games in 2002', *The New Zealand Herald*,
    1 January 2003

Romanos, Joseph, *Winning Ways: Champion New Zealand coaches
    reveal their secrets*, Wellington: Trio Books, 2007

Rutherford, Jenni, 'Bitter taste of defeat', NZPA/*The New Zealand Herald*, 9 September 2002

——'Bring on Puerto Ricans say Tall Blacks', NZPA/*The New Zealand Herald*, 6 September 2002

——'Don't waste team's sweat, warns Tall Blacks' coach', NZPA/*The New Zealand Herald*, 10 September 2002

——'Tall Blacks soar to new heights', NZPA/*The New Zealand Herald*, 7 September 2002

——'They've got tabs on our Mr Baldwin', NZPA/*The New Zealand Herald*, 7 September 2002

Saker, John, *Tracing the Arc*, Montana Estates Essay Series, series ed. Lloyd Jones, Wellington: Four Winds Press, 2003, quoted in Gilbert Wong, 'The coach', *Metro*, April 2003

'Shortie team thinking tall', NZPA/*The New Zealand Herald*, 30 August 2002

'Tall Black "old man" raring to do battle', NZPA/*The New Zealand Herald*, 21 September 2001

'Tall Blacks no match for red-hot Germany', NZPA/*The New Zealand Herald*, 9 September 2002

'Tall Blacks slip back to sixth', NZPA/*The New Zealand Herald*, 10 September 2001

Wong, Gilbert, 'The coach', *Metro*, April 2003

'Yugoslavia end Tall Blacks' dream run', NZPA/*The New Zealand Herald*, 8 September 2002

22 Michael Campbell

'Campbell: Golf's mercurial master', *The New Zealand Herald*, 25 June 2005

Campbell, Michael, interview, transcript and recording at 'U.S. Open Championship', ASAP Sports, <www.asapsports.com>, 19 June 2005

'Campbell player of year on European Tour', *The New Zealand Herald*, 6 December 2005

'Campbell's stunning comeback from nowhere', *The New Zealand Herald*/Agencies, 21 June 2005

Crowe, Martin, & Craig Tiriana, *Michael Campbell: Celebration of a champion*, Auckland: Reed Publishing, 2005

Davidson, Martin, 'Campbell: Standing up when it matters', NZPA/*The New Zealand Herald*, 21 June 2005

Golf Today, <www.golftoday.co.uk>

Juliano, Joe, 'Campbell's coronation: With princely play he put his past behind him', *The Inquirer* (Philadelphia, PA), 20 June 2005

Mair, Lewine, 'Malaysian Open: Campbell in his element despite heat and rain', *The Telegraph* (London), 16 February 2001

'Michael Campbell wins 2005 US Open! vs Tiger Woods', video, YouTube, <www.youtube.com>, uploaded 10 June 2013

New Zealand, <www.newzealand.com>

PGA, <www.pga.com>

Rude, Jeff, '2005 US Open: Staying power', *Golfweek*, 12 September 2005

Shipnuck, Alan, 'Kiwi surprise', *Sports Illustrated*, 27 June 2005

Tiriana, Craig, 'After a long road to the top, Campbell can finally enjoy the view', *Rotorua Daily Post*, 21 June 2005

Willis, George, 'Persistence pays off at Pinehurst', PGA, <www.pga.com>, n.d.

23 The 2008 Kiwis

Borley, Craig, 'Look what we got in Australia', *The New Zealand Herald*, 24 November 2008

Deane, Steve, 'Great whingeing land', *The New Zealand Herald*, 28 November 2008

Donaghy, Dave, 'England, be afraid: Lockyer tips Roos to improve', *The Daily Telegraph* (Sydney), 30 October 2008

Gould, Phil, 'Memo organisers: Note the World in World Cup', *The Sydney Morning Herald*, 19 October 2008

Jackson, Glenn, 'How Benji got his groove back', *The Sydney Morning Herald*, 21 November 2008

——'Joke becomes a choke', *The Sydney Morning Herald*, 23 November 2008

——'Kiwis know all the Kangaroos' secrets: Jones', *The Sydney Morning Herald*, 19 November 2008

Jessup, Peter, 'Arch-rivals keep the faith for World Cup decider', *The New Zealand Herald*, 20 November 2008

——'Error-ridden semifinal means hard training for New Zealanders', *The New Zealand Herald*, 17 November 2008

——'Joke World Cup slips further into farce', *The New Zealand Herald*, 28 October 2008

——'Kiwis open era of "no regrets"', *The New Zealand Herald*, 24 November 2008

——'Marshalling his troops', *The New Zealand Herald*, 22 November 2008

——'Stuart says the hardest word', *The New Zealand Herald*, 29 November 2008

Kilgallon, Steve, 'Benji's redemption helped bring down Roos', <www.stuff.co.nz>, 24 November 2008

——'It doesn't get better than this, baby', *Sunday Star Times*, 30 November 2008

——'Kiwis upset Aussies in cup final stunner', *Sunday Star Times*, 23 November 2008

Lonergan, Dean, 'Kiwis will have to catch the Kangaroos having an off day', *The New Zealand Herald*, 21 November 2008

Lowe, Robert, 'Marshall's sights set firmly on title', *The New Zealand Herald*, 17 November 2008

McKewen, Trevor, 'Kiwis laugh off "wrestling" rumours', <www.stuff.co.nz>, 23 October 2008

Magnay, Jacquelin, & Glenn Jackson, 'Stuart blames officials for shock loss', *The Age* (Melbourne), 24 November 2008

——'Stuart's conspiracy claim rattles Carr', *The Sydney Morning Herald*, 24 November 2008

Marshall, Benji, with Glenn Jackson, *Benji: My story—the authorised biography*, Auckland: Hodder Moa, 2011

Matheson, John, *Benji Marshall: A tribute to a rugby league genius*, Auckland: HarperSports, 2011

Naylor, Grant, 'Upset puts smile on bookies' faces', *The Sydney Morning Herald*, 23 November 2008

Prichard, Greg, 'Game over: Australia win', *The Sydney Morning Herald*, 27 October 2008

Rattue, Chris, 'God or guru, it's time to take a hike, Benny', *The New Zealand Herald*, 29 October 2008

Ritchie, Dean, 'Ricky Stuart quits as Australian league coach', *The Daily Telegraph* (Sydney), 8 December 2008

Rugby League World Cup, Australia 2008: New Zealand—the final, DVD, Visual Entertainment, 2008

Smith, Tony, 'Kiwis deliver victory at cup', *The Press*, 27 December 2008

Stuart, Ricky, 'Biggest mistake of my life: Ricky Stuart', *The Daily Telegraph* (Sydney), 28 November 2008

Walter, Brad, 'Wayne's world smells like team spirit', *The Age* (Melbourne), 24 November 2008

Wilson, Andy, 'New Zealand stun Australia to secure World Cup glory', *The Guardian* (London), 22 November 2008

Worthington, Sam, 'Kiwis stun rugby league world', <www.stuff.co.nz>, 23 November 2008

——'Marshall rejects underdogs label', *The Dominion Post*, 11 October 2008

——'Nelson College old boy a world champ', *The Nelson Mail*, 24 November 2008

——'On top of the world', *The Dominion Post*, 24 November 2008

——'Remember this', *The Dominion Post*, 21 November 2008

24 The 2010 All Whites

'2010 World Cup: Italy vs New Zealand (full highlights)', video, YouTube, <www.youtube.com>, uploaded 20 June 2010

'All Whites' $10m World Cup goal', *Sunday Star Times*, 15 November 2009

'All Whites light up Cup: World press', *The New Zealand Herald*, 16 June 2010

'All Whites qualify for World Cup', NZPA/*The New Zealand Herald*, 14 November 2009

'All Whites v Italy: And the Oscars go to . . .', NZPA/*The New Zealand Herald*, 21 June 2010

'All you need to know about All Whites v Slovakia', *The New Zealand Herald*, 15 June 2010

Brown, Michael, 'All Whites face impossible dream', *Herald on Sunday*, 20 June 2010

——'All Whites hold on for stunning draw', <www.nzherald.co.nz>, 21 June 2010

——'All Whites with nothing to lose against Italy—Smeltz', <www.nzherald.co.nz>, 18 June 2010

——'Future of football starts now', *Herald on Sunday*, 13 June 2010

——'Herbert walking in the footsteps of giants', *The New Zealand Herald*, 9 May 2010

——'Our World Cup stunner', *The New Zealand Herald*, 16 June 2010

——'Ref ruined match—Nelsen', *The New Zealand Herald*, 21 June 2010

Cornaga, Andrew, *One Shot for Glory: The All Whites in South Africa*, Auckland: Photosport/Penguin, 2010

Dickison, Michael, 'Michael Jones: All Whites' run NZ's greatest sporting achievement', *The New Zealand Herald*, 25 June 2010

Dye, Stuart, 'Battle of the haves and the have nots', *The New Zealand Herald*, 19 June 2010

——'That's a handball. That'll be a red card. What a twat', *The New Zealand Herald*, 18 June 2010

Falconer, Phoebe, 'All Whites watch out: Here come the world champs', *The New Zealand Herald*, 17 June 2010

Glendenning, Barry, 'World Cup 2010: Paraguay v New Zealand—as it happened', *The Guardian* (London), 24 June 2010

'Highlights from the 0–0 draw between the All Whites–Paraguay at the FIFA World Cup', video, <www.youtube.com>, uploaded 26 February 2013

Holloway, Steven, & Daniel Richardson, with Michael Brown & Kris Shannon, 'One night in November', *The New Zealand Herald*, November 2013

Kay, Simon, 'An eligible batch of talent', *Herald on Sunday*, 20 June 2010

——'Modest Paston praises defence', *The New Zealand Herald*, 20 June 2010

'Kiwis score history against Italy', video, FIFA TV/YouTube, <www.youtube.com>, uploaded 27 September 2012

Long, Gideon, 'All White Nelsen steals Cannavaro's limelight', Reuters, <in.reuters.com>, 20 June 2010

McCarra, Kevin, 'Winston Reid's late header seals draw for New Zealand against Slovakia', *The Guardian* (London), 15 June 2010

Maddaford, Terry, 'Equation simple for Kiwis—beat Paraguay', *The New Zealand Herald*, 22 June 2010

Matheson, John, *All White Fever: New Zealand's road to the World Cup*, Auckland: HarperCollins, 2010

Nelsen, Ryan, with Tony Smith, *Ryan Nelsen's Road to the World Cup*, Auckland: Hachette New Zealand, 2010

Neville, Alice, & Michael Dickison, 'Experts, fans give NZ fighting chance', *The New Zealand Herald*, 15 June 2010

'New Zealand v Slovakia: Ryan Nelsen has his sights set on a shock All Whites win', *The Telegraph* (London), 15 June 2010

'New Zealand vs Slovakia (FIFA World Cup 2010)', video, <www.youtube.com>, uploaded 25 May 2012

New Zealand, <www.newzealand.com>

'One shot for glory', *Sunday*, television programme, TVNZ, <tvnz.co.nz>, 15 November 2009

'Paraguay or bust for All Whites', *The New Zealand Herald*, 21 June 2010

Phillips, Antony, 'Editorial: We'll take a draw despite the referee', *Hawke's Bay Today*, 21 June 2010

Rattue, Chris, 'Adshead realistic yet still positive', <www.nzherald.co.nz>, 15 June 2010

——'All Whites: Goalkeeper's heroics keep world champs at bay', *The New Zealand Herald*, 21 June 2010

——'All Whites make history with late goal', <www.nzherald.co.nz>, 16 June 2010

——'Herbert slams critics after shock result', <www.nzherald.co.nz>, 21 June 2010

——'Italy game battle of hopes and dreams', *The New Zealand Herald*, 19 June 2010

——'Mighty task for All Whites to take on giants', <www.nzherald.co.nz>, 18 June 2010

——'Paston enjoying the good times', <www.nzherald.co.nz>, 23 June 2010

——'Pressure to perform rests with the reigning world champions', <www.nzherald.co.nz>, 18 June 2010

——'Smith about to realise his dream', *The New Zealand Herald*, 19 June 2010

———'We can go further, says ecstatic Nelsen', <www.nzherald.co.nz>,
      16 June 2010
'Self-belief the key, says Herbert', NZPA/*The New Zealand Herald*,
      15 November 2009
Silkstone, Dan, 'Fighting All Whites make one more point', *The Sydney
      Morning Herald*, 21 June 2010
'Slovakia sharpening knives for All Whites', NZPA/*The New Zealand
      Herald*, 15 June 2010
Smith, Tony, 'Nelsen: Gee whiz that ref was bad', <www.stuff.co.nz>,
      21 June 2010
Tan, Lincoln, '"Australian" victory plunges Bahrain into darkness at
      noon', *The New Zealand Herald*, 16 November 2009
Undefeated: The All Whites' World Cup story, DVD, New Zealand
      Football/New Zealand Professional Footballers' Association, 2010
'Watch highlights of the All Whites win against Bahrain at Westpac
      Stadium in Welling', video, <www.youtube.com>, uploaded
      28 February 2013
'White hot', *Hawke's Bay Today*, 16 November 2009
'Written off already', *The New Zealand Herald*, 12 June 2010

25 Stephen Donald
'Better players than Donald: Henry', *The New Zealand Herald*, 22 June
      2011
Chadband, Ian, 'Rugby World Cup 2011', *The Telegraph* (London),
      23 October 2011
———'Stephen Donald was New Zealand's accidental hero when kicking
      the winning points in the Rugby World Cup final', *The Telegraph*
      (London), 18 November 2011
Cleaver, Dylan, 'All Blacks crying out for a hero? Step up Stephen
      Donald', *The New Zealand Herald*, 24 October 2011
Dickison, Michael, 'All Blacks pressure? Just leave it to Beaver', *The New
      Zealand Herald*, 25 October 2011
———'New Year's Honours: Sir Graham Henry', *The New Zealand Herald*,
      31 December 2011
Donald, Stephen, interview with Barry Guy, *Morning Report*, Radio
      New Zealand National, 24 October 2011

Donnell, Hayden, & Andrew Koubaridis, 'Mum: "He proved them wrong"', *The New Zealand Herald*, 24 October 2011

Gilhooly, Dan, 'Live blog commentary: World Cup final', <www.stuff.co.nz>, 23 October 2011

Gray, Wynne, 'All Blacks: Stephen Donald's Rugby World Cup call up lesson in depth', *The New Zealand Herald*, 25 October 2011

——'All Blacks win Rugby World Cup: Angst is over', *The New Zealand Herald*, 24 October 2011

——'Rugby World Cup: Donald never relinquished dream', *The New Zealand Herald*, 12 October 2011

Henry, Graham, with Bob Howitt, *Graham Henry: Final word*, Auckland: HarperCollins, 2012

Hewett, Chris, 'Can star of New Zealand save Bath?', *The Independent* (London), 31 December 2011

Hinton, Marc, 'Stephen Donald delighted to answer the call', *Sunday Star Times*, 25 October 2011

——'Stephen Donald ruled out over chest tear', *Sunday Star Times*, 1 June 2010

——'Stephen Donald's omission no surprise', *Sunday Star Times*, 23 June 2011

Ihaka, James, & Vaimoana Tapaleao, 'Beaver fever in All Black Donald's hometown', *The New Zealand Herald*, 29 October 2011

Johnstone, Duncan, 'Carter always confident in "Beaver" Donald', <www.stuff.co.nz>, 25 October 2011

——'Donald's world-beater tag a perfect fit', <www.stuff.co.nz>, 25 October 2011

——'Unlikely replacement Donald wins high praise', <www.stuff.co.nz>, 24 October 2011

Jones, Chris, 'Stephen Donald's rise from beers on a boat to toast of his nation', *London Evening Standard*, 24 October 2011

Jones, Nicholas, 'All Blacks give time for elation after epic Rugby World Cup struggle', *The New Zealand Herald*, 24 October 2011

Knowler, Richard, 'Stephen Donald turns criticism on its head', *The Press*, 25 October 2011

Lewis, Paul, 'Henry loyalty is misplaced', *Herald on Sunday*, 7 November 2010

Loe, Richard, 'All Blacks must smash Wallabies early and game is in the bag', *The New Zealand Herald*, 16 October 2011

McCaw, Richie, with Greg McGee, *Richie McCaw: The open side*, Auckland: Hachette New Zealand, 2012

Mulvenney, Nick, 'Donald's net gain is surprise World Cup call-up', Reuters, <uk.reuters.com>, 11 October 2011

'New Zealanders turn on Donald after Test loss', *The Daily Telegraph* (Sydney), 31 October 2010

'New Zealand hero Stephen Donald delights in "unreal" World Cup journey', BBC, <www.bbc.com>, 23 October 2011

Paul, Gregor, 'Blackened reputations', *Herald on Sunday*, 24 April 2011

——*Top 10 of Everything Rugby*, Auckland: Exisle Publishing, 2012

Pearce, Nick, 'Rugby World Cup 2011 final: New Zealand v France live', *The Telegraph*, 23 October 2011

Savage, Jared, 'Cold Bath for Beaver after field of dreams', *The New Zealand Herald*, 20 October 2012

'Stephen Donald ducks his chorus of critics', *The Dominion Post*, 1 November 2010

'Stephen Donald: Leave it to Beaver', *Waikato Times*, 31 December 2011

Weepu, Piri, with Heather Kidd, *Piri: Straight up—cups, downs and keeping calm*, Auckland: Hachette New Zealand, 2012

ABOUT THE AUTHORS

BRONWYN SELL is an award-winning journalist, a freelance writer and a bestselling author. Her previous books include *Lawbreakers and Mischief Makers: 50 notorious New Zealanders*, and *Kiwi Heroes: 50 courageous New Zealanders*, both published by Allen & Unwin. She has worked in the media for twenty years, and is a regular contributor to *The New Zealand Herald*. CHRISTINE SHEEHY is a freelance writer and author, whose work has featured in *The Guardian* (UK), *The Listener, The New Zealand Herald, Canvas, New Zealand House & Garden* and *The School Magazine* (NSW). A former lawyer, Christine spent several years advising journalists at the BBC in London on the finer points of media law before turning her pen to more creative pursuits. In 2012, she was shortlisted for the Storylines Joy Cowley Award. Christine and Bronwyn both write from their respective homes in seaside villages north of Auckland.